Property of:

Mrs. Lois Merideth
102 Dennis Dr # B
Eureka, IL 61530-1611

Christmas present 2001
from my Granddaughter
Penny Ann Kossesky

D1478797

The warrior's name,
Tho' peal'd and chimed on all the tongues of fame,
Sounds less harmonious to the grateful mind,
Than his who fashions and improves mankind.

Columbiad Book 8.th line 126.

JOEL BARLOW.

Painted by R. Fulton.   Engraved by J. Smith A.R.A

THE HISTORY

OF

REDDING, CONN.,

FROM ITS

FIRST SETTLEMENT TO THE PRESENT TIME.

WITH NOTES ON

THE ADAMS, BANKS, BARLOW, BARTLETT, BARTRAM, BATES, BEACH, BENEDICT,
BETTS, BURR, BURRITT, BURTON, CHATFIELD, COUCH, DARLING, FAIRCHILD,
FOSTER, GOLD, GORHAM, GRAY, GRIFFIN, HALL, HAWLEY, HILL, HERON,
HULL, JACKSON, LEE, LYON, LORD, MALLORY, MEADE, MEEKER,
MERCHANT, MOREHOUSE, PERRY, PLATT, READ, ROGERS,
RUMSEY, SANFORD, SMITH, AND STOW FAMILIES.

BY

CHARLES BURR TODD,

AUTHOR OF "A HISTORY OF THE BURR FAMILY"

NEW YORK:
THE JOHN A. GRAY PRESS AND STEAM TYPE-SETTING OFFICE,
CORNER OF FRANKFORT AND JACOB STREETS.

1880.

A Facsimile Reprint
Published 1999 by

HERITAGE BOOKS, INC.
1540E Pointer Ridge Place
Bowie, Maryland 20716
1-800-398-7709
www.heritagebooks.com

ISBN 0-7884-1220-5

A Complete Catalog Listing Hundreds of Titles
On History, Genealogy, and Americana
Available Free Upon Request

PREFACE.

An interest is attached to the place of one's birth which change of scene rather enhances than removes, and which increases rather than diminishes in intensity as one approaches the later stages of life : this home feeling has been largely instrumental in the production of this work, and to it is due nearly every thing of interest or value that the book possesses.

A history of Redding has been long contemplated by the author as a service due his native town, and as long shrunk from because of the labor, the expense, and the difficulty of its compilation. Whether well or illy done, it is now completed, and goes out to the somewhat limited public for whom it was written.

The materials for the work have been drawn largely from the ancient records of the town and parish, from the records of the colony, and from the files of musty papers in the State Library at Hartford. Tradition and oral information have not been neglected, and every reasonable effort has been made to render the work as far as possible a thorough and reliable history of the town. That errors and discrepancies will be found, is to be expected ; but it is not believed that they are sufficiently numerous or important to destroy its historical value. In the preparation of the book the compiler has aimed to preserve the character of a local historian, and has confined himself chiefly to the narration of local facts and incidents. In harmony with this principle, an extended biography of Joel Barlow, at first intended for this work, has been excluded. The sketch of the poet so grew on the author's hands, that it was found it would make a volume by itself, and contained so much of general interest and detail that it could not be made to harmonize with the local character of this work. A concise sketch of the poet's life, however, and the original portrait from Fulton's oil-painting, that formed the frontispiece of the Columbiad, are included in its pages.

The compiler has not aimed at making a large book : many facts in few words is what a busy age demands of the historian, and in deference to this demand only such matter as was of real value and interest has been admitted. The church histories and the genealogical notes are, perhaps, the most important, if not the most interesting, portions of the work. It would have added to the value of the ecclesiastical history, no doubt, if it had been prepared by the pastors of the different churches represented ; but, with one exception, these had so recently assumed the care of their charges, that they did not feel at liberty to undertake it, and the task fell to the lot of the compiler. If this department is not what it might have been, the cause may be found in the disadvantages which a layman must labor under in attempting to write ecclesiastical history. The Rev. Mr. Welton, rector of Christ Church, very kindly consented to prepare the history of that church, and his paper will be read with interest by our citizens.

In preparing the notes on the early families of the town, it was the writer's intention at first to make them much more complete and extensive. But the little interest in the matter manifested by the families concerned, and the great labor and expense involved in compiling any thing like a complete history of the thirty or forty families mentioned, led him to abridge the work, and to give the matter in the form of notes taken chiefly from the town and parish records. The fact that the record of some families is given more fully than that of others, is not owing to any partiality on the author's part, but to the fact that these families interested themselves enough in the matter to furnish the data called for.

By reference to the title-page it will be seen that the modern method of spelling the name of the town—Redding —is adopted rather than the ancient—Reading. Legally, no such town as *Reading* exists in Connecticut, since, both in the act of incorporation and on the probate seal, the name is spelled Redding ; and inquiry elicits the fact that the majority of the citizens prefer the latter method of spelling. It is the opinion of the writer, however, that the original name of the town was Reading, and that if historical precedents are to be followed it should be so named now. In all old documents among the State archives, and in the ancient records of Fairfield (where the name first occurs), the orthography is *Reading.* In the town and society records it is spelled either Redding or Reding, rarely Reading. Rev. Moses Hill, a gentleman well versed in the antiquities of the town, informs me that at the time of its incorporation, in 1767, a meeting was held, at which it was voted that the name of the new town should be Redding ; and the fact that in the original bill incorporating it the name Reading has been crossed out and that of Redding substituted, would seem to point to some such action on the part of the town. I find no entry of any such action, however, in the town records.

The books consulted in the preparation of the volume have been Barber's " Historical Collections of Connecticut," Hollister's " History of Connecticut," De Forrest's " Indians of Connecticut," Teller's " History of Ridgefield," the Congregational Year-Book, and Stevens'

" History of Methodism.'' The author's thanks are due Mr. Lemuel Sanford, our efficient town-clerk, for ready access to the town records, and for many valuable hints and suggestions ; also to Messrs. Thomas Sanford, William E. Duncomb, Daniel Sanford, David S. Bartram, James Sanford, and David H. Miller, for efficient aid in the preparation of the work. He is also indebted to Rev. Moses Hill, of Norwalk, for data of the Hill and Barlow families ; and to Mr. A. B. Hull, of Danbury, for many papers and documents relating to the history of the town.

C. B. T.

REDDING, March 1, 1880.

CONTENTS.

—◆—

PHYSICAL HISTORY.

"READING, 60 miles south-west of Hartford, about 5 miles long by 6½ wide, with an area of 32 square miles. The Saugatuck River crosses it through the middle, north and south ; and the Norwalk River is in the west part. The forest trees are oak, nut trees, etc. Population in 1830, 1686."—*United States Gazetteer*, 1833.

" Like many of the New England villages, it is scattered, and beautifully shaded with elms, maples, and sycamores."—Lossing, *Field-Book of the Revolution.*

" The geological character of the town, as throughout Western Connecticut is *metamorphic.* Granitic and porphyritic rocks, and especially micaceous schists, predominate. The minerals are such as are familiar in such rocks—hornblende, garnet, kyanite, tremolite, etc. In the western part of the town are deposits of magnesian limestone (or dolomite), much of which is quite pure, though some of it contains tremolite and other impurities. The other mineral features of the town are not specially noteworthy, or of general interest. The soil is probably, in the main, the result of the disintegration of the underlying rocks."—*Notes of Rev. John Dickinson.*

HISTORY OF REDDING.

CHAPTER I.

PRELIMINARY SETTLEMENT.

THE history of the early settlement of Redding differs radically from that of any of the neighboring towns. A new settlement was generally formed by a company of men, who purchased of the Indians a tract of land in the wilderness, had it secured to them by a charter from the General Assembly, and also surveyed and regularly laid out, and then removed to it with their wives and families. Danbury, Newtown, and Ridgefield were settled in this manner ; but Redding at the time of its first settlement was a part of the town of Fairfield, and so continued for nearly forty years—a fact which makes it much more difficult to collect the fragments of its early history and to accurately define its original metes and bounds. Fairfield formerly extended to the cross highway leading from the Centre to Redding Ridge, and the entire southerly portion of Redding was given by that town on the erection of the former into a parish in 1729. This portion of Redding was probably surveyed as early as 1640, being included in the purchase made by the proprietors of Fairfield in 1639. Between Fairfield north

2

bounds and the towns of Ridgefield, Danbury, and
Newtown was an oblong tract of unoccupied land,
whose bounds were about the same as those that
now exist between Redding and the towns above
named : this tract was variously called, in the early
records, the " oblong," the " peculiar," and the
" comon lands." It was claimed by a petty tribe
of Indians, whose fortified village was on the high
ridge a short distance south-west of the present residence of Mr. John Read. This tribe consisted of
disaffected members of the Potatucks of Newtown,
and the Paugussetts of Milford, with a few stragglers
from the Mohawks on the west.

Their chief was Chickens Warrups, or Sam Mohawk, as he was sometimes called. President Stiles
says in his " Itinerary" that he was a Mohawk
sagamore, or under-chief, who fled from his tribe
and settled first at Greenfield Hill, but having killed
an Indian there he was again obliged to flee, and
then settled in Redding. All the Indian deeds to
the early settlers were given by Chickens, and
Naseco, who seems to have been a sort of sub-chief.
The chief, Chickens, figures quite prominently in
the early history of Redding ; he seems to have been
a strange mixture of Indian shrewdness, rascality,
and cunning, and was in continual difficulty with
the settlers concerning the deeds which he gave
them. In 1720 he was suspected by the colonists
of an attempt to bring the Mohawks and other
western tribes down upon them, as is proved by the
following curious extract from the records of a
meeting of the governor and council held at New
Haven, September 15th, 1720 :

" It having been represented to this board that an Indian living near Danbury, called Chickens, has lately received two belts of wampumpeag from certain remote Indians—as it is said, to the west of Hudson River—with a message expressing their desire to come and live in this colony, which said messenger is to be conducted by aforesaid Chickens to the Indians at Potatuck, and Wiantenuck, and Poquannuck, in order to obtain their consent for their coming and inhabiting among them ; and that hereupon our frontier towns are under considerable apprehensions of danger from Indians, fearing that the belts have been sent on some bad design :

" *It is Resolved,* That Captain John Sherman, of Woodbury, and Major John Burr, of Fairfield, taking with them Thomas Minor, of Woodbury, or such other interpreter as they shall judge meet, do repair immediately to said Indians at Potatuck and Wiantenuck, and cause the said Chickens, to whom the belts and messengers were sent, to attend them, and to make the best inquiry they can into the truth of said story, and what may be the danger of said message, and as they shall see cause, take proper order that the said Indian with the belts, and the principal or chief of the Potatuck and Wiantenuck Indians, attend the General Court at its next session, to receive such orders as may be useful to direct them in their behavior in relation thereunto ; and that Major Burr return home by way of Danbury, that the inhabitants there and in those western parts may be quieted as to their apprehensions of danger from the Indians, if upon inquiry they find there is no just ground for them."

The first deed or grant of land in the " oblong" within my knowledge was given to Mr. Cyprian Nichols in 1687. This grant, in Secretary Wylly's handwriting, reads as follows :

"*At a General Court held at Hartford, October* 13, 1687.

"This Court grants Mr. Cyprian Nichols two hundred acres of land where he can find it, provided he take it up where it may not prejudice any former grant to any particular person or plantation; and the surveyors of the next plantation are hereby appointed to lay out the same, he paying for it.

"CALEB STANLEY."

Captain Nichols "took up" his grant in that part of the "oblong" which is now Lonetown, as is shown by the following document:

"MARCH 1, A.D. 1711.

"Then laid out ye Grant of two hundred acres of land granted by ye General Court to Capt. Cyprian Nichols, Oct. 13, 1687, as follows, viz., beginning at a great Chestnut tree marked on ye south and west side, and J. R. set upon it, standing at ye south end of Woolf Ridge, a little below Danbury bounds, thence running west one hundred rods to a Walnut tree marked on two sides, then running south one mile to a red oak tree marked, then running east one hundred rods to a black oak tree marked, then running north one mile to the Chestnut tree first mentioned. An heap of stones lying at ye root of each of ye trees. We say then thus laid out by us,

THOMAS HOYT,
DANIEL TAYLOR,
Surveyors of ye Town of Danbury.

"Entered in ye public book of Entrys for Surveys of Land, folio 14, per Hezekiah Wyilys, Secretary, March 21, 1711."

The next two grants in this tract of which we have any record were made, the first, May 7th, 1700, to Mr. Daniel Hilton, and the second October 10th,

1706, to Mr. Richard Hubbell. They were laid out nearly at the same time, and side by side with the preceding grant, as follows :

" MARCH 3RD, A.D. 1711.

" Then laid out ye Grant of two hundred acres of land made by ye General Court to Mr. Daniel Hilton, May 7, 1700, and ye Grant of one hundred acres, granted October 10th, 1706, by ye General Court to Mr. Richard Hubbell, all in one piece as followeth, viz., Beginning at a Walnut tree marked, and J. R. upon it, standing a little way North East from ye Hog Ridge, between Danbury and Fairfield, thence running two hundred and eighty rods northerly to a Red Oak tree marked, on ye West 'side of Stadly Ridge, thence running easterly one hundred and eighty-four rods to the Little River at two Elm Staddles and a Red Oak, marked, thence running Southerly, west of ye river, and bounded upon it, two hundred and eighty rods to a bitter Walnut tree marked, thence running one hundred and sixty rods westerly to the Walnut tree first mentioned, thus and then laid out by us,

THOMAS HOYT,
DANIEL TAYLOR,
Surveyors of the Town of Danbury."

These grants were purchased, probably before they were laid out, by Mr. John Read, one of the earliest actual settlers of Redding. Mr. Read was a gentleman of education, and later became an eminent lawyer in Boston. He was withal something of a wag, as is proven by an Indian deed given him about this time, which he drew up, and which was—what rarely happens—a humorous as well as a legal production.* It reads as follows :

---

* For this paper and several others that follow, I am indebted to Mr. George Read, of Redding, a lineal descendant of Colonel Read.

"Know all men by these crooked Scrawls & Seals, yt. we Chickens, alias Sam Mohawk, & Naseco, do solemnly declare yt. we are owners of yt tract of land called Lonetown, fenced round between Danbury and Fairfield, and Jno. Read, Govr. & Commander in Chief there of, & of the Dominions yr-upon depending, desiring to please us, having plied the foot, and given us three pounds in money, & promised us an house next autumn. In consideration yr' of, we do hereby give and grant to him and his heirs the farm above mentioned, corn appertaining, & further of our free will—motion & soverain pleasure make ye land a manour, Indowing ye land with ye privileges yr of, and create the sd. John Read, Lord Justice and Soverain Pontiff of the same to him and his heirs forever : Witness our crooked marks and borrowed Seals, this seventh day of May, Anno Regni, Anno Dei, Gratia Magna Brittannia, and Regina Decimo Tertio, Anno Dom'r, 1714.

                                                          his
              " CHICKENS, *alias*   ×
                   SAM MOHAWK,   mark.

                                          his
                         NASECO   ×
                                        mark.
Sealed and delivered in presence of
                   his
       WINHAM,   ×
                 mark.
                   his
       LIACUS,   ?
                 crook.
       NATHAN GOLD.
                         her
       MARTHA HARNEY,   ×
                       mark.

"The above mentioned Chickens & Naseco—personally appeared & acknowledged ye above

Instrument yr free act and chearful deed in Fairfield, ye 7th of May, 1714,

> before me.
> N. GOLD,
> *Dept. Govr.*"

About 1723 Captain Samuel Couch of Fairfield appears as a large landholder in Redding, and his operations there seem to have caused the settlers no little uneasiness. The General Court of 1712 had ordered that all the lands lying between Danbury and Fairfield, not taken up by actual settlers, should be sold in Fairfield at public vendue. The land, however, was not sold until the August of 1722, when it was bid off by Captain Couch for himself and Nathan Gold, Esq. No notice of the vendue was given to the settlers at Redding, and when news of the sale reached them they became very much excited and indignant, and Mr. Read at once drew up the following protest and petition, which was signed by the farmers and presented to the next General Court at New Haven. It is noteworthy from the fact that the Quaker system of dates is used.

" At a General Court held at New Haven, 8th, 10th, 1723.

" *To the Honor'ble the General Court:*

" John Read in behalf of himself and the rest of the farmers or proprietors of farms between Danbury and Fairfield, humbly sheweth,

" That the Hon'ble Nathan Gold, Esq., late deceased, and Peter Burr, Esq., as Agents for ye Colony, held a Vandue lately at Fairfield about ye time of ye Superior Courts sitting yr in August last, and sold to Capt. Samuel Couch, who bid for himself and

for s'd Nathan Gold, Esq., all ye land between Fairfield and Danbury not before disposed of for the sum
of —— ——. Yr humble pet'rs conceive the same
ought not to be ratified : because ye same was done so
unexpectedly, and without sufficient notice, none of
us most nearly concerned knew any thing of it : if ye
order of ye General Court had been freshly passed,
ye less notice was need full, but lying ten or twelve
years, sufficient notice was not given, and well considered it cant be good. The inconveniences are in-
tolerable ; the place is now growing to be a village
apace. Ye lands purchased are but ye ——————
over and over for farms.

"The remaining Scraps will be a very lean and
scanty allowance for a comon, and (are) absolutely
necessary to accommodate the place with hiways,
and some strips left on purpose for ye use and ye
surveying of the farms—Several farms interfere
through mistakes and such interfers must be supplied elsewhere ; now in such circumstances it was
never the hard fate of any poor place to have ye
shady Rock at their door, and ye path out of town
or about town sold away from them by ye General
Court. Therefore humbly praying ye Hon'ble
Court to grant ye same to ye proprietors of farms
there in proportion for a common and hiways, or
if the same seem too much, since some persons have
bid a sum for our hiways we pray to buy them at
first hands, and will pay this Hon'ble Court for the
same as much as ye Court shall sett upon, and
remain your honor's most obedient servants.

                              "JNO. READ."

When the matter came before the Court, Mr. Read
produced several witnesses to show that the vendue
was conducted in an unseemly and illegal manner ;
among them Mr. Jonathan Sturges, who deposed as
follows :

" Some of the Company began to bid for s'd land, and some of the Company desired that Mr. Stone who was there present, would pull out his watch and that the time for bidding should be but ten minutes, and the watch was laid down on the table ; for a little time the people bid but slowly ; but when they perceived the ten minutes to be near out, they began to bid very briskly, and when it come to the last minute, the people bid more quickly, and at the last they bid so quick after one another that it was hard to distinguish whose bid it was ; at the very minute the tenth minute ended ; but I, standing near the watch, spoke and said, ' the time is out, and it's Capt. Couch's bid,' but I am certain Thomas Hill bid twenty shillings more.' "

Mr. Read did not succeed in his attempt to have the sale set aside, and the lands were adjudged to the purchasers. Captain Couch seems to have disposed of an interest in a part of his purchase to Thomas Nash, of Fairfield, and in 1723 the two received a joint patent for the same : this patent is a curious and valuable document and is given entire :

" Whereas, the Governor and Company of the English Colony of Connecticut, in General Court assembled at Hartford, the 8th day of May Anno Domini 1712, did order and enact that all those lands (lying within the said Colony) between Danbury on the north, and the towns of Fairfield and Norwalk on the south, should be sold at Public Vendue, and by said act did fully authorize and empower the Honble Nathan Gold and Peter Burr Esq. both of the town of Fairfield aforesaid, to make sale and dispose of the s'd same lands accordingly, and whereas the s'd Nathan Gold and Peter Burr in pursuance and by force and virtue of the aforesaid act, did by their deed in writing, executed in due form

bearing date this first day of May, Anno Domini,
1723, for a valuable sum of money paid by Samuel
Couch and Thomas Nash, both of the town afores'd,
Grant, sell, and convey unto them the s'd Samuel
Couch and Thomas Nash, one hundred acres of s'd
land bounded and butted as follows, that is to say,
lying within six rods of the north bounds line of the
townships afores'd, and on both sides of the road
that leads from Norwalk to Danbury, and lying the
whole length of the one hundred acres formerly
laid out to s'd Thomas Nash and bounded westerly
by the s'd Thomas Nash, and from the north east
corner of s'd Nash, his bound being a black oak
stump, that stands on the land, and a small box
wood tree marked in course, running northerly, sixty
eight degrees, eastwardly thirty two rods to a white
oak staddle, thence South forty three degrees and
thirty minutes, eastwardly fifty rods to a rock, and
stones on the same, that stands on the eastward side
of a brook that runs by the southerly end of
Umpawaug Hill, between the s'd brook and Danbury
road, and from s'd Rock to run North sixty eight
degrees, Eastwardly eighty six rods to a mass of
stones, then South twenty two degrees, Eastwardly,
one hundred and thirteen rods to a white oak sap-
ling, marked, standing on the aforementioned North
bounds line of Fairfield, then by s'd line one
hundred and forty rods up to the South East corner
of s'd Nash, his one hundred acres, Danbury road
being allowed in above measure of six rods wide, and
the hiway by the Township's line of six rods wide,
and whereas the s'd Samuel Couch, and Thomas
Nash, have humbly desired that they may have a
particular grant of s'd Governor and Company made
(by Patent) unto them, their heirs and assigns for
the same land bounded butted and described, under
the seal of the s'd Colony, know ye therefore, that
the Governor and Company of the s'd Colony, in
pursuance, and by virtue of the powers granted unto

them by our late Sovereign Lord, King Charles the
Second of blessed memory, in, and by his Majestie's
letters patent under the great seal of England bearing date the three and twentieth day of April, in the
fourteenth year of his s'd Majestie's Reign, have
given and granted, and by these presents, for them
their heirs and successors do give grant, ratifie, and
confirm unto them the s'd Samuel Couch and Thomas
Nash, their heirs and assigns forever, all the s'd
peice or parcell of land containing one hundred acres
be the same more or less, butted and bounded as
afores'd, and all and singular, the woods, timber,
under woods, lands, waters, brooks, ponds, fishings,
fowlings, mines, minerals and precious stones, upon
or within the s'd piece or parcell of land, here by
granted or mentioned, or intended to be granted as
afores'd, and all and singular, the rights, members,
hereditaments and appurtenances of the same, and
the reversion or reversions. remainder or remainders,
—profits, privileges whatsoever, of and in the s'd
peice or parcell of land or every or any part thereof.
To have and to hold the s'd one hundred acres of
land hereby granted with all and singular, its appurtenances unto them the s'd Samuel Couch and Thomas
Nash, their heirs and assigns to and for their own
proper use, benefit, and behoof from the day of the
date hereof, and from time to time, and at all times
forever here after, as a good, sure, lawful, absolute,
indefeasible estate of Inheritance in Fee simple,
without any condition, limitation, use, or other
thing to alter change, or make void the same. To
be holden of our Sovereign Lord, King George, his
heirs and successors, as of his Majestie's Manor of
East Greenwich, in the county of Kent, in the Kingdom of England, in free and common soccage and
not in cappitee, nor by Knight service ; they yield-
ing and paying therefor to our Sovereign Lord the
King, his heirs and successors forever, only the fifth
part of all the oar of Gold and Silver, which from

time to time, and at all times hereafter shall be got-
ten, had or otherwise obtained ; in lieu of all rents,
services, duties and demands whatsoever according to
charter.   In witness whereof, we the s'd Governor
and Company have caused the Seal of the s'd Colony
to be hereunto affixed, the fourteenth day of May,
Anno George, Magna Brittanniæ &c. Annoque Domini 1723.

G. SALTONSTALL,
Governor.

" By order of the Governor,
        HEZEKIAH WYLLYS,
                Secretary."

Subsequently Captain Couch purchased of the Indians a tract of land lying in Lonetown, contiguous
to the estate of Mr. John Read, and which a few
years later he sold to that gentleman. The deed
was given by Chickens, and some of its provisions
caused considerable trouble to the colonists in later
years. This deed is as follows :

" Know all men whom it may concern that I
Chicken an Indian Saggamore living between Fairfield, Danbury, Ridgefield and Newtown, at a place
called Lonetown in the county of Fairfield in the
Colony of Connecticut, in New England, for and in
consideration of twelve pounds, six shillings, already paid unto me by Samuel Couch of Fairfield,
husbandman, have given, granted, bargained, sold,
confirmed, and firmly made over unto said Samuel
Couch, his heirs and assigns forever, all the lands,
lying, being and situate between the aforesaid towns
of Danbury, Fairfield, Newtown, and Ridgefield,
except what has been by letters patent from the
Governor and Company of this Colony of Connecticut made over unto any person or persons or for
any particular or public use. To have and to hold

unto the said Samuel Couch, and to his heirs and
assigns forever the aforesaid granted and described
lands or unpatented premises, with all the privileges and appurtenances thereunto belonging, or any
manner of way appertaining, affirming myself to be
the true owner, and sole proprietor of said land and
have just, firm, and only right to dispose of the
same. *Reserving in the whole of the same, liberty
for myself and my heirs to hunt, fish and fowl
upon the land and in the waters, and further
reserving for myself, my children, and grand
children and their posterity the use of so much land
by my present dwelling house or wigwam as the
General Assembly of the Colony by themselves or
a Committee indifferently appointed shall judge
necessary for my or their personal improvement,
that is to say my Children, children's children
and posterity,* furthermore I the said Chickens
do covenant, promise, and agree, to and with the
said Samuel Couch, that I the said Chickens, my
heirs, executors, and administrators, the said described lands and bargained premises, unto the said
Samuel Couch his heirs etc. against the claims and
demands of all manner of persons whatever, to warrant and forever by these presents defend. In con-
firmation of the above premises I the said Chickens
set to my hand and seal this 18th day of February
Anno Domini one thousand seven hundred and
twenty four five Annoque Regis. etc."

his

CHICKENS,   ✕   *Saggamore.*

mark

But the proprietors of Redding could not long rest
satisfied with the sale that had placed in the hands
of two men nearly all the unoccupied lands lying in
the " peculiar," and in 1725 made a second and, so
far as appears, unsuccessful attempt to reverse the for-

mer decision of the Court. This attempt took the shape of a petition, and was as follows :

" *To the Honorable the General Court to be holden at Hartford on the Second Thursday of May,* 1725. THE EARNEST PRAYER

Of the inhabitants, and of those that have farms in a certain tract of land lying between Fairfield and Danbury, Newtown and Richfield, with whom the Proprietory of a certain division of Land in Fairfield importunately joins—

" WHEREAS the Honorable General Assembly of this Colony hath in several of their Sessions, been pleased out of their great goodness & generosity to give unto some of your humble Petitioners & to others of them to sell certain Parcells of Land between the aforesaid towns & many of your Petitioners that they might get a comfortable maintenance & thereby be better able to serve their country have removed from their former habitations with great families of Children unto sd Land where we by ye blessing of God on our Industry have (passed) through (the) many difficulties that generally attend such new & Wooden Habitations and have now yet to go through, which are by us insuperable—but reflecting upon your Honor's accustomed Goodness, ready protection, and willing encouragement towards all such that have been under ye like circumstances as we now are, makes us far from despairing of Living like rational Creatures and Christians in a very few years, and under our present Circumstances we have often the neighboring Ministers preaching ye word of God to us, and when your Honors shall be pleased to grant this our earnest & necessary request our number of Inhabitants will immediately be greatly renewed & we soon able to obtain a Minister & give him an honorable support—and that is to grant the vacant land that lies in slips and pieces between ye Land already given and sold to your

Petitioners to lye for a perpetual Comon for ye good
of ye Parish : otherwise your poor Petitioners living
at a great distance from any place where the public
worship of God is attended, must be obliged and
their Posterity after them to be soon as the Hathen
are—without the outward and ordinary means of Sal-
vation, the Thought of which makes us now most
importunately address your Honors with this our
Request making no doubt but yt ye desire your
Honors have & the great care you have always taken
to promote & encourage Religion—will also now be
moved to grant your poor Petitioners their Request,
it being no more than your Honors have often done
even unto every new Plantation, many of which are
not nor never will be comparable unto this. Your
Honors, granting us this our Request, and it will
be as we humbly conceive the most profitable way
for ye good of this Colony to dispose of ye land for
a perpetual comon, for ye good of a Parish than any
other way whatsoever : for a flourishing and large
Parish such as we are assured this will make will
soon pay more into ye Public Treasury than the
whole of the Land would do if it were now to be
sold : and not only so, but your poor Petitioners &
their Posterity preserved from Heathenism & Infidel-
ity : for if your Honors should not grant the Land
for a common for the good of a Parish your poor
Petitioners—the most of us at least, must be shut
within the compass of our own land, & cant possibly get off unless we trespass, or gain the shift yt
the birds of the air have, neither to market nor meeting & we & our Posterity forever unable to have a
settled Minister & your Honors may easily conceive
how greatly disadvantageous to our Temporal Interest, which is so great an act of cruelty and hard-
ship that never yet was experienced from your Honors & your Petitioners humbly beg they may not :
but yt they may be sharers with their neighbors in
your Honor's thoughtful care and regard for them—
" And if your Honors in their Prudence and Wis-

dom shall think it best to sell the aforesaid Land
your Petitioners humbly beg they may have the
first offer of it, who are always ready to give as
much as any shall or will let it lye for a perpetual
Common, & your humble Petitioners beg and most
earnestly desire the Land may not be sold from
their doors or confirmed to any yt pretend they
have bought it : for whatever pretended sale there
has been made thereof already we humbly conceive
that it was not with the proper Power & Legality
that it ought to be confirmed : and as for its being
purchased of the Indian (who both English and Indian acknowledge has a good Indian title to it viz.
Chicken, is by what we can learn by the Indian himself & ye circumstances of, a sligh peice of policy &
we fear Deceit, ye latter of which the Indian constantly affirms it to be, for his design as he saith,
and being well acquainted with him, living many of us
near him have great reason to believe him, was to
sell but a small Quantity, about two or three hundred
acres, but in ye deed ye whole of the land is compre-
hended, which when the Indian heard of it he was
greatly enraged, and your Petitioners humbly beg
yt such a sale may not be confirmed, lest it prove
greatly disadvantageous to this Colony & cause
much bloodshed, as instances of ye like nature have
in all Probability in our neighboring Provinces—

"Your Petitioners most earnestly & heartily beg
that your Honors would think on them & grant them
their request, & your Petitioners as in duty bound
shall ever pray—

JOHN READ,	WILL'M HILL,
THOMAS WILLIAMS,	DAN'LL CROFOOT,
STEPHEN MOREHOUSE,	EBENEZER HULL,
BENJAMIN HAMBLETON,	ASA HALL,
BENJAMIN FRANKLIN,	JOSEPH MEEKER,
MOSES KNAPP,	DAN'L LYON,
NATHAN LYON,	THOMAS HILL,
BENAJAH HALL,	GEORGE HULL.

"And we, ye Proprietors of a certain Division of

Land in Fairfield called ye Longlots most heartily join with your Honor's above Petitioners in their needful Request to you, & as we your humble petitioners being well acquainted with the circumstances of them—they being our Children Friends & Neighbors & concerned greatly for their welfare do earnestly beg that your Honors would consider how melancholy a thing it is, that these poor people should live destitute of the means of grace for want only of your small encouragement which to give them would not only be most certainly very pleasing to Almighty God but would likewise enrich this Colony if a large & Rich Parish will any ways contribute thereto, & as your Petitioners Land runs to & adjoyns to ye aforesaid Vacant Land, We for the good of a Parish, thereby to advantage your above poor Petitioners are willing & very ready to give in Two miles of our land adjoining to the afores'd Vacant Land to be within the Parish ; & are assured if your Honors would grant the afores'd Land to be for a Comon there soon would be a Flourishing Parish ; & being so well acquainted with the Circumstances of the above Petitioners that we cant but earnestly & Pathetically entreat your Honors to grant their Request.

"& your Petitioners as in Duty bound shall ever Pray :"

MOSES DIMON,
JOHN HIDE,
THO. HILL,
CORNELIUS HULL,
ELIZABETH BURR,
JONA STURGIS,
JOHN SMITH,
THAD'S BURR,
ANDREW BURR,
SAMUEL WAKEMAN,
SAMUEL SQUIRES,
EZEKIEL SANFORD,
ROBERT TURNEY, JR.,

JOSEPH WILSON,
JOHN WHEELER,
JOHN STURGES,
JOSEPH WHEELER,
THOMAS SANFORD,
JOHN MOREHOUSE,
JOSEPH ROWLAND,
WILLIAM HILL,
NATHAN GOLD,
JOHN GOLD,
ROBERT SILLIMAN,
DANIEL MOREHOUSE.

3

The settlement of Georgetown seems to have been begun at about the same time as the other portions of the town, though the present village has had but a short existence.

The first settlers in that section seem to have been Benjamin and Isaac Rumsey, one of whom lived in a house that stood in the old orchard east of Aaron Osborne's, and the other near the site of the present homestead of Mr. S. M. Main. As early as 1721 Robert Rumsey, of Fairfield, bought of John Applegate a large tract of land located in what is now the village of Georgetown. In 1724 he willed this land to his three sons, Benjamin, Isaac, and Robert. Benjamin and Isaac were actual settlers on this tract, and the former's estate was inventoried and distributed in 1744.

The earliest settlers located their houses on the three fertile ridges that now form the most striking as well as beautiful features of our landscape. The valleys were avoided, as being literally in the shadow of death from the miasms which they engendered ; the hills, according to the early writers, were open, dry, and fertile, and, being comparatively healthful, were in almost all cases selected as sites for the infant settlements. At that day they were covered, like the valleys, with continuous forests of oak, chestnut, hickory, and other native woods, from which every autumn the Indians removed the underbrush by burning, so that they assumed the appearance of natural parks : Indian paths wound through the forest, often selected with so much engineering skill as to be followed later by the highways of the settlers. There were " long-drawn aisles and fretted vaults" in these verdant temples, nooks of outlook, and open, sunny glades, which were covered with tufts of long coarse grass ; groves of chestnut and hickory afforded shelter to whole colonies of squirrels—black, gray, and red. Other game was abundant. Deer, wild turkeys. water fowl, quail, partridges, an occasional bear, and, in the autumn, immense flocks of wild pigeons darkened the air with their numbers. Panthers were seen rarely ; wolves were abundant, and the otter and beaver fished and builded in the rivers. Both tradition and the written accounts agree in ascribing to the rivers an abundance of fish : Little River is especially mentioned as being the favorite home of the trout, and tradition asserts that scarcely four generations ago they were so abundant in that stream that the Indian boys would scoop them up in the shallows with their hands.

According to tradition, the three first houses in the town were built nearly at the same time. One was in Boston district, where Mr. Noah Lee's house now stands, the second in the centre, on the site of Captain Davis's present residence, and the third in Lonetown, built by Mr. John Read, and which occupied the site of Mr. Aaron Treadwell's present residence. It is related of the lady of the house in the Boston district, that, becoming frightened one day at the conduct of a party of Indians who entered her house bearing an animal unmentionable to ears polite, which they ordered her to cook, she seized her babe, and fled with it two miles through the forest path to her nearest neighbor at the Centre, arriving there safely, though breathless and exhausted. It is fair to assume, however, that erelong neighbors were nearer. Settlers began to flock in from Stratford, Fairfield, and Norwalk ; several families moved here from Ridgefield and Danbury, and the settlement began to assume quite the appearance of a populous community. It is not, however, until 1723 that we get any authentic record of the names of the inhabitants or of their entire number. In that year a petition was presented to the General Court praying that the settlement might be constituted a parish ; and which bears the signatures of twenty-five of the planters or settlers of Redding. This invaluable paper has been preserved in the State Archives at Hartford, and is as follows :

"May 9th, 1723. At a General Court in Hartford.

" *To the Hon'ble the Gov'nr, Assistants and Deputies in Gen'll Court Assembled.*

" To this Hon'ble Court yr hon'rs most humble pet'rs hereunto subscribing, settlers and well wishers to the settlement of a plantation between Fairfield and Danbury, Humbly Shew, That there is a Tract of land lying between Fairfield and Danbury, Ridgefield and Newtown and without all ye claims of the largest pretenders of those towns, containing about two miles wide, north and south, and six miles long East and West, mostly laid out in particular farms, so that when the farms that casually interfere on others are made up, there will not be one hundred acres of any value left in the whole.

" On these farms are one half dozen housen set up, and many more going to be set up, and therefore we humbly conceive it is of great necessity for ye use of them, that are come and coming, and for ye incouragement of others to come, to take some prudent care for the establishment of Divine service in that place. That forasmuch as the distance from this land to Fairfield church measures about fourteen miles or better, that is the part on which will cer-

tainly be most of the inlargement made, and on that
side the bounds of those lands uncertain ; for the
grant of 12 miles from the sea given to Fairfield, as
far as we can learn has never yet been measured, as
it ought long since to have been done. Your hon'rs
pet'rs therefore humbly pray that a Com'tee may
be appointed to measure out the twelve miles granted
to Fairfield from the —— and put the vacant land,
if any shall then appear into the hands of a Com'tee
of ye Court to be dealt out to such as will settle on
and improve the same, at such price as will bear ye
charge of ye Com'tee therein, first laying out a farm
of 200 acres for ye ministry, 200 for a school, and as
much for the first minister that shall settle there,
and annex the whole to the town of Fairfield. Settling the bounds of the parish to comprehend so
much of the west end of ye long lots of Fairfield as
may make it near square at ye discretion of ye
Com'tee upon ye view of it when ye proprietors of
the long lots shall settle their end they may pay
their dues there (if they will not be so good as to
fling up the west end to a public use, which would
doubtless be their private advantage also.

      " Yr hon'rs most humble pet'rs,

NATHAN PICKET,
GERSHOM MOREHOUSE,
JOHN HALL,
FRANCIS HALL,
ROBERT CHAUNCEY,
WOLCOTT CHAUNCEY,
DANIEL ——*
WILLIAM HILL, JR.,
PHILLIP JUDD,
NATHAN ADAMS,
STEPHEN MOREHOUSE,
BENJAMIN FAYERWEATHER,
THOMAS BAILEY,"

THOMAS WILLIAMS,
ASA HALL,
JOSHUA HULL,
DAVID CROFUT,
JNO. READ,
ISAIAH HULL,
MOSES KNAPP,
BENJAMIN STURGES,
SAM'L HALL,
JOHN READ, 2d,
BURGESS HALL,
ISAAC HALL.

* Illegible.

Fairfield, as was to be expected, opposed the petition, and her potent influence defeated the measure, and although it was agitated year by year, it was not until 1729 that the petitioners effected their object, and the little settlement blossomed into the dignity of a parish.

The action of the General Court constituting it a Parish is thus recorded in the Colonial Records, vol. vii. pp. 231-2 :

" Upon the memorial of John Read, in behalf of himself and the rest of the inhabitants of Lonetown, Chestnutt Ridge, and the peculiar between Fairfield and Danbury, shewing to this Assembly, the great difficulty they labor under in attending on the publick worship of God, and the forwardness of the town of Fairfield to encourage them to set up the publick worship of God among themselves, by conceding that two miles of the rear end of their long lots be added to them, in order to the making them a parish, and praying this Assembly that they may be allowed to be a society for the worship of God, with the privileges usually granted to such societies or parishes, and that said society or parish may comprize those lands that lie encirculed betwixt the townships of Fairfield, Danbury, Newtown and Ridgefield, together with the aforesaid two miles of Fairfield long lots ; and that they may have remitted to them their country rate during the pleasure of this Assembly ; and that all the lands aforesaid may be taxed by the order of said Assembly, and that said parish may be annexed to Fairfield, and that it be named *Redding.* This Assembly grants that the said Lonetown, Chestnutt Ridge and the peculiar thereof, be a society or parish by themselves, and to have all the privileges usually granted to societies or parishes, and that said society or parish shall comprize all those lands that lie encirculed betwixt the townships of Fairfield, Danbury, Newtown, and Ridgefield, together with two miles of the rear end of Fairfield long lots. Furthermore this Assembly doth remit to them their country rate for four years, excluding those only who decline to joyn with them for what is prayed for, of being released of country tax ; and that all the laid out, unimproved lands within the limits of said parish be taxed at six shillings a hundred acres per year for four years, and that the money raised thereby be improved for the defraying the ministerial charges among them in that place ; and that said parish be named Redding."

CHAPTER II.

REDDING AS A PARISH.

THE parish history of Redding covers a space of thirty-eight years, and for this period the only materials we have for our history—except a few entries in the records of the colony—are found in the record book of the First Church and Society. These records seem to have been kept with the most pitiless brevity ; only the barest details were set down, and if one desires more than the dry facts of this era, he must draw on his imagination for material. During this period events happened of the greatest moment to the colony. Three of the terrible French and Indian wars occurred, to which Redding contributed her full share of men and money, although Fairfield received the credit. Then there were constant alarms of Indians on the border—there were hunting and exploring parties into the wilderness, under the guidance of the friendly Indians, and the usual incidents of pioneer life ; all of which would have been vastly entertaining to the men of to-day, and which a hundred years ago might have been taken down from the lips of the actors themselves, but which has passed away with them forever. Things spoken vanish, while things written remain, and the unfriendliness to the pen, of the early settlers, has entailed a sad loss upon their descendants. It is evident, however, that this was the busiest period in the history of the town. The men were abroad in the clearings from morn till night, felling the trees, burning, ploughing, sowing, and reaping, or building churches, school-houses, mills, highways, and bridges. The women remained in the rude cottages, preparing the simple food, carding and spinning wool, weaving it into cloth, fashioning the homely garments of linsey-woolsey and homespun, and rearing their large families of rosy, healthful children. This is the picture in the barest outline ; the imagination of the reader will fill it out at pleasure : but, as before said, for our details— acknowledged facts—we must turn to the quaint and musty records of the Society.

The first Society meeting was held June 5th, 1729 —less than a month after the parish was organized. A fuller account of this meeting will be found in the history of the First Church and Society. The three first committee-men of the parish, elected at this meeting, were John Read, George Hull, and Lemuel Sanford. At this time, too, the " places for setting up warnings for Society meetings" were de-

termined on as follows : " In the lane by Ebenezer
Hull, and a Chestnut tree by Mr. John Reads, and
a post set up by Moses Knaps :" These were the first
sign-posts in the town. Ebenezer Hull's house I am
unable to locate. Mr. John Read's house has already been located. Mr. Knap lived probably where
James Kerwick now lives.

The next February a parish rate or tax of 2d.
2 far. on the pound was laid, and John Hull was appointed the first tax-collector ; he received for gathering the rate fourteen shillings. The next year,
February 23d, 1730–1, the rate had risen to 9d. on
the pound, and John Read appears as collector.
The next year, 1732, the first " pound" was built by
Mr. John Read, near his house, and at a Society
meeting held January 25th, 1732, he was appointed
" key-keeper." May 8th, 1732, they petitioned the
General Court to have their north-west corner
bounds settled, Captain Couch bearing the charges.
The same meeting they voted " that there shall be
but one sign-post in this society," and voted that
this sign-post should be by the meeting-house,
which had been built the preceding year on the common. Mr. Hun, the first minister, was settled early
in 1733, and the rates that year rose to the high figure of one shilling on the pound. A very important
entry appears on the records of a meeting held October 17th, 1734, wherein Stephen Burr and Thomas
Williams were appointed a committee to the County
Court to desire the court to choose a committee to
lay out the county road from Chestnut Ridge to
Fairfield town. This road was probably the first
ever laid out through the town, and passed through

Lonetown, the Centre, and Sanford town, and thence nearly direct to Fairfield.

December 10th, 1735.—Stephen Burr was appointed a committee to go to the County Court, and desire them to send a committee to lay out necessary highways in that part of the parish above the long lots.

January 26th, 1737.—" Joseph Sanford and Samuel Sanford were appointed a committee to take charge of the parsonage money belonging to said parish, giving a receipt to said parish, and to let the same at their discretion, and to the best advantage, taking double security in land, and not to let less than fifty pounds to one man, and for no longer time than five years, and said committee shall be accountable to the parish committee for the interest of said money, and also at the period of abovesaid term of five years, for the principal."

December 26th, 1737.—It was " voted to have a parish schole, voted to maintain s'd schole by a parish rate voted that John Read, Joseph Lees, Joseph Sanford, John Hull, Matthew Lion, Stephen Morehouse, and Daniel Lion, shall be a com'tee for s'd schole, also that s'd schole shall be divided into three parts, that is to say, five months in that quarter called the Ridge, and five months in the west side of the parish near the mill, and two months at Lonetown, understanding that the centre of division is the meeting hous, and likewise that Stephen Burr belongs to the west side." Thus was established the first school. Subsequent action of the parish in this direction will be found in the chapter on Schools.

At the above meeting, John Read, Esq., was chosen to represent the society, " to pray for to be relest from paying county rates.'' The action of the General Court on this petition is given in Colonial Records, vol. viii., p. 176, as follows : '' Upon the memorial of the Presbyterian society in the parish of Reading in Fairfield County setting forth to this Assembly their low circumstances, and praying a remission of their country tax : this Assembly do grant unto the said society their country tax for the space of four years next coming.''

It will be remembered that the bill organizing the parish in 1729 exempted it from country rates for four years. In 1733 the Assembly granted them a further release of four years, and also imposed a '' tax of three shillings per one hundred acres, on all unimproved lands laid out in said society ,for the space of four years, to be exclusive of those lands belonging to persons of the episcopal persuasion (who) by our law are discharged from paying taxes for the support of the ministry allowed by the laws of this Colony.''

When the next quadrennium began in 1741, the parish seems to have been on a better financial footing, and no further taxes were remitted. Apropos to the above, it may be remarked that in 1737 the parish rates had risen to 1s. 1d. on the pound. Continuing our extracts from the parish records, we find at a meeting held August 22d, 1738, that '' it was voted to try for town privileges in s'd Society,'' and Stephen Burr was chosen agent '' to see if the town (*i.e.* Fairfield) will consent that s'd Society shall have town privileges.''

This entry gives a hint of the rapid growth of the settlement, and of the energy and enterprise of its inhabitants. There were many reasons why they desired a separation : Fairfield was fourteen miles distant, and the interests of the two were distinct ; then they must go to Fairfield to vote, to pay taxes, and to record deeds and conveyances. They could not even have their necessary highways laid out without the consent of that town ; hence we find them making early and persistent efforts for town privileges, so effectually opposed, however, by the mother town, that it was not until twenty-nine years after that the town was organized.

In this year, 1739, the place for putting up warnings for the society's meetings was changed from Umpawaug to the mill-door. In the vote establishing a school in 1737, reference is made to the mill, and it is evident that it was erected at 'a very early date. The miller and the blacksmith were very necessary artisans in a new settlement, and grants of land were in many cases made to induce them to settle : if such was the fact in Redding no record of it remains. According to tradition, the first miller was Jabez Burr, and the first mill stood on the Saugatuck, near the present dwelling of Stephen Burr, a short distance above where the Nobbs Crook road crosses the stream.

October 1st, 1740, it was voted to try and get liberty to have the north of Redding set off for a town, and in December " to have a pound erected on the highway southwest of Ebenezer Ferry's barn provided he will build it on his own charge," also voted that " Ebenezer Ferry be key keeper of the pound and have the profits of it." This was the second pound erected in the parish, the first being at Mr. John

Read's. In 1741 they again voted to ask the consent of the town, that "we may have town privileges."

No further entries of importance appear until 1746, when Joseph Sanford was appointed agent for the parish to "petition the Superior Court now sitting in Fairfield to appoint a committee to lay out highways through the lands granted to Capt. Couch and Company in s'd parish" (these lands were in Umpawaug). In 1747 a list of the parish officers is given. They were as follows : Lemuel Sanford, selectman ; Adam Clark, constable ; Daniel Meeker, David Knapp, grand-jurymen ; Thomas Taylor, James Gray, James Morgain, Joseph Hawley, Joseph Bradley, Jabez Burr, surveyors of highway ; Ebenezer Couch, Thomas Taylor, listers ; William Burritt, John Mallory, tithing men ; Lieutenant Stephen Burr, Joseph Hawley, fence viewers ; Allen Lee, key-keeper for the pound.

January 23d, 1749, it was voted that "Ephraim Jackson shall procure a copy of the doings of the General Assembly concerning highways in the country in this parish," and at the same time complaint was made against Daniel Deane, the Society's collector for the year previous, for his "mismanagement" in collecting the rate, and it was voted "that the committee shall prosecute him in case he shall not satisfy them." This action seems to have been carried to Mr. Deane at once, for he the next day makes this humble apology :

" REDDING, January 24, 1749.

" *To Mr. Jehu Burr, Mr. Stephen Betts, and Mr. Samuel Sanford, Committee men for said Redding :*

" GENTLEMEN, I understand you have declared

that there is some mismanagement in the rate that I have to gather in the year 1748, and you seem to think that I have done the same, and if you insist upon it, I desire your forgiveness : in so doing you will much oblige your humble servant.

"DANIEL DEANE."

In 1754 the parish again applied for town privileges without success, and again in 1757 with a like result.

The next attempt in 1766 was successful, and the Assembly of 1767 passed the long-desired act of incorporation.

It will be noticed that nothing is said in the records concerning the tribe of Indians inhabiting the parish, but from other sources we learn that quite important changes had taken place among them. Their chief, Chickens, after causing the settlers no little trouble concerning the deeds which he had given them, had been induced in 1749 to remove with most of his tribe to Scattacook, in New Milford, and there were now but a few scattered families remaining in the town. No less than three petitions of Chickens, complaining of the injustice of the settlers, are preserved in the Colonial Records. The first, presented to the General Court of May, 1735, asked that in accordance with the provisions of his deed to Samuel Couch in 1725, the Assembly would appoint a committee to lay out to him, his children, children's children, and their posterity, so much land near his wigwam as they should deem necessary for his and their personal improvement ; and the Assembly appointed such a committee.

No report of the action of this committee is preserved in the archives ; but ten years later, in 1745, Chickens again petitioned the Assembly to appoint a committee to view his lands for the same purpose, and the Assembly appointed such a committee " to repair to and upon said land, and having due regard to said deed of conveyance, with the savings and reservations therein contained, to survey and by proper meets and bounds set out for, and to the use of the memorialist and his children, such and so much of said lands as they shall be of opinion—(on hearing all parties or persons therein concerned) ought to be allowed and set out to said memorialist and his children. The third and last memorial, presented in 1749, is a very interesting document, and is given in full.

" The memorial of Capt. Chicken *alias* Sam. Mohawk of Reading in Fairfield county, shewing to this Assembly that in his deed formerly made to Capt. Samuel Couch, late of Fairfield, deceased, of his land lying between the township of said Fairfield, and Danbury, Ridgefield and Newtown, he had reserved to himself so much of said land as a committee, appointed by this Assembly, should judge should be sufficient for himself, his children and posterity, for their personal improvement, which said reserve has since been set out by proper meets and bounds in two pieces, containing in the whole about one hundred acres as per the surveys thereof may appear, reference thereunto being had : and showing also that John Read Esq. late of Boston deceased, had surveyed, and laid out to him two hundred acres of land by the appointment of this Assembly, at a place called Scattacook bounded as in the survey thereof on record : and also shewing that the land aforesaid, laid out to the said John Read Esq. is much more convenient and advantageous for him, the said Chicken, being

well situated for fishing and hunting, and that he
had made and executed a deed of exchange of his
aforesaid hundred acres, lying in two pieces as aforesaid in the parish of Reading to the said John Read
Esq. and to his heirs, which said deed bears date
October 11th, A.D. 1748, and in consideration thereof
did receive of the said John Read Esq. a deed
bearing date the day aforesaid well executed to him
the said Chicken and to his heirs by his attorney
John Read Esq. of said Reading, being fully authorized thereunto, of the aforesaid two hundred
acres ; praying this Assembly that said deeds, executed as aforesaid, may be allowed of, ratified, and
be admitted as good evidence in the law for conveying and fixing the title to the several pieces of land
aforesaid."

This petition the Assembly granted, and Chickens
and his tribe soon after removed to the reservation
at Scattacook. His grandson, Tom Warrup, however, remained in Redding, as will be more fully related.

CHAPTER III.

TOWN HISTORY.

THE Act of the General Assembly incorporating
the town was as follows :

" AN ACT FOR MAKING AND FORMING THE PARISH
OF REDDING INTO A DISTINCT TOWN BY THEM-
SELVES.

" *Whereas* this Assembly are informed that the
Parish of Redding in the northwesterly part of the
township of Fairfield is very remote from the main
body of that town, and that they are by their situa-

tion almost entirely prevented from attending the
publick meetings of said town, and that they suffer
very great inconveniences thereby, and that for them
any longer to continue as a parish of said Fairfield
is very inconvenient : Therefore,

" Be it enacted by the Governor and Council and
Representatives in General Court assembled and by
the authority of the same, That said Parish of Redding be and they are hereby erected, made and constituted within the limits and bounds of said parish
a distinct Town by themselves with all the liberties,
privileges and immunities which by law the other
towns in this Colony have and do enjoy, and that
said new constituted town shall hereafter be called
by the name of the Town of *Redding*, with this limitation and restriction, that but one Representative
which said new constituted town shall at any time
chuse to attend the General Assemblies shall be at
the publick expence.

" And be it further enacted by the authority aforesaid, That said Town of Redding shall have and
hold their first Town Meeting for the choice of their
town officers for the present year some time in the
month of June next, which meeting shall be warned
by a warrant signed by any justice of the peace in
the county of Fairfield, to be directed to some in-
different person to serve, which warrant shall appoint the time and place at which said meeting is to
be held, and shall be served at least five days before
the day appointed for the holding said meeting."

It was passed at the May session, 1767, and a
meeting was held, June 15th, 1767, in accordance with
its provisions. Colonel John Read was chosen Moderator. Lieutenant Stephen Mead was chosen clerk
for the year, and the following town officers elected.
Stephen Mead, Ephraim Jackson, Daniel Hill, selectmen ; David Lyon, Asahel Fitch, Daniel Hull, con-

4

stables ; Benjamin Hamilton, Zalmon Read, fence
viewers ; Peter Fairchild, Lemuel Sanford, Jr.,
David Jackson, listers ; Thomas Fairchild, Jonathan Couch, grand-jurymen ; Gurdon Merchant,
town treasurer ; Paul Bartram, Thomas Fairchild,
Eleazer Smith, Jr., tithing-men ; Ebenezer Williams, Ebenezer Couch, pound keepers ; Gershom
Morehouse, sealer of leather ; Benjamin Meeker,
Jonathan Mallory, sealer of weights ; Ephraim
Jackson, Captain Henry Lyon, and Gurdon Merchant, a committee to take all proper and lawful
methods to clear the highways. The town by vote
made the pound by Elizabeth Sanford's the "Town
pound," and voted " to use the school house by the
old meeting house for ye place for holding ye town
meetings in ye future." The second town meeting
was held September 28th, the same year, at which
" it was voted and agreed that whereas the people
being within one mile of the Southeasterly end of
this Township, and in the Northwesterly end of the
town of Fairfield, are about to petition the General
Assembly to be held at New Haven in October next,
to be annexed to this town, we are willing and desirous to receive them, and that we will assist them
to endeavor to have them annexed to this town by
appointing an agent for that purpose," and Colonel
Read was appointed such agent. Shortly after they
began agitating the question of building a town-
house, and in November a meeting was called to
provide " for the building or purchase of a Town
house and pound. The first mention of a turnpike
in the town is found in the records of a town meeting held in 1768, wherein the Highway Committee

are instructed " to lay out a road from the School-
house in Lonetown, so called, east, through Col.
John Read's land to consort with a highway lately
laid out from the road that leads from Danbury to
Fairfield, west, through Andrew Fairchild's land, to
s'd read's land," and Colonel Read was given liberty
to keep a gate at the west end by the school-house,
" he having given land to the town." The same
year the town offered a bounty of 3s. on every
" wile cat" killed, and of 2s. for every grown fox,
and 1s. for every young fox. A meeting held September 20th, 1768, appointed a committee to act with
a committee of the Superior Court to lay out a highway in Redding from west to east, in rear of the
long lots. This will be recognized as the road leading from Boston District to Hopewell, though portions of it must have been in use long ere this. In
the records of a meeting held October 6th, 1768, we
find a striking example of the towering ambition
of the town fathers : this meeting appointed a committee to " present a memorial to the General Assembly, praying that Redding be made a *County
town.*" December 26th, 1768, the selectmen were instructed to " set the districts for the law books belonging to this town, and to enter the names of
those persons in each district that hath a right by
law to said books, in said books."

Several highways were laid out during this year,
and the next : one across Sturgis' long lot, beginning
at the upright highway above Ebenezer Andrus'
barn, " to run southerly slanting down in some suitable way until it comes to the cross highway Southeasterly from said barn." The county road from

Danbury to Fairfield, originally laid out six rods wide, was reduced to four rods, and Stephen Mead, Gurdon Merchant, and Lemuel Sanford were appointed a committee "to lay out the County road, four rods wide, exchanging where it shall be thought necessary, and all at the Proprietor's cost." A highway was also laid out from Samuel Smith's, southerly to the bridge below Daniel Perry's gristmill.

The following interesting entry appears in the records of a meeting held March 6th, 1771 : "Voted and agreed, that whereas a Plan hath been proposed of moving to the General Assembly in May next for the erecting a new county, to consist of the towns of Danbury, Newtown, Ridgefield, Redding, and New Fairfield, we are willing and desirous that said towns shall be erected a county, and that we will assist them to endeavor to have said county established." The committee appointed for this purpose were David Lyon, Gershom Morehouse, and James Rogers.

In October, 1773, the General Assembly passed a resolution, "to assert, and in some proper way support their claim to those lands contained within the limits and bounds of the charter of this Colony westward of the Province of New York"—an act strongly disapproved by the people at large.

Town meetings were called to protest against it, and a convention comprising delegates from twenty-three towns met in Middletown, and adopted a petition and remonstrance to the General Assembly against the proposed action.

Redding's attitude in the matter is shown by the

following extract from the doings of a town meeting held March 14th, 1774 : '' Whereas it is the opinion of many of the freemen and other inhabitants of this Colony (and of this meeting in particular) that if ye abovesaid Resolve be carried into execution it will inevitably involve the inhabitants of Connecticut in a long, expensive, and fruitless Litigation with Mr. Penn, therefore this meeting appoints and delegates Messrs. William Hawley and Peter Fairchild to attend a meeting to be held at Middletown on the last Wednesday of Instant March, to concert some Proper Methods in order to put a stop to so disagreeable a procedure.'' But the project of the Assembly was never carried into execution : within a few months an invading army was hovering about its coasts, and the sturdy, belligerent little Colony found other vents for its pugnacious spirit.

In the Revolutionary War, to which period we are now come, Redding played an important part : her people were fully alive to the importance and direfulness of the conflict, and bore their full share of the burdens it imposed ; but the town records during this period refer but rarely, and then briefly, to the great conflict.

The first action of the town in regard to the war is found in the records of a town meeting held April 2d, 1777, when a committee consisting of Messrs William Hawley, Zalmon Read, Thaddeus Benedict, David Jackson, Gershom Morehouse, Stephen Betts, Jr., William Heron, and Daniel Mallory was appointed '' to hire a number of Soldiers to serve in the Continental army.'' It was also voted that the '' sum or sums the said Committee promise to, or do pay, to those soldiers that do enlist themselves as soldiers to serve in said army, as a bounty over and above what the Government bounty is, shall be paid by way of town rates, and the Selectmen are ordered and desired to make a rate to collect the money.'' In the records of the same meeting is the following significant entry : '' Hezekiah Sanford, Seth Sanford, Daniel Mallory, S. Samuel Smith, William Hawley, Stephen Betts Jr. Jonathan Couch, Stephen Gold, and Hezekiah Read, are appointed a committee to take care of the families of those soldiers that are in the service of their country ;'' and this also, under date of May 5th, 1777 : '' David Jackson, Seth Sanford, Thaddeus Benedict and John Gray are chosen Selectmen in addition to, and to supply the place of Stephen Betts and James Rogers taken prisoners by the enemy in their expedition to Danbury.''

The above-named gentlemen were released when the British re-embarked at Norwalk. September 18th, 1777, it was voted '' that the injunction or request from his Excellency the Governor and the Council of Safety be complied with, and that the Committee procure and get double the articles if they can, mentioned in the Governor's said request, and that said Committee be paid by the town, the extra charges that the said articles may cost more than they are set at in said request.'' March 23, 1778, David Jackson, Zalmon Read, and Ephraim Robbins were appointed a committee to provide clothing for the army. May 8th, 1778, Asahel Fitch appears as committee, '' to take care and provide as the law directs for Nathan Coley's family.'' At the same time he, with Capt. Zalmon Read,

was appointed a committee to provide " shirts, shoes,
stockins and other articles of clothing for the Continental soldiers." December 17th, 1778, another
committee was appointed to care for the families of
soldiers as follows : Nehemiah Hull, for Nathan
Colcy's ; Elijah Burr for Stephen Meeker's ; Ebenezer Couch for Elias Bixby ; Nehemiah Sherwood
and John Read for Jeremiah Ryan, and William
Hawley for Samuel Remong. July 30th, 1779, Micayah Starr, Thaddeus Benedict, and Stephen Betts
were appointed a committee to prepare clothing for
the soldiers, and a tax of 2s. on the pound was levied to pay for the same. Several of the records are
very annoying from their incompleteness ; the following for instance of a meeting held September 2d,
1779 : " Voted, to ratify the proceedings of the
County Convention held Aug. 10th, 1779, and to appoint a Committee to carry into effect what was recommended in the first resolve of said Convention."
Not a word is said as to the object of the Convention, nor is any report of its proceedings given.
From other sources, however, we learn that it was
called to devise measures to prevent further depreci-
ation of the paper currency, and also to consider
what course should be pursued in dealing with the
Tories among them.

No record of the proceedings of this convention,
interesting and important as it would have been, is
found. It was held at the dwelling-house of Captain Stephen Betts, on Redding Ridge. January
23d, 1780, the town voted to appoint a committee
of nine " to procure and hire nine soldiers to enlist
into the Connecticut Line in the Continental army,

for the town of Redding." This committee consisted
of Stephen Betts, Ezekiel Sanford, David Jackson,
Nathaniel Barlow—brother of the poet—Asahel
Fitch, Hezekiah Read, Elijah Burr, Ephraim Robbins,
and Hezekiah Sanford. The committee were also instructed " to use their utmost diligence to hire nine
able bodied efficient men to enlist as aforesaid, during the war or for three years, or six months, and
that they enlist them at such sum or sums of money
in any price, or such quantity of provisions of any
kind as they shall judge reasonable and just." Six
months later, June 26th, they voted to instruct their
committee to give to each soldier they enlist for six
months, ten bushels of wheat per month or the
value in hard money when paid, besides they shall
receive the bounty the state offers, but the town
shall receive their wages." The same offer was made
to the drafted men. This course was probably
taken in the belief that the town could more readily
collect the wages of the soldiers than they could
themselves.

November 20th, same year, it was voted, " that
the town will lay a tax on provisions to supply their
quota of provisions for the Connecticut Line in the
Continental Army, and that a rate bill be made ap-
portioning to each individual his proportion of each
kind of provision to be raised, viz. flour, beef, and
pork, according to his list for the year 1779. George
Perry was appointed Receiver of the flour collected
by the town, and sworn to a faithful discharge of his
trust. Russell Bartlett was appointed Receiver of
pork and beef, and was also sworn. At the same
meeting a committee was appointed " to repair to

the camp and ascertain the number of soldiers of the
town now in camp." This order was several times
repeated, but none of the reports of the committees
are preserved. The following significant entry appears in the records of a meeting held February 5th,
1781 : " Voted not to abate assessments for purposes
aforesaid (*i.e.* tax, on provisions) on Enos Lee, James
Morgan, Hezekiah Platt, Daniel Lyon, Abigail
Lyon, Sarah Phinney, David Knapp, James Gray,
Abigail Morehouse, Ezekiel Hill, Andrew Fairchild,
and Sarah Burr, who have each of them a son or
sons, or a son or sons in law gone over to the enemies of the United States." At this meeting several
who had refused to pay the tax levied for hiring soldiers were assessed double rates. March 28th, 1781,
Captain Gershom Morehouse and Lieutenant Nehemiah Hull were appointed a committee " to collect
the tents belonging to this town"—probably those
furnished for the winter encampment of the troops ;
at the same time a committee was appointed " to
vindicate our claims to the Connecticut Soldiers."
April 16, 1781, it was voted " to divide the people
into eight classes according to their several lists in
order to raise seven soldiers, and one Light Horseman to serve for one year as coast guards." It was
voted " that the sixth class (for procuring men to
serve in the guards at Horse Neck till ye first of
March next) shall procure a light horseman and
horse, and that the town shall pay said class all it
shall cost them more to procure a man and horse,
than it shall cost the other seven classes on a
medium."

July 5th, same year, a tax of three pence on the

pound was laid " to pay last year's six months men, to be paid in Silver, or Gold, or wheat at six shillings a bushel, and to be collected and paid to the selectmen before the 10th of July Inst."

The next fall, October 30th, 1781, George Perry was chosen " Receiver of Grain and flour on the half crown Tax, Benjamin Meeker and Isaac Meeker to receive the grain and flour on the two sixths tax, and William Hawley Esq. to receive the Beef and Pork on said tax, and to provide casks and salt said provisions as the law directs."

The last entry referring to the war appears August 11th, 1783, some nine months after the Provisional Articles of Peace had been signed at Paris. It is as follows : " Voted that the select men of this town be desired to move out of this town all those persons that have been over and joined the enemy, and have returned into this town, and that they pursue the business as fast as they conveniently can according to law." The selectmen on whom this task devolved were, Seth Sanford, James Rogers, Stephen Betts, Hezekiah Sanford, and John Gray.

Several items that next follow are important as denoting the progress of events. December 18th, 1781 : " Voted, that the select men be instructed to petition the General Assembly to annex this town to Danbury Probate District," and the road committee was instructed to sell the highway from Nobb's Crook to Captain Grays, and also the " upright highway" west of Micayah Starr's, from Nathan Rumsey's to the rear of the long lots.

August 9, 1782, the town appointed delegates to a County Convention held in Greenfield " to inquire into the progress of illicit trade :" also a Committee of Inspection to assist the informing officers in putting the laws into execution.

August 11th, 1783 : It was voted " that the town will set up a singing school," and a tax of one penny on the pound was laid to pay the singing master.

March 13th, 1797 : " Voted not to admit Small Pox by innoculation ; voted to admit Small Pox by innoculation next fall."

December 14th, 1791, a committee was appointed to apply to the proprietors of the mile of commons for a title to the land in Redding left by said proprietors for a parade." (This " parade," familiar to all old inhabitants of Redding, was in the large field adjoining the Congregational parsonage now owned by Mr. Joseph Squires ; it was the scene of many militia trainings in later days.)

December 19th, 1792 : " Voted to reduce the highway from Danbury to Norwalk to four rods wide, and to sell two rods." In 1795 : " Voted that the selectmen prosecute those persons that cut timber on the highways."

The first town-house was built early in 1798. It stood nearly in the centre of the common, a few yards west of the present building.

From the plan submitted December 27th, 1797, by the building committee, we learn that it was " 36 feet in length, and 30 feet wide, with 12 foot posts, covered with long cedar shingles, the sides with pine." There was a chimney in each end, and fifteen windows with twenty lights in each. Peter Sanford, Ezekiel Sanford, Samuel Jarvis, Aaron Sanford, Andrew L. Hill, and Simon Munger were appointed

" to receive proposals and contract for building the aforesaid Town House." The builder was Daniel Perry. In 1807 there was a movement to petition the General Assembly, " that Redding be made the shire town of Fairfield County." In 1809 it was voted unanimously," That we will prefer a petition to the Congress of the United States for the establishment of a Post Road through this town," and William Heron, Lemuel Sanford, and Billy Comstock were appointed to draft the petition. This was successful, and the first post-office in the town was shortly after established. It was kept in the dwelling-house of Billy Comstock, who was the first postmaster ; his house stood where Mr. Dimon Finch now lives, at the fork of the Danbury road, and that leading to Redding Centre, *viâ* Nobb's Crook. There are old people in town who remember this first post-office, and the excitement attendant upon the arrival of the weekly mail, carried by the great lumbering Danbury stage, which, with its four horses, its red-faced driver, and crowd of dusty, sweltering passengers, was the great tri-weekly event of the villages through which it passed.

There is evidence that in early times the town exercised considerable influence in public affairs. In the *Farmer's Journal* (Danbury) for April 8th, 1793, appears a circular letter " sent by a committee appointed to correspond with the different towns in the county of Fairfield," from Reading, as follows :

" READING, Apr. 2, 1793.

" GENTLEMEN : We are, by the inhabitants of this town, in a town meeting legally warned for that purpose, appointed a committee to correspond with the other towns in Fairfield County respecting the list of persons entered on the records of Congress, a number of whom this town apprehend are really undeserving. We are ordered to ask of you to adopt a similar mode of appointing a committee to correspond accordingly, and if by due enquiry any person, or persons shall be found to be put on the pension list, who are undeserving, to adopt proper means for redress at a proper board.

Signed :

THADDEUS BENEDICT,
WILLIAM HERON,
LEMUEL SANFORD,
S. SAMUEL SMITH,
JAMES ROGERS.

To the Selectmen of———

And in the *Farmer's Chronicle* (Danbury) for January 6th, 1794 :

" At a Town Meeting held in Reading, by adjournment, on the 23rd day of December A.D. 1793, " Voted unanimously, That this Town will exert ourselves in every legal and constitutional method in our power to prevent the sale of the western lands at present, and to obtain a repeal of the act of this state appropriating the avails thereof for the support of the ministry and schools in this state, as we conceive the same to be impolitic. And that a committee be appointed to correspond with the other towns in this county to effect the purpose aforesaid, and that this vote be sent to the committee appointed to sell those lands, with our request that they will omit to make any contract or sale of them till the sitting of the next General Assembly."

And in the records of a town meeting held April 20th, 1818 :

" Voted, That our Representatives to the General Assembly to be holden at Hartford in May next, be, and hereby are, instructed to use their influence that measures be taken preparatory to forming a written constitution for the Government of this State. That it is the opinion of this meeting, that the State of Connecticut is without a written constitution of Civil Government, and we believe it very important for the security of the Civil, and Religious rights, and privileges of the Citizens, that the powers and authorities of the Government should be distinctly defined.''

The present town-house was erected in 1834. At a town meeting held March 3d, 1834, Mr. Thomas B. Fanton made a proposition '' that he would engage to build a new Town House, same dimensions as the old one, of. good materials, covering to be of pine, with shutters to the windows, outside of house to be painted, and the whole inside and out, to be finished in a workman like manner, to be erected near the old one, on land belonging to the town, provided the town will give him $400, and the old house,'' and engaged to save the town from any expense on account of materials provided by the committee to repair the old town house. This proposition was accepted, and John R. Hill, Gershom Sherwood, and Aaron Burr, 2d, were appointed a committee '' to superintend building said House.'' There were objections, however, to having the new house built on the old site, and a meeting held shortly after voted '' to relocate the house in the building owned by Thaddeus M. Abbott recently occupied for a school house.''

But other parties objected to this plan, and a third meeting was held before a site satisfactory to all parties could be agreed on.

This meeting voted to locate it " on the Southeast corner of Thaddeus M. Abbott's homelot, fronting the public parade on the South, and on the west the Lonetown highway, provided that nothing in this vote interferes with the contract made with Thomas B. Fanton for building said house, and that it be no additional expense to the town." The building belonging to Mr. Abbott which stood on this site was moved away, and the present townhouse erected in the summer of 1834.

From this point until the opening of the civil war the records indicate only the usual routine of town business, and may be profitably passed over in order to make room for the valuable and interesting Revolutionary history of the town.

CHAPTER IV.

REVOLUTIONARY HISTORY AND INCIDENTS.

Two years had passed since the opening of the War of Independence—years of alternate victory and defeat to the colonists—when a hostile armament of twenty-five vessels bearing two thousand men, the flower of the British army, appeared off Compo, in Westport, on the Connecticut shore. It was the 26th of April, 1777. A few days before, news had come to Lord Howe, commanding in New York, that a magazine of munitions of war had been formed by the rebels in Danbury, and which afforded him a pretext for a descent on Connecticut —a step which he had long meditated. The region of country covered by the proposed campaign had been swept of its able-bodied men, who were in the Continental ranks keeping a careful watch on his lordship's regulars ; but that there might be no balk in the operations, an overwhelming force of two thousand picked men was detailed for the expedition. For commanders, Howe chose a nondescript genius, one Governor Tryon, and two military men of ability, General Agnew and Sir William Erskine. Tryon had been Governor of New York ; he had the further merit of being intimately acquainted with Connecticut, and of being consumed with an inveterate hatred for, and thirst for revenge on, the Yankees ; he had a special grudge too against Connecticut, the sturdy little colony having thwarted him in a variety of ways. Her dragoons had scattered the types of his newspaper organ through the streets of New York ; her "Sons of Liberty" had plotted against him even in his own city, and she had treated with contempt his proclamations, inviting her to return to her allegiance, even printing them in her gazettes as specimens of the governor's pleasant humor.

Furthermore, he was well acquainted with the country to be traversed. He had been as far inland as Litchfield, had probably visited Danbury, and had been dined and fêted at Norwalk, Fairfield, and New Haven. He seems to have acted as guide to the expedition while his two advisers attended to its military details. The troops disembarked at Compo at four in the afternoon, and the same day marched to Weston, about eight miles distant, where they encamped for the night. To oppose these troops there was only a militia corps of old men and boys, not equal in number to one half the invading force.

Colonel Cook was in command at Danbury with a company of unarmed militia. General Silliman at Fairfield, General Wooster at Stratford, and General Arnold at Norwalk could not muster, all told, more than eight hundred raw, undisciplined men. Under these circumstances Tryon's expedition can only be viewed as a picnic excursion into the country, and as such no doubt he regarded it. Cn the morning of the 26th his army was early astir, and reached Redding Ridge, where the first halt was made, about the time that the inhabitants had concluded their morning meal. What transpired here is thus narrated by Mr. Hollister in his admirable " History of Connecticut," vol. ii., chap. 12:

" On the morning of the 26th, at a very seasonable hour, Tryon arrived at Reading Ridge, where was a small hamlet of peaceful inhabitants, almost every one of them patriots, and most of them farmers, who had crowned the high hill, where they had chosen to build their Zion, with a tall, gaunt church, which drew to its aisles one day in seven the people that dwelt upon the sides of the hills, and in the bosom of the valleys, within the range of the summons that sounded from its belfry. By way of satisfying his hunger with a morning lunch, until he could provide a more substantial meal, he drew up his artillery in front of the weather-beaten edifice that had before defied every thing save the grace of God, and the supplications of his worshippers, and gave it a good round of grape and canister, that pierced its sides through, and shattered its small-paned windows into fragments. The only spectators to this heroic demonstration were a few women and

little children, some of whom ran away at the sight
of the red-coats, and others faced the invaders with
a menacing stare.''

Mr. Hollister is in the main a careful and accurate
historian, but a due regard for the truth of history
compels us to say that he was misinformed in regard
to the above facts. The following account is believed to be correct, our principal informant being
an aged inhabitant of Redding, and a competent
authority :

During the halt the main body of the troops remained under arms on the green in front of the
church. Tryon, Agnew, and Erskine were invited
into Esquire Heron's, who lived in the first house
south of the church, and which is still standing,
though in a ruinous condition. Here they were hos-
pitably entertained with cake and wine, and with
many hopeful prognostications of the speedy col-
lapse of the '' rebellion.'' Across the street from
the church, in a house a few yards south of the one
now occupied by Thomas Ryan, lived Lieutenant
Stephen Betts, a prominent patriot, and at whose
house it will be remembered the county convention
was held in 1779. A file of soldiers entered the
house, seized him, and he was taken with them on
their march. James Rogers, another prominent
patriot, and Jeremiah Sanford, a lad of ten years,
son of Mr. Daniel Sanford, met a like fate. The
lad, we may remark, was carried to New York and
died in the prison ships, June 28th, 1777. Shortly
before the army resumed its march, a horseman was
observed spurring rapidly down the Couch's Hill
road toward them, and approached within musket-

shot before discovering their presence ; he then
turned to fly, but was shot, and severely wounded
in the attempt. He proved to be a messenger from
Colonel Cook in Danbury, bearing dispatches to
General Silliman, by name Lambert Lockwood.
Tryon had formerly known him in Norwalk, where
Lockwood had rendered him a service, and seems to
have acted on this occasion with some approach to
magnanimity, as he released him on parole, and
allowed him to be taken into a house that his
wounds might be dressed.

The statement concerning the firing into the
church is a mistake, and I am assured that the reverse is true. It is said that the church was not molested at all (except that a soldier with a well-di-
rected ball brought down the gilded weathercock
from the spire), and the fact that the pastor, the
Rev. John Beach, as well as several of its most
prominent members, among them the Squire Heron
above referred to, were most pronounced loyalists,
strengthens the assertion.

The British army, after halting an hour or two in
the village, resumed its march to Danbury, with the
capture and burning of which the reader is no doubt
acquainted.

Meanwhile the patriots in Redding anxiously
waited the approach of the Continental army in
pursuit. At length it came in view, marching
wearily, with dusty and disordered ranks, a little army of five hundred men and boys, led by
Brigadier-General Silliman in person. They had
marched from Fairfield that day, and were fully
twenty-eight hours behind the foe, who was then ly-

ing drunken and disorganized at Danbury. A muster-roll of the little band would have shown a most pathetic exhibition of weakness. There were parts of the companies of Colonel Lamb's battalion of artillery, with three rusty cannon, a field-piece, and part of the artillery company of Fairfield, and sixty Continentals; the rest were raw levies, chiefly old men and boys. It was eight o'clock in the evening when the troops arrived at Redding Ridge—an evening as disagreeable as a north-east rain-storm with its attendant darkness could make it. Here the troops halted an hour for rest and refreshment. At the expiration of that time a bugle sounded far down the street; then the tramp of horsemen was heard, and presently Major-General Wooster and Brigadier-General Arnold, at the head of a squadron of cavalry, dashed into the village.

On hearing that the British were so far ahead, it is said that Arnold became so enraged that he could scarcely keep his seat, and his terrible oaths fell on his auditors' ears like thunder-claps. Wooster at once assumed command, and the column moved forward through the mud as far as Bethel, where it halted for the night. At Danbury, but three miles distant, Tryon's force was sleeping in drunken security, and might have been annihilated by a determined effort, but the command was too much exhausted for the attempt.

Tryon the next morning was early astir, being aware that the militia were closing in on him on all sides, and commenced a retreat to his ships, taking the circuitous route through Ridgefield. On learning this move, General Wooster at Bethel divided his command, one detachment under Generals Arnold and Silliman marching rapidly across the country and taking post at Ridgefield, while the other, commanded by himself, pressed closely on Tryon's rear. The succeeding fortunes of the patriots—how they met the foe at Ridgefield, how Wooster fell gallantly leading on his men, how Arnold performed prodigies of valor, and how the enemy were pursued and harassed until they gained the cover of their ships—has become a part of our national history, and needs no recounting.

News that the British had landed at Compo, that they were encamped at Weston, and would march through Redding the next day, was conveyed to this town at an early hour, and occasioned the greatest consternation and excitement.

Money and valuables were hastily secreted in wells and other places of concealment ; horses and cattle were driven into the forests, and the inhabitants along the enemy's probable route held themselves in readiness for instant flight. Herod's emissaries could not have excited livelier emotions of terror in the hearts of Judean mothers than did Tryon's invasion in the breasts of the mothers of Redding. He seems to have warred pre-eminently on women and boys. The latter especially he made prisoners of, and consigned to the horrible prison-ships, either holding them as hostages, or on the plea that they " would very soon grow into rebels." The women of Redding had heard of this propensity, and at his approach gathered all the boys of thirteen and under—the older ones were away under arms—and conveyed them to a secluded place near the Forge, where they were left under the charge of one Gershom Barlow ; here they remained until the invader had regained his ships, provisions being cooked and sent in to them daily.

Many other incidents of the invasion are current in the town.

On receiving intelligence of the landing at Compo, Captain Read mustered his company of militia, and forthwith marched to intercept the invaders. At a place called Couch's Rock, in Weston, they came suddenly upon the entire force of the enemy and were taken prisoners. Timothy Parsons, one of the militiamen, had a fine musket which he particularly valued ; this a grenadier took, and dashed to pieces on the stones, saying it should waste no more rebel bullets.

Mrs. Thankful Bradley, living in Weston, near the Redding line, was milking by the roadside when the troops surprised her. An officer told her to remain quiet, and they would not molest her. She followed his advice and continued milking while the entire army filed by. With the exception of kidnapping the lad Sanford, the British behaved with praise-worthy moderation during their march through Redding. No buildings were burned, and no such enormities committed as marked their descent on Fairfield and New Haven two years later.

After their departure nothing further of a warlike nature occurred in the town, until the encampment in Redding in the winter of 1778-9 of General Putnam's division of the Continental Army. This division comprised General Poor's brigade of New Hampshire troops, the two brigades of Connecticut troops, the corps of infantry commanded by Hazen,

and that of cavalry by Sheldon. This division
had been operating along the Hudson during the
fall, and as winter approached it was decided that it
should go into winter quarters at Redding, as from
this position it could support the important fort-
ress of West Point in case of attack, overawe
the Cow Boys and Skinners of Westchester
County, and cover the country adjacent to the
Sound. Accordingly, early in November, General
Putnam arrived with several of his general officers
to select sites for the proposed camps. Three were
marked out : the first in the north-eastern part of
Lonetown, near the Bethel line, on land now owned
by Aaron Treadwell. The second also in Lonetown,
about a mile and a half west, on the farm of the late
Sherlock Todd, a short distance south-west of his
dwelling-house. The third camp was in West Redding, on the ridge lying east of Uriah Griffin's, on
land now owned by him, and about a quarter of a
mile north of Redding Station. The sites of all
three camps may be easily distinguished by the ruins
of the stone chimneys which formed one side of the
log huts in which the troops were sheltered. The
ruins of the first camp are most distinct, and form
perhaps one of the best preserved, as well as most
interesting, relics of the Revolution within the reach
of the antiquary. This camp was laid out with admirable judgment, at the foot of the rocky bluffs which
fence in on the west the valley of the Little River.
The barracks were so disposed as to form an avenue
nearly a quarter of a mile in length, and several
yards in width. At the west end of the camp was a
mountain brook, which furnished a plentiful supply

of water ; near the brook is a heap of cinders which probably marks the spot where a forge was erected. The camp was until recently covered with heavy forests, which explains perhaps the secret of its preservation. The present owner is clearing up the underbrush which has overgrown the ruins, rendering it easy of access to visitors, and it will in time no doubt become a favorite place of resort. Only a few heaps of stone mark the site of the second camp, which was also laid out on the southerly slope of a hill, with a stream of running water at its base. The same may be said of the camp at Long Ridge.

As to the exact location of Putnam's headquarters at this time, authorities differ, but all agree in placing it on Umpawaug Hill. Mr. Barber, in his " Historical Collections," says it was the old house that stood until recently on the corner of the road leading down to Sanford's Station, a short distance north of Andrew Perry's present residence. Mr. Lossing, in his " Field Book of the Revolution," makes the same statement ; but I am informed by an aged resident, whose father was an officer in the Revolutionary army, and visited General Putnam at his headquarters, that they were in an old house that then stood between the residence of the late Burr Meeker and that now occupied by Mr. Brady, and that the first-named was his guard-house. The question is one of little importance perhaps, except to those who demand the utmost possible accuracy in the statement of fact.

Some of the officers were quartered in the house now occupied by Seth Todd, then owned by Samuel Gould ; others in a house that stood on the site of the one recently occupied by Sherlock Todd. General Parson's headquarters were on Redding Ridge.

While the army lay at Redding several events of importance occurred, which are worthy of narrating with some degree of particularity. The troops went into winter quarters this year in no pleasant humor, and almost in the spirit of insubordination. This was peculiarly the case with the Connecticut troops. They had endured privations that many men would have sunk under—the horrors of battle, the weariness of the march, cold, hunger, and nakedness. What was worse, they had been paid in the depreciated currency of the times, which had scarcely any purchasing power, and their devoted families at home were reduced to the lowest extremity of want and wretchedness.

The forced inactivity of the camp gave them time to brood over their wrongs, until at length they formed the bold resolve of marching to Hartford, and presenting their grievances in person to the Legislature then sitting. The two brigades were under arms for this purpose before news of the revolt was brought to Putnam. He, with his usual intrepidity and decision of character, threw himself upon his horse and dashed down the road leading to his camps, never slacking rein until he drew up in the presence of the disaffected troops. "My brave lads," cried he, "whither are you going? Do you intend to desert your officers, and to invite the enemy to follow you into the country? Whose cause have you been fighting and suffering so long in—is it not your own? Have you no property, no parents, wives, or children? You have behaved like

men so far—all the world is full of your praises, and
posterity will stand astonished at your deeds ; but
not if you spoil all at last. Don't you consider how
much the country is distressed by the war, and that
your officers have not been any better paid than
yourselves ? But we all expect better times, and
that the country will do us ample justice. Let us
all stand by one another then, and fight it out like
brave soldiers. Think what a shame it would be for
Connecticut men to run away from their officers.''
When he had finished this stirring speech, he
directed the acting major of brigades to give the
word for them to shoulder, march to their regimen-
tal parades, and lodge arms, which was done ; one
soldier only, a ringleader in the affair, was confined in the guard-house, from which he attempted
to escape, but was shot dead by the sentinel on duty
—himself one of the mutineers. Thus ended the
affair, and no further trouble was experienced with
the Connecticut troops.

Nothing had so much annoyed Putnam and his
officers during the campaign of the preceding summer on the Hudson than the desertions which had
thinned his ranks, and the Tory spies, who fre-
quented his camps, under every variety of pretext,
and forthwith conveyed the information thus gathered to the enemy. To put a stop to this it had been
determined that the next offender of either sort captured should suffer death as an example, and according to the usages of war. The time for putting
this determination into execution soon arrived. One
day some scouts from Putnam's outposts in Westchester County captured a man lurking within their

lines, and as he could give no satisfactory account of himself he was at once haled over the borders, and into the presence of the commander-in-chief. In answer to his queries, the prisoner said that his name was Jones, that he was a Welshman by birth, and had settled in Ridgefield a few years before the war commenced : that he had never faltered in his allegiance to the king, and that at the outbreak of hostilities he had fled to the British army, and had been made a butcher in the camp ; a few weeks before, he had been sent into Westchester County to buy beeves for the army, and had been captured as above narrated. He was remanded to the guard-house and a court-martial at once ordered for his trial. The result is to be found in the following document found among the papers of the late Lieutenant Samuel Richards, paymaster in Colonel Wylly's regiment : *

" Feb. 4, 1779. Was tried at a General Court Martial Edward Jones for Going to and serving the enemy, and coming out as a spy—found guilty of each and every charge Exhibited against him, and according to Law and the Usages of Nations was sentenced to suffer Death.

" The General approves the sentence and orders it to be put in Execution between the hours of ten and eleven A.M. by hanging him by the neck till he be Dead."

Two days after another court-martial was held for a similar offence, as the following proves :

---

* Many other papers from the Richards Collection, both interesting and valuable, will be found in this work. The originals are in the possession of Hon. D. B. Booth, of Danbury, who has kindly allowed me to copy them.

" Feb. 6, 1779. At a Gen'l Court Martial was tried
John Smith of the 1st Connecticut Regiment for desertion and attempting to go to the Enemy, found
guilty, and further persisting in saying that he will
go to the Enemy if ever he has an opportunity, Sentenced to be shot to death, and orders that it be put
in Execution between the hours of ten and twelve
A.M."

General Putnam having two prisoners under sentence of death determined to execute them both at
once, or as he expressed it, " make a double job of
it," and at the same time make the spectacle as
terrible and impressive as the circumstances demanded. The lofty hill dominating the valley and
the camps (known to this day as Gallows Hill) was
chosen as the scene of the execution, the instrument of death being erected on its highest pinnacle.
The details of the execution, for reasons which will
appear, I prefer to give in the words of the three
different historians who have chronicled it. Mr.
Barber, in his " Historical Collections of Connecticut," p. 399, says :

" The scene which took place at the execution
of these men is described as shocking and bloody.
The man on whom the duty of hangman devolved
left the camp, and on the day of execution could
not be found. A couple of boys about the age
of twelve years were ordered by General Putnam to perform the duties of the absconding hangman. The gallows was about twenty feet from the
ground. Jones was compelled to ascend the ladder, and the rope around his neck was attached to
the cross-beam. General Putnam then ordered Jones
to jump from the ladder. ' No, General Putnam,'
said Jones, ' I am innocent of the crime laid to my

charge ; I shall not do it.' Putnam then ordered the boys before mentioned to turn the ladder over. These boys were deeply affected by the trying scene ; they cried and sobbed loudly, and earnestly entreated to be excused from doing any thing on this distressing occasion. Putnam, drawing his sword, ordered them forward, and compelled them at the sword's point to obey his orders. The soldier that was shot for desertion was but a youth of sixteen or seventeen years of age. Three balls were shot through his breast : he fell on his face, but immediately turned over on his back ; a soldier then advanced, and putting the muzzle of his gun near the convulsive body of the youth, discharged its contents into his forehead. The body was then taken up and put into a coffin ; the soldiers had fired their pieces so near, that they set the boy's clothes on fire, which continued burning. An officer with a drawn sword stood by, while every soldier of the three brigades who were out on the occasion was ordered to march by and look at the mangled remains.''

Mr. Barber says in a foot-note that the above particulars were derived from an aged inhabitant of Reading, who was present on the occasion, and stood but a few feet from Jones when he was executed. Mr. Hollister, in his '' History of Connecticut,'' takes exception to the above account. In Vol. ii., page 375, of his work, he has the following note :

'' The Rev. Nathaniel Bartlett, who was pastor of the Congregational church in Redding for a period of fifty years, officiated as chaplain to the encampment during the winter, and was present at the execution. He interceded with General Putnam to defer the execution of Smith until Washington could be consulted—the offender being a youth of seventeen years ; but the commander

assured him that a reprieve could not be granted.
Mr. Bartlett was an earnest and fearless Whig,
and openly talked and preached 'rebellion'—so
much so, that the Tories, who were numerous in
the eastern part of the town, threatened to hang him
if they could catch him. In consequence of these
threats he often carried a loaded musket with him
when on his parochial visits. His son and successor
in the ministry at Redding—the Rev. Jonathan
Bartlett, now (1855) in his ninety-first year—well re-
members the Revolutionary encampment at Redding and frequently visited it. He is sure that the
story in Barber's 'Historical Collections' about
Putnam's inhumanity at the execution of Smith and
Jones is incorrect. Though not present himself, he
has often heard his father relate the incidents of the
occasion ; and furthermore he once called the attention of Colonel Asahel Salmon (who died in 1848,
aged ninety-one), who was a sergeant in attendance
upon the execution, to the statement, and he declared that nothing of the kind took place."

Another historian, Rev. Thomas F. Davies, in an
historical sermon delivered at Green's Farms in 1839,
also takes exception to Mr. Barber's statement. He
says :

"Mr. Barber must have been misinformed.
Reading is my native town, and from my boyhood
I have heard the history of the proceedings on the
occasion referred to, and was much surprised at the
statements in the 'Historical Collections.' The
Rev. Mr. Bartlett, whose father was chaplain on that
occasion, informs me that General Putnam could
not have been guilty of the acts there charged.
"That Mr. Barber may have something to substitute for the narrative to which I object, I give the
following :

"When General Putnam occupied the house of which Mr. Barber has given an engraving, a scene occurred which presents the General in a very amiable light. A poor man with a family needing support, and who lived in the neighboring town of Ridgefield, was told by one acquainted with his wants, that if he would visit General Putnam and hold a conversation with him, he would on his return, and on proof of the fact, give him a bushel of wheat. The temptation in that time of scarcity and taxes was great, and so also was the fear of intruding upon so distinguished an individual ; but the stern necessities of his condition at length induced the poor man to venture. He accordingly presented himself at headquarters, and requested the servant to solicit for him an interview with the General. Putnam promptly summoned the man to his presence, directed him to be seated, and listened with interest while the man with great trepidation gave the statement which accounted for the liberty he had taken. The General directed the servant to bring some wine, conversed for a time very pleasantly with his needy visitor, and then calling for pen and ink, wrote a certificate in which he gives the name of the individual, and stated that he had visited and conversed with General Putnam, who signed it in his official character. Thus furnished with the means of giving bread to his family, the distressed individual returned to his humble roof ; and this anecdote, which I have on the very best authority, is proof that Putnam was not destitute of those kind and gentle affections which are so desirable an ornament of the most heroic character."

This diversity of statements has led the writer to investigate the matter more thoroughly than he would otherwise have done ; and the weight of proof seems to be in favor of the correctness of Mr. Barber's statement. His version of the affair is the one generally prevalent in the town, with the exception of Putnam's forcing the boys to become executioners. Nor is there any thing in the story inconsistent with Putnam's known character and temperament. He had been a man of war from his youth, in perils often from wild beasts, the elements, the wilderness, and the Indians.

Long service in the bloody French and Indian wars had scarcely taught him amiability. Boldness, firmness, promptness, decision—these were the chief elements of his character, and at this particular crisis all were needed. There was disaffection and insubordination in the army, as has been seen. Desertions were frequent, and spying by the Tories was almost openly practised. To put a stop to these practices was vitally necessary to the safety of the army ; and as the prisoners had been tried and sentenced to death by a competent tribunal, it was Putnam's duty to see that the sentence was carried into effect. If the execution was bunglingly done, the fault was with the executioners, and not with the General.

As was to be expected, the citizens of 'Redding felt quite honored by the selection of their town for the army's winter quarters, and welcomed heartily the dusty battalions as they filed into camp ; but a few months' acquaintance opened their eyes to some of the ways of soldiers, and caused them to speed the army in the spring as heartily as they had welcomed it in the autumn. The soldiers argued that as they were fighting the country's battles it devolved on the latter to furnish the sinews of war, and plundered the neighboring farmers, whether Whig or

Tory, with the utmost impartiality. To them a well-stocked poultry yard or a pen of fat porkers offered irresistible inducements. A milch cow never failed of a circle of devoted admirers, while bands of merry reavers occasionally stole over the borders into the neighboring towns, and harried in under cover of night droves of fat cattle, which were killed and eaten with as little formality as they were taken. With the morning would come the owner complaining of these little peccadilloes, but as he could never prove property nor identify the rogues, they usually escaped punishment. After a time, however, the wary farmers foiled the depredators by herding their live-stock over night in the cellars of their houses and in other secure places.

The ringleader in all these forays was Tom Warrups, an Indian, grandson of the chief Chickens, whose story is given in the earlier pages of this work, and one of Putnam's most valued scouts and messengers. Tom possessed a great deal of individuality, and impressed himself on a succeeding generation to the extent that numberless anecdotes are remembered and told about him to this day. Some of these, illustrating the Indian character, are worthy the attention of the grave historian. Tom had a weakness for liquor, which would have caused his expulsion from the camp had it not been for his services as scout and guide. One day he was seen deplorably drunk, and the officer of the day in disgust ordered him to be ridden out of the camp. A stout rail was brought, Tom was placed astride of it, four men hoisted it upon their shoulders, and the cavalcade started. On their way they met General Put-

6

nam with his aids, making the rounds of the camp.
" Tom," ' said the General sternly, " how's this ?
Aren't you ashamed to be seen riding out of camp
in this way ?"   " Yes," replied Tom, with drunken
gravity.   " Tom is ashamed, vera mooch ashamed,
to see poor Indian ride and the Gineral he go afoot.' '
Tom had a house on the high ridge back of Captain
Isaac Hamilton's, now owned by William Sherwood.
It was built, it is said, in primitive Indian style, of
poles set firmly in the ground, then bent and fas-
tened together at the top.   This framework was covered with bark, and roofed with reeds and rushes.
Its furniture consisted of framework bedsteads, with
bedding of skins, wooden bowls fashioned from pep-
perage knots, huge wooden spoons, baskets made of
rushes or long grass, pails of birch bark, and an iron
pot and skillet begged or borrowed from the settlers.
His sister Eunice was his housekeeper.   Except in
war he was a worthless, shiftless fellow, and lived
chiefly by begging ; hunting and trapping were his
recreations.   He would often absent himself from
his hut for weeks at a time, sleeping in barns or in
the forest.   A huge overhanging rock about a mile
north of Georgetown often sheltered him on these
occasions, and is still known as Warrup's Rock.
    Tom's neighbor and landlord before the war was
Colonel John Read, son of the early settler of that
name.   On one occasion the colonel had a company
of gentlemen from Boston to visit him, and planned
a grand hunt in their honor.   Tom was always master
of the revels at such times, and piloted the party on
this occasion.   In their rambles through the forests
they came to a spring, and being thirsty one of the

party lamented that they had left their hunting cups behind. Tom at once slipped off his shoe, and filling it with water offered it to the guest to drink ; whereupon Colonel Read reproved him sharply for his ill-breeding. Tom drank from the vessel while the homily was being delivered, and then replaced the shoe, observing with the haughtiness of a king, " Good enough for Indian, good enough for white man too.''

After the war Captain Zalmon Read and Tom were near neighbors, and the former had a cornfield in dangerous proximity to Tom's cabin ; he missed the corn and suspected Tom, and watching, not only discovered him to be the thief, but also his ingenious plan of procedure. About midnight the Indian would come, basket in hand, and seated on the top rail of the fence would thus address the field : " Lot, can Tom have some corn ?" " Yes, Tom," the lot would reply, " take all you want ;" whereupon Tom would fill his basket with ears and march off. The next night, as the story goes, the captain armed himself with a grievous hickory club and lay in wait behind the fence. Presently Tom came, repeated his formula, and proceeded to fill his basket, but when he returned with it to the fence, it was occupied by the captain, who proceeded to repeat Tom's formula with a variation. " Lot, can I beat Tom ?" " Yes," the lot replied, " beat him all he deserves ;" whereupon the fun-loving captain fell upon the culprit and gave him the thorough beating which his roguery deserved.

One more anecdote of Tom must suffice. One day he went to a neighbor's house and demanded whiskey. No, the neighbor was of the opinion that

whiskey was bad for Tom. " Rum, then." " No."
" Cider." " No, cider was bad too ; food he might
have to keep him from starving, but no fire-water."
Tom ruminated. " Well," said he at length, " give
me toast and cider"—a favorite dish in those days—
and in this way won the desired stimulant.

Some years after, when age was creeping on, Tom
and his sister removed to the Indian reservation at
Schaticook, in Kent, whither his tribe had preceded
him, and the time and manner of his death was un-
known to his white brethren in Redding.

This is a long digression, pardonable in this connection only because its subject was one of the brave
defenders of his country.

Among the papers in the " Richards Collection"
are some that are interesting as detailing little epi-
sodes of camp life, as well as some that possess considerable historic value. They are as follows :

" HEADQUARTERS, READING, May 28, 1779.

" Daniel Vaughn and Jonath'n Gore of the 8th
Connecticut Regt Tryd by a Brigade C. M.
whereof Lt. Col. Sumner was President, For Steal-
ing a Cup from Capt. Zalmon Read of Reading,
The Court are of Opinion the charges against Vaughn
and Gore are not supported.

"B. O."

" CAMP, 2ND HILL, Nov. 14, 1778.

" The General having obtained permission of the
Commander In Chief to be Absent a few days from
the Division, the Command will devolve upon Brig-
adier Gen'l Huntington. Gen'l McDougal is happy
that it falls upon a Gentleman in whose care for and
attention to the Troops he has the utmost Confidence.
The Orders will be issued as usual at the Headquarters of the Division."

GENERAL PUTNAM'S ORDERS.

" READING, Dec. 18, 1778.

" Lieut. Col. Butler of Wylly's Reg. is promoted to the command of the 2nd Company Battalion and is to be obeyed as such. Col. Meigs is appointed Inspector to the Division and to do the duty of Adjt. General for the same until further Orders—Quartermaster Belding of the First Conn. Brigade is appointed Quartermaster of the Division and is to do that duty until further Orders. David Humphrey Esq. late Brigade Major to Gen'l Parsons is appointed aide de camp to Gen'l Putnam till further Orders."

" FEB. 13, 1779.

" The Gen'l Directs that no person be permitted to visit the Prisoners under sentence of Death Unless at their Request as frequent Complaints have been made that they are interrupted in their Private Devotions by persons who came for no other Purpose but to Insult them."

" *At a Gen'l Court Martial held at Bedford Oct.* 3 *1778, By order of Gen. Scott whereof Lt. Col. Blaisden was President.*

" Elisha Smith a private in Capt. Stoddard's Co. 2d Regt. Light Dragoons was tryed for Deserting to the Enemy last August and Piloting them into and against the troops of this State Defrauding the publick, by selling his horse and Accouterments in a Treasonable Manner to the Enemy and for Menacing and Insulting his officers while a Prisoner, found Guilty, and Sentence Him to Suffer the pains of Death—His Excellency the Commander in Chief Approves the Sentence and Orders s'd Elisha Smith to be Executed next Monday the 12th Inst. at 11 O Clock A.M. at or near Bedford as Gen. Scott shall Direct."

No date : " Divine Service will be performed to morrow at the Church, to begin at 11 O Clock A.M.

Those off Duty are to March from Camp so as to be at the Church by that time.''

The '' Church'' was the Congregational at the Centre, and the preacher the Rev. Nathaniel Bartlett.

"HEADQUARTERS, May 27, 1779.
'' Major General Putnam being (about) to take command of one of the Wings of the Grand Army, before he leaves the Troops who have served under him the winter past, thinks it his Duty to Signify to them his entire approbation of their Regular and Soldier like Conduct, and wishes them (wherever they may happen to be out) a Successful and Glorious Campaign.''

Hazen's command seems to have been the first to break camp in the spring, as the following proves :

"HEAD QUARTERS, READING, March, 21, 1779.
'' Col. Hazen's Regt. will march to Springfield in 3 Divisions by the shortest notice : the first Division will march on Monday next, and the other two will follow on Thursday and Friday next, Weather permitting, and in case the detached parties join the Regt. Col. Hazen will take with him one peice of Cannon and a proportionable Number of Artillery men.''

April 11th, the following order was issued :

"HEAD QUARTERS, Apr. 11th, 1779.
'' The officers are Requested to lose no time in Preparing for the field, that they may be ready to leave their present Quarters at the Shortest Notice. The Q. M. Gen'l—as far as it is in his power will supply those with Portmanteaus, who have not been furnished before, and those who have or shall be provided are on no account to carry chests or Boxes into the field. The portmanteaus are given by the publick to Supersede those of such Cumbersome articles

in order to contract the Baggage of the Army and lessen the Number of Waggons, which besides saving the Expense, is attended with many obvious and most Important Military Advantages. The General also thinks it necessary to give explicit notice in time with a View to have the army as little Encumbered as possible in all its movements, and to prevent burthening the public and the farmers more than can be avoided. No officer whose Duty does not Really require him to be on horseback—will be permitted to keep horses with the Army—It ought to be the pride of an officer to share the fatigues, as well as the Dangers to which his men are exposed on foot. Marching by their sides he will lessen every inconvenience and Excite in them a spirit of patience and perseverance. Inability alone can justify a Deviation from this necessary practice. Gen. Washington strongly recommends to the officers to Divest themselves as much as possible of Every thing Superfluous—Taking to the field only what is Essential for Dining and Comfort. Such as have not particular friends within reach with whom they would choose to confide their Baggage, will apply to the Q. M. Gen'l who will appoint a place for their Reception and furnish Means of Transportation."

" READING, May 24, 1779.

" Gen. Parsons orders the Brigade to be Ready to March to Morrow at 6 o Clock A.M. Complet for Action."

This brigade seems to have returned to the Highlands *via* Ridgefield and Bedford, as General Parsons dates his next order at Ridgefield, May 30 :

" That Col. Wyllys furnish a Sergt. Corp. and 12 privates to be posted as a Guard this Night one quarter of a Mile in front of where his Regt. is quartered on the road leading to Bedford. That Col. Meigs furnish a Guard of the Same Number

and Distance on the road leading to Norwalk. The
Revielle to be beat to-morrow morning at the Dawn
of Day, the troops to parade at 4 o'clock half a mile
below the meeting house, on the road leading to
Bedford, for which place they will march immediately after in the same order as this day.''

" BEDFORD, May 31st, 1779.

" The troops of Gen. Parson's Brigade to have
two Days . . . per man from Capt. Townsend . . .
refresh themselves, and be ready to march in two
hours to Parade near the Meeting house."

" FISHKILL, June 2, 1779.

" Gen. Parsons orders that Com'sr Sturm deliver
one gill of Rum per man, and two Days provision
to the troops of his Brigade, this Day.—The Qr. master to make return for the same."

" HD. QUARTERS, HIGHLANDS, June 6, 1779.

" General McDougal Orders a Detachment of 150
Men Properly Officered from Gen. Parson's and
Huntington's Brigades to parade at 12 o clock, with
arms, ammunition, accouterments, Blankets and
three days Provisions in front of Gen. Hn. Bd."
(Huntington's Brigade).

" HD. QR. June 7th, 1779.

" The Grand Parade in front of Gen. Hn. Bd.
100 men properly Officered from Hn. Bd. will parade
for piquet at 3 o'clock for the future. The Relief
will parade at 8 o'clock in the morning. No person
will pass the piquet who cannot give a Good Ac'ct.
of himself."

" The Signal of Alarm will be three cannon fired
Distinctly by the Artillery in the front line."

The following orders show the route taken by
the army in the fall of 1778 from the Highlands to
Redding :

" HEAD QUARTERS, FREDERICKSBURG, Oct. 16, 1778.

"To morrow being the Anniversary of the Sur-
render of Gen'l Burgoynes and his Troops to the
Arms of America under the Command of Major
Gen'l Gates, it will be Commemorated by the firing
of thirteen cannon from the Park of Artillery at 12
o : Clock."

" HEAD QUARTERS, Oct. 22, 1778.

" Nixon's, Parson's and Huntington's Brigades
are to.march to morrow morning at 7 'o'clock from
the Line under the command of Major Gen'l Mc-
Dougall—Orders of March—Gen'l Nixon's Brigade
leads, Huntington's follows, Parson's brings up the
Rear, Commanding Officers of Corps will be an-
swerable for the conduct of their men while on the
March. Artillery to March in Centre of each Brigade—the Baggage of Gen'l Officers to March in
Rear of the Troops, the other Baggage will march
in the same order. Forage and Commissary Waggons in the rear of the Whole."

" NEW MILFORD, Nov. 5, 1778.

" The Honorable, the Continental Congress having on the 12th of October passed a Resolution to
discourage prophaneness in the Army it is inserted
in this Division for the information of Officers, and
Gen. McDougall hopes for their aid and Counte-
nance in Discouraging and Suppressing a Vice so Dis-
honorable to human Nature, to the commission of
which there is no Temptation enough."

" CAMP, NEW MILFORD, Oct. 26, 1778.

" His Excellency the Commander in Chief has
Directed the troops to remain here till further or-
ders—and be in Readiness to March at the shortest
Notice as Circumstances shall require. While the
Division is Reposed, two days bread will be on store
Continually, Baked."

These interesting extracts might fitly conclude the story of the army's encampment in Redding ; there are, however, some entries in the parish records, proving that amid the horrors of war sly Cupid found a chance to inflict his wounds, that are worthy of insertion. They are given as entered by the Rev. Nathaniel Bartlett :

"Feb. 7, 1779. I Joined together in marriage James Gibbins a soldier in the army and Ann Sullivan."

"March 18th, 1779. I joined together in marriage John Lines, a soldier in the army, and Mary Hendrick."

"March 30, 1779. I joined in marriage Daniel Evarts a soldier, and Mary Rowland."

"Apr. 15, 1779. I joined in marriage Isaac Olmsted a soldier, and Mary Parsons."

"Apr. 28, 1779. I joined in marriage Jesse Belknap an artificer in the army, and Eunice Hall."

"May 4, 1779. I joined in marriage William Little, Steward to Gen. Parsons, and Phebe Merchant."

"May 23, 1779. I joined in marriage Giles Gilbert an artificer in the army, and Deborah Hall."

"March 9, 1780. I joined in marriage William Darrow a soldier, and Ruth Bartram."

In the month of June, 1781, Count de Rochambeau and the Duke de Lauzun marched a column of French troops across Connecticut and took post in Ridgefield, within supporting distance of Washington's army on the Hudson.

They passed through Redding on the march, and encamped over night, it is said, on the old parade-ground.

Their supply-train numbered 810 wagons, most of

them drawn by two yoke of oxen and a horse. The column attracted much attention as it moved with flashing arms and soldierly precision over the hills and through the valleys on its way to Ridgefield.

No complete list of the soldiers furnished by Redding to the Continental army can be prepared. The following names appear on the town list of Revolutionary pensioners : Colonel Asahel Salmons, Captain Zalmon Read, Captain John Davis, Joel Merchant, Ezra Bates, Calvin Jenkins, Ezra Hull, Stephen Batterson, Jacob Patchen, and Abraham Parsons ; and in the town records those whose families were aided were Nathan Coley, Stephen Meeker, Elias Bixby, Jeremiah Ryan, and Samuel Remong.

CHAPTER V.

THE CONGREGATIONAL CHURCH, 1729–1879.

THE Congregational church was the first religious body organized in the town. Deeply impressed as were our Puritan forefathers with the value of religion to the soul, they were equally impressed with its value to the state, and were careful to rear, side by side with their civil structure, the church, in which, as they believed, the pure Gospel of Christ was preached, and the soundest principles of morality inculcated. Proof of their pious care in this respect is to be found in the history of Redding, as in that of almost every New England town. As

early as August, 1729, but three months after they
had wrung a reluctant consent from the mother
town to assume parish privileges, we find them
providing for the settlement of a minister among
them in the following manner :

" At a Society Meeting held in the Society of Redding, Deacon George Hull chosen Moderator. It was
voited that s'd Society would give for the settlement
of a minister in s'd society the sum of seventy
pounds, and a house, and his wood, and bring it up,
and the next year eighty pounds, and raise five
pounds a year till it comes to one hundred pounds a
year. It was voted, that Edmond Luis, esquire,
shall decide the matter as to seting the meeting
hous, it was voited that s'd Mr. Luis should come
the first week in October to decide the matter afore-
s'd."

No minister was settled, however, until 1733 ; the
first church edifice was erected early in 1732. It
stood a few yards west of the present Methodist
church, and nearly in the centre of the public square
or common.* A photograph or rough sketch even,
of this the first church in Redding, would be invaluable to men of the present day : we are certain,
however, that it was a much more elegant and finished edifice than was common in the new settlements. It was two stories high, as we shall see, and
of quite respectable dimensions. It was also lathed
and plastered, and furnished with galleries, and windows of imported glass, but further details are lack-
ing. All that is to be found in the church records

---

* The corner-stone of the old church may still be seen on the common, a little south of a line drawn from Deacon Abbott's to the store
lately occupied by Mr. Mandeville.

concerning the building is contained in the following extracts :

November 12th, 1730.—It was voted " that we will build a meting-hous in said society for the worship of God in the Presbyterian way. Voted that the meting-hous shall be thirty feet long, twenty eight feet wide, and two stories high, voted, that Lemuel Sanford, Thomas Williams, and Daniel Lion, (be) chosen committee for (building) s'd meting hous."

Feb. 23d, 1730–1.—" You that are of the minds that all those persons that do, or hereafter may inhabit in this parish, which profess themselfs to be of the Church of England, shall have free liberty to come into this meting hous that is now in building, and attend the Publick worship of God there, according to the articles of faith agreed upon by the assembly of Divines at Seabrook, and established by the laws of this Government, and be seated in s'd hous according to their estats."

November 3d, 1732.—" Stephen Burr hath undertaken to cart stones and clay for the underpinning the meting hous for 1 lb. 10s. 00d. Daniel Lion hath undertaken to underpin the meting hous and tend himself for 2 lbs. 4s. 0d. Daniel Lion hath undertaken to get the lath and lay them on for 3 lbs. 0s. 0d. Stephen Burr and Theophilus Hull are chosen committee to take care of the parsonage" (probably to secure a parsonage for the expected preacher, as it is not likely that one was then built).

It was as yet, however, a church without a pastor. Mr. Elisha Kent had been called in October, 1730, but had declined, as we infer from the silence of the records on the subject. A Society meeting held May 8th, 1732, extended a similar call to the Rev. Timothy Mix, and deputed Deacon George Hull " to go to the association at Stanford to ask advice concerning the settlement of Mr. Mix ;" but this call, as in the case of Mr. Kent, seems to have been declined. At length a unanimous call was made to the Rev. Nathaniel Hun, as follows :

Jan. 31, 1732–3.—" At a society meeting held in the parish (of) Reading, George Hull chosen Moderator for s'd meting, Mr. Nathaniel Hunn by a voit *nemine contradicente* was made chois of for the minister of s'd parish, furthermore it was voited at s'd meting to settle upon the s'd Mr. Hunn's yearly sallery as followeth, that is, for the first year of his administration, seventy pounds current money or bills of Public Credit in New England, the second year, seventy-five pounds, for the third year, eighty pounds, for the fourth year, eighty five pounds, the fifth year ninety pounds, the sixth year, ninety five pounds, the seventh year, a hundred pounds, all in currant money as afores'd, and so on a hundred pounds a year during the term of his continuance in the ministry in s'd parish, and also to give the s'd Mr. Hunn the whole and sole priviledge of all the parsonage land belonging to s'd parish, and to provide him his firewood, during the term aboves'd, also to find him a convenient dwelling hous for the first five years, also to give the s'd Mr. Hunn, a hundred acres of land on or before the day of his ordination."

Feb. 20th, 1732–3.—" It was voited that the ordination of Mr. Hunn shall be on the 21st day of March next," and John Read and George Hull were chosen a committee " to represent the parish concerning the ordination of Mr. Hunn." From this point we have for a guide the church records in the handwriting of Mr. Hunn, its settled pastor. It is called " A Book of Records Wherein is an account, 1st of the transactions of the church, 2d of persons re-

ceived to communion, 3rd of persons baptized, 4th
of marriages, 5th of deaths, 6th of persons who re-
new the covenant."

The Rev. Sidney G. Law, in his Centennial Sermon, delivered at Redding, July 6th, 1876, thus
speaks of Mr. Hunn's pastorate :

" His first record is very brief for so important a
matter, viz.: ' March 21st, 1733, I was separated to the
work of the ministry by prayer and fasting, and the
laying on of the hands of the Presbytery.' The
next record gives the choice of deacons, viz.: ' At a
church meeting March 29, 1733, we made choice of
Stephen Burr for a deacon, and some time after we
chose Theo. Hull to the same service. . . .' The
next records relate to the adoption of Tate and
Brady's version of the Psalms, first for one month,
and then for the indefinite future. The first members of the church enumerated by Mr. Hun were as
follows : Col. John Read and wife, Theophilus Hull
and wife, George Hull and wife, Peter Burr and
wife, Daniel Lion and wife, Daniel Bradley and
wife, Stephen Burr and wife, Ebenezer Hull and
wife, John Griffen, Nathaniel Sanford, Thomas Fairchild, Lemuel Sanford, Benjamin Lion and wife,
Mary wife of Richard Lion, Isaac Hull, Esther wife
of Thomas Williams, Esther wife of Benjamin Hamilton. Thus it appears that the church was organized with twenty-six members, including the two
deacons, about the time that Mr. Hun was ordained,
viz., the 21st of March, 1733. Mr. Hunn married
Ruth, a sister of Col. Read.* He was pastor of the
church sixteen years. During this time he received

---

* She was a daughter of the Hon. John Read, who settled at Lonetown in 1714. Both Mr. Law and Mr. Barber are in error in suppos-
ing that the original John Read lived and died in Redding. He removed to Boston in 1722, and his son John succeeded to his title, and
to the manor at Lonetown. The latter is the one mentioned in these
records.

about ninety-two members into the church, the
most of them by letter of recommendation from
neighboring churches. He performed thirty-five
marriages and one hundred and ninety-two baptisms. He died while on a journey, and was buried
in Boston in 1749. His widow, Ruth Hunn, died
in 1766, and was buried near her brother, Col. John
Read, in the cemetery west of the parsonage."

Mr. Hunn's administration seems to have been a
happy and prosperous one, and few events of importance occurred during its continuance. The records are taken up with cases of church discipline,
with additions to his salary, providing his firewood,
and with repairs to the meeting-house.

In 1738 it was voted " to finish glassing the meting hous, and to finish seating the meting hous as is
begun, and do something to the pulpit." In 1739,
" voted, that Sergt. Joseph Lee shall get Mr. Hun's
wood, and have seven pounds for it." " Voted that
the place for putting up warnings for society meetings be changed from Umpawaug to the mill door."
In 1740, " voted to rectifie the meting hous in the
following articles, viz. to put in new glass where it
is wanting, and to mend the old. To lay some
beams in the gallery and double floor. To fasten
the meting hous doors ; to make stairs up the gallery ; to put a rail on the foreside of the gallery,"
and " that the place for parish meeting shall be at
the school house, by the meting hous for the
future." In 1741, " voted, to seat the meting hous
in the lower part with plain strong seats." In
1742, " voted to impower the parish committee to
agree with a person to beat the drum as a signal to

call the people together on the sabbath." Again
Feb. 15, 1743–4, " It was voted that the timber and
boards provided for seating the meeting house, shall
be improved to that end for the use of the Parish."
These entries though unimportant in themselves give
us pleasant glimpses of the healthy and active life
of the church. Mr. Hunn died in the summer or
fall of 1749, and for the four following years the
church was without a pastor. A call was extended
to Mr. Solomon Mead in March, 1751, without success, and in November of the same year to the Rev.
Izrahiah Wetmore, with a like result. The interim
was improved by the people, however, in building a
new church, which stood nearly on the site of the
present edifice.

The first action in this important matter was taken
at a Society meeting held Feb. 9,1748, when it was
put to vote " whether it be necessary to build a new
meting hous in s'd Parish," and passed in the affirmative ; whereupon " Left. Joseph Sanford " was
appointed agent for the Society to prefer a memorial to the next General Assembly, " to affix the
place whereon the meeting house should be built."
The successive stages by which the building grew to
completion are defined in a very interesting manner
in the records." Dec. 29th, 1799, " It was voted that
Deacon Burr and others be a committee to see that
there is timber got, and sawmill logs for a meeting
house in this Parish, s'd timber to be 37 ft in width
and 46 ft in length." Jan. 17th, 1750, the County
Court in session at Fairfield, on the memorial of
Redding, appointed Thomas Benedict, Esq., and
Capt. Josiah Starr, of Danbury, and Samuel

7

Olmsted, Esq., of Ridgefield, a committee to affix
the place whereon the meeting-house should be
built ; to act with these, the Society appointed a
committee composed of John Read, Stephen Burr,
Joseph Sanford and Ephraim Jackson. Jan. 29th,
1751, a committee was appointed " to agree with
some persons to build the new meting hous." It
would appear that ground had not been broken for
it as early as April 25th, 1751, for at that date a
committee was appointed to meet the County Court's
committee " to find a place for the meeting house."

It was probably completed and ready for use
early in the summer of 1752, as on the 22d of June
of that year a call was extended to the Rev. Mr.
Tammage to be their preacher, and the old meeting house was sold to Jehu Burr for £34. The
manner in which this meeting-house was " seated"
(which did not occur until 1763) is an interesting
commentary on the manners and customs of the
day, and has the further merit of novelty, it being
doubtful if another record can be found in New
England detailing so minutely the method of assign-
ing pews in the early Puritan churches. We copy
from the records of a Society meeting held at
Widow Sanford's, June 23d, 1763 :

" Put to vote whether the meeting house of s'd
society shall be seated in ye form following viz. a
com'te being appointed to Dignify ye pews and other
seats in s'd Meeting House the Respective members
of s'd society shall sit in s'd pews and seats according to their Rank and Degree to be computed by
their several lists and age, viz. upon ye two last
years lists, and to allow three pound per year to be
added to a person's List for his advancement in a

seat, and all at ye discresion of s'd com'te who shall be appointed to Dignify s'd pews and seats, and to inspect the Respective lists and ages of s'd mem- bers."

The committee appointed was Joseph Sanford, Ebenezer Couch, and Stephen Burr ; but Messrs. Sanford and Burr declining to act, Ephraim Jackson and Joseph Banks were chosen in their place." This committee was unable to settle the question satisfactorily, and a meeting was held August 11th, 1763, at which the following action was taken :

" It was put to vote whether the Dignity of ye pews and seats in ye meeting house should be in the following manner viz. ye pew adjoining ye pulpit stairs first in Dignity : ye Pew adjoining ye grait doors, west side, second in Dignity : the fore seat third in Dignity, the second pew west of ye pulpit, fourth, the second seat, fifth : the second pew north from the west door, sixth : the fifth pew north of ye west door seventh : the third pew north of the west door, eighth : the second pew west of ye grait doors ninth : the first pew south of ye west door, tenth : the third seat, eleventh : the second pew south of the west door twelfth : the fourth seat, thirteenth the front seat in ye gallery, fourteenth : the fore seat on ye side of the gallery, fifteenth : the pews and seats upon ye east end of ye meeting house of Equal Dignity with those upon the west side in the same manner and order as they are above mentioned. Passed in the negative."

Three months later another meeting was called, and adopted the following plan :

" The respective members of the society shall sit in ye pews and seats of the meeting house of s'd Society according to their rank or degree, to be com-

puted by their respective lists and ages, viz. upon
the lists given in upon the years 1751 and 1761 and
1762, and to allow three pounds per year to be
added to a person's list for his advancement in a seat
or pew the Respective lists and ages of s'd members
are to be inspected, also to give the committee
chosen at this meeting power to seat those that are
new comers, and have not . . in s'd society, to seat
them at s'd committee's discresion.

" Likewise to seat ye Widows in s'd Society at the
best of ye Committee's judgment, which method of
seating s'd meeting house shall continue until s'd
Society at their meeting shall order otherwise.

" Also voted that s'd com'te shall seat those women
whose husbands belong to the Church of England at
their discresion."

The Rev. Nathaniel Bartlett, the second pastor of
the church, was ordained May 23d, 1753, the next
year after the church was built. From the record
in his own handwriting, we learn that the ministers
who assisted at his ordination were as follows :

" The Rev. Mr. White of Danbury made the first
prayer. The Rev. Mr. Todd of East Guilford
preached the sermon. Rev. Mr. Kent made the
ordaining prayer. Rev. Mr. Mills of Ripston gave
the charge, Rev. Mr. Judson, of Newtown gave the
right hand of fellowship, and Rev. Mr. Ingersoll of
Ridgefield made the concluding prayer."

Mr. Bartlett came to Redding when a young man
fresh from his collegiate studies, and continued pastor of the church over which he was ordained for
fifty-seven years—the longest pastorate, it is said,
known to the New England churches. He is described as a gentleman of the old school, kind and
considerate, of an equable temper, a just man, a fine

scholar, and an eloquent preacher. During his term
of service the crude settlement in the wilderness
assumed the dignity of a town. The church grew
from infancy to manhood and the country passed
from the position of dependent colonies to that of
free and sovereign states. In the War of Independence Mr. Bartlett's sympathies were entirely with
the patriot cause ; two of his sons entered the army,
munitions of war were stored in his house, and he
himself frequently officiated as chaplain during the
encampment of Putnam's division in the town in the
winter of 1779. Like many of the New England
clergymen of that day, he was the teacher of such
youths in his charge as might desire a liberal education, and among the many whom he thus fitted for
usefulness was the celebrated poet and statesman,
Joel Barlow. Mr. Bartlett died Jan. 11, 1810, and
was buried in the old cemetery west of the church.
The simple inscription upon his tombstone reads as
follows :

THE REV. NATHANIEL BARTLETT.
Died, January 11, 1810, *aged* 83 *years.*

"I am the resurrection and the life ; he that believeth in me,
though he were dead, yet shall he live."—JESUS CHRIST.

During the entire period of Mr. Bartlett's ministry
we have in the church records but one entry of importance, and that is of interest as marking the organization of the Episcopal Society in the town.
This entry is as follows :

" To Seth S. Smith of Redding, in Fairfield Co.
Greeting, Whereas by law the Episcopal Church in
said Redding is become a distinct society whereby

the members of the Presbyterian church in said Redding have become the first society in said town. These are therefore by authority of the State of Connecticut to command you to warn and give notice to all the members of said first society, and all others who by law are obliged to contribute toward the support, and the worship, and the ministry with the same, to meet at the meeting house in said Redding on Monday the 20th of December at 12 in order to choose a moderator and necessary officers.

" Redding, December 14, 1785."

The Rev. Jonathan Bartlett, third minister of the church, was ordained as colleague with his father, Rev. Nathaniel Bartlett, in 1796. The first of the church records in his handwriting is as follows :

" Feb. 3, 1796. I was separated to the work of the ministry and ordained as colleague with my father Nathaniel Bartlett over the Congregational church in Redding in Gospel order and form. The ministers who performed the work were as follows viz. the Rev. Israhiel Wetmore chosen Moderator, Robert Ross made the ordaining prayer, Elisha Rexford made the introductory prayer, David Ely preached the sermon. Imposition of hands by N. Bartlett, R. Ross and Rexford. John Ely gave the right hand of fellowship, Samuel W. Stebbins made the concluding prayer."

Of the life and ministry of this most excellent man, one who knew him intimately, the Rev. Thomas F. Davies, thus wrote :

" In February, 1796, Mr. Bartlett was ordained colleague with his father, and after a faithful ministry of thirteen years, greatly esteemed and beloved by his people, was dismissed on account of ill-health, and by his own request. His heart was gladdened near the close of his pastoral life by a powerful and general revival of religion among the people of his charge. After his dismission, and when his health had been in a degree restored, he preached from time to time to destitute congregations in the vicinity, and at different periods, as occasion required, to the church of which he had been pastor, with great acceptation and usefulness. As a preacher he was eminently distinguished, for he was a man ' mighty in the Scriptures.' Large portions of the Word of God, entire epistles even, dwelling in his memory, and when an impaired vision rendered the perusal of a book difficult or painful, he reviewed in his own mind, and often rehearsed to others, portions of the Scriptures with comments which rendered his society delightful and instructive. He was a man of native eloquence, and great skill in the examination and exhibition of the subjects which came before him. He was a scribe, ' well instructed in the things of the kingdom, a workman that needed not to be ashamed, rightly dividing the word of truth.' While aiding other societies, he was eminently a benefactor to the church and society of which he had been a pastor, for in addition to the ministerial services gratuitously rendered, he gave in money in his various benefactions more to the society than the entire amount received from it during the whole period of his ministry, and has also left it a legacy of three thousand dollars. Useful, honored, and beloved he lived in his native town, inhabiting for nearly a century the same residence, for he was born in the house in which he died. With a calm and humble trust in God, in the entire possession of his mental powers, and with little apparent suffering, he fell asleep in Jesus."

Rev. Daniel Crocker, of Bedford, N. Y., was called in August, 1809, as colleague with Rev. Nathaniel Bartlett. He was a good man and a successful pastor, and served the church fifteen years, being dismissed in 1824. The Rev. Charles De Witt Tappen was called, but not settled. The next pastor chosen was Mr. William C. Kniffen in 1825. He was dismissed in 1828. The Rev. Burr Baldwin was next called, but not settled. The next pastor was the Rev. William L. Strong, formerly pastor at Somers, Tolland Co., Conn. He was installed June 23d, 1830, and dismissed Feb. 26th, 1835. In September, 1835, following Mr. Strong's dismissal, a subscription was commenced for the erection of the present church edifice, which was built in 1836. The expense was not to exceed $2500 with the old meeting-house. In December of the same year a unanimous call was extended to the Rev. David C. Comstock, but was not accepted at that time. In March, 1837, Rev. Daniel E. Manton was called, but not settled. In June of the same year the Rev. Jeremiah Miller was called, and was installed July 12th, 1837. Mr. Miller was dismissed in 1839. In the following year, 1840, Mr. David C. Comstock was ordained and installed pastor of the church. He was dismissed in 1845. After him Daniel D. Frost, after preaching as stated supply for eighteen months, was ordained December 30th, 1845. He continued pastor ten years, being dismissed October 13th, 1856. In 1857 the pulpit was supplied by the Rev. Mr. Root. In 1858 the Rev. Enoch S. Huntington supplied the pulpit one year. He presented the communion service to the church, for which he received its thanks. In 1859 the church was remodelled and painted, receiving the beautiful fresco which still adorns it. In 1860 Rev. W. D. Herrick became pastor, and so continued until 1864. After him Rev. E. B. Huntington, and also Rev. Mr. Barnum, preached for a short time. Rev. S. F. Farmer supplied in 1865. Rev. K. B. Glidden was installed September 12th, 1866 ; resigned December, 1868. In 1869 the Rev. Charles Chamberlain became acting pastor. He resigned in September, 1871. Rev. Sidney G. Law, to whom I am indebted for the above summary of the later history of the church, became acting pastor June 1st, 1872, and after a prosperous ministry of six years resigned in 1878. Rev. W. J. Jennings, the present pastor, was installed December 17th, 1879. Some statistics of this ancient church ready gathered to my hand will prove interesting and valuable. The complete list of those who have served it as pastors, with the date of their ordination and dismissal, is as follows :

MINISTERS.	SETTLED.	DISMISSED.	DIED.
Nathaniel Hunn	Mar. 21, 1733		1749
Nathaniel Bartlett	May 23, 1753		Jan. 11, 1810.
Jonathan Bartlett	Feb. 3, 1796	June 7, 1809	Mar. 22, 1858 .
Daniel Crocker	Oct. 4, 1809	Oct. 24, 1824	
William C. Kniffen	June 8, 1825	Dec. 17, 1828	
William L. Strong	June 23, 1830	Feb. 26, 1835	
Jeremiah Miller	July 12, 1837	July 23, 1839	
David C. Comstock	Mar. 4, 1840	April 8, 1845	
Daniel D. Frost	Dec. 30, 1846	Oct. 15, 1856	
Enoch S. Huntington	1858	1859	
W. D. Herrick	1860	1864	
K. B. Glidden	Sept. 12, 1866	Dec., 1868	
Charles Chamberlain	1869	Sept., 1871	
Sidney G. Law	June 1, 1872	June 1, 1878	

DEACONS.	APPOINTED.	DEACONS.	APPOINTED.
Stephen Burr	1733	Lemuel Sanford	1808
Theophilus Hull	1733	Aaron Read	1808
Lemuel Sanford	1740	Joel Foster	1820
Daniel Mallory	1740	Lemuel Hawley	1832
Joseph Banks	1776	Samuel Read	1832
Simon Couch	1776	Charles D. Smith	1854
Lemuel Sanford	1785	Rufus Meade	1854
Stephen Betts	1785	Thaddeus M. Abbott	1854

REVIVALS.

YEAR.	CONVERSIONS.	YEAR.	CONVERSIONS·
1808–9	75	1838	30
1823	40	1852	24
1829	8	1855	12
1831	20		

The present membership of the church is 119. Males, 40 ; females, 79.

CHAPTER VI.

CHRIST CHURCH.

1722–1879.

BY REV. ALANSON WELTON.

THE present town of Redding is one of the few places in the old Colony of Connecticut where the Episcopal ministry is entitled to the distinction of having been first on the ground, laying foundations, and not building upon those already laid. The Church of England was not planted in New England without strenuous and bitter opposition from the Puritans, who were first in the field. By old English law, indeed, that church was established in all the plantations ; yet it is manifest from the records of the colonial legislation of the charter government of Connecticut, that previously to 1727, the church of which the king was a member was not recognized as having a right to exist. Congregationalism was the established religion. " in opposition to which there could be no ministry or church administration entertained or attended by the inhabitants of any town or plantation, upon penalty of fifty pounds for every breach of this act ;" and every person in the colony was obliged to pay taxes for the support of this establishment.

In this uncongenial soil the Anglican Church of Connecticut was planted—strange to say, not by foreign-born missionaries, but by seceders from the ministry of the Congregationalists. The pioneers in this movement were Timothy Cutler, Rector of Yale College, Daniel Brown, Tutor ; James Wetmore, of North Haven ; and Samuel Johnson, of West Haven, a former tutor in the college. These gentlemen, after a professedly careful and prayerful examination of the subject of church order, discipline, and worship, which resulted in a conviction that the English Church followed most closely the teaching of the Scriptures and the practice of the church of the first ages, sent to the trustees of the college a formal statement of their views, and declared for Episcopacy—-to the no small surprise and consternation of their colleagues in the college and church. The four went to England for Episcopal ordination, where Brown died. The three survivors returned in 1722, as missionaries of the " Society for the Propagation of the Gospel in Foreign Parts," Johnson only being sent to Connecticut. The ante-Revolutionary history of the church at Redding Ridge is mostly to be found in the archives of this Society, as published in the " Documentary History of the Protestant Episcopal Church in Connecticut," and the Rev. Dr. Beardsley's " History of the Episcopal Church in Connecticut"—from which sources, mainly, this sketch has been compiled.

A letter was addressed to the secretary of the S. P. G., dated October 19th, 1722, signed by John Glover and twelve other heads of families in Newtown, Thomas Wheeler, of Woodbury, and Moses Knapp, of Chestnut Ridge, thanking the Society for the services of the Rev. George Pigot, missionary at Stratford, and earnestly soliciting the appointment of a missionary for themselves at Newtown.

The next year, 1723, Mr. Pigot was transferred to Newport, R. I., and the Rev. Samuel Johnson, his successor at Stratford, " accepted all his missionary duties in Connecticut."

In 1727, the Rev. Henry Caner [pronounce *Canner*] was sent to Fairfield, of which town Chestnut Ridge was a part. After having named in his report the several villages or hamlets in the vicinity of his station, he says : " Besides these, there is a village northward from Fairfield about eighteen miles, containing near twenty families, where there is no minister at all, of any denomination whatsoever ; the name of it is Chestnut Ridge, and where I usually preach or lecture once in three weeks." In 1728 he says there are four villages " about Fairfield,—Green Farms, Greenfield, Poquannuck and Chestnut Ridge, three of them about four miles distant, the last *about sixteen.* The same year, the name of Moses Knapp appears as a vestryman of the church at Fairfield.

In 1729, " Moses Knap, Nathan Lion, and Daniel Crofoot" objected, in a meeting of the [Presbyterian] " Society of Redding " "against" the " hiering" any other than a minister of the Church of England. These three names appear again in the list of Mr.

Beach's parishioners in 1738. The Rev. Dr. Bur-
hams [*Churchman's Magazine*, 1823] says : "The
first Churchman in Reading was a Mr. Richard Lyon,
from Ireland, who died as early as 1735." He also says
on the authority of " an aged member of the Church
in Reading," that " Messrs. [Richard ?] Lyon,
[Stephen] Morehouse, [Moses] Knapp, [Joshua]
Hall, [William] Hill, [Daniel] Crofoot, and [Lieut.
Samuel] Fairchild, appear to have composed the
first Church in Reading." *Nathan* Lyon died in
1757, in the fifty-fourth year of his age. Mr. Caner
reported in 1728 *seven* families at Chestnut Ridge ;
the number reminding us of the " House of Wis-
dom" with its " Seven Pillars," as the first Puritan
organization at New Haven was named.

Mr. Caner was succeeded at Chestnut Ridge, in
1732, by the Rev. John Beach, a pupil of Johnson in
Yale College, and afterward Presbyterian minister
at Newtown for several years. As Mr. Beach was a
resident of East Redding for about twenty years, and
pastor of this church full half a century, his history
is substantially that of the parish, or mission, over
which he presided. His pastorate was the longest
of all the ante-Revolutionary clergy. He was born
in Stratford, October 6th, 1700 ; graduated from Yale
at the age of twenty-one, and licensed to preach
soon afterwards. He is said to have been selected for
the Presbyterian pastorate at Newtown as a " popular and insinuating young man," well fitted to check
the growth of Episcopacy, which was there thriving
under the ministry of Caner and Johnson. Many
Churchmen must have " joined in settling him with
Presbyterian ordination," for in 1722 they claimed

to be a majority of the population, whereas, for some-
time *after* his " settlement," Mr. Johnson ministered
to only about five families. "From these visits
. . . frequent and earnest discussions resulted between the two teachers, the influence of which was
soon evident to Mr. Beach's congregation. After
two or three years of patient study and meditation he
alarmed his congregation by his frequent use of the
Lord's Prayer; and still more by reading whole
chapters from the Word of God. Next he ventured
to condemn a custom, common in their meetings, of
rising and bowing to the minister, as he came in
among them, and instead of which he begged them
to kneel down and worship God. At length [in
January, 1731], " after he had been a preacher more
than eight years, he told them from the pulpit that,
' From a serious and prayerful examination of the
Scriptures, and of the records of the early ages of
the Church, and from the universal acknowledgment
of Episcopal government for fifteen hundred years,
compared with the recent establishment of Presbyterian and Congregational discipline,' he was fully
persuaded of the invalidity of his ordination, and of
the unscriptural method of organizing and governing
congregations as by them practised. He therefore,
' In the face of Almighty God,' had made up his
mind to ' conform to the Church of England, as being Apostolical in her ministry and discipline, ortho-
dox in her doctrine, and primitive in her worship.'
He affectionately exhorted them to weigh the subject well; engaged to provide for the due administration of the sacraments while absent from them,
and spoke of his intended return from England in

holy orders. So greatly was he beloved, that a large proportion of his people seemed ready to acquiesce in his determination." But the others, in evident alarm and consternation at this " threatened defection from their ranks," held a town meeting " to consult" as to " what was possible to be done with the Rev. Mr. John Beach, under present difficulties ;" " voted to have a [day of] solemn fasting and prayer ; . . . to call in the Ecclesiastical Council of Fairfield to direct and do what they shall think proper, under the . . . difficult circumstances respecting the Rev. Mr. Beach, and the inhabitants of the town of Newtown—also that the first Wednesday of February [1732] be appointed for the fast."

The council met, and in spite of Mr. Beach's remonstrances proceeded to depose him from the ministry. " From this resulted a printed discussion" between him and his deposers, which ultimately helped rather than hindered the Church of England.

Mr. Beach returned from England in Episcopal orders, and took charge of the Newtown and Redding mission in the autumn of 1732. From this period his history and that of his mission may be more accurately told in the language of his own letters to the Secretary of the S. P. G.

" NEWTOWN IN CONNECTICUT, August 7th, 1735.

" REVEREND SIR, I think it my duty to acquaint the venerable Society with the present state of my parish, although the alteration since my last has not been very considerable. I have baptized twenty-nine children and admitted twenty-five persons more to the communion, so that the number . . .

now at Newtown, Reading, and the places adjacent,
is ninety-five. I preach frequently and administer
the Sacrament at Ridgefield . . . about eighteen miles distant . . . where there are about
fourteen or eighteen families of very serious and
religious people who have a just esteem of the
Church of England, and are very desirous to
have the opportunity of worshipping God in that
way. I have constantly preached, one Sunday at
Newtown ; and the other at Reading ; and after I
have preached at Reading in the day-time, I . . .
preach at Newtown in the evening ; and although I
have not that success I could wish for, yet I do, and
hope I always shall, faithfully endeavour (as far as
my poor ability will allow,) to promote that good
work, that the venerable Society sent and main-
tained for me. I am, Rev. Sir,
            " Your most humble servant,
                    " JOHN BEACH."

As a specimen of his manner of defending himself
against personal attacks we have the following from
a controversial pamphlet, in reply to John Dickinson, of New Jersey, in 1736 :

    " I have evened the scale of my judgement as much
as possibly I could, and to the best of my knowledge,
I have not allowed one *grain* of worldly motive on
either side. I have supposed myself on the brink
of eternity, just going into the other world, to give
up my acccount to my great Judge ; and must I be
branded for an antichrist or heretic, or apostate, because my judgement determines that the Church of
England is most agreeable to the Word of God ? I
can speak in the presence of God, who knows my
heart better than you do, that I would willingly turn
Dissenter again, if you, or any man living will show
me reason for it. But it must be reason (whereby I
exclude not the Word of God, which is the highest

reason.) and not sophistry and calumny, as you have
hitherto used, that will convince a lover of truth and
right."

In 1739 he says: "I have one hundred and
twenty-three communicants, but they live so far distant from each other, that commonly I can administer to no more than about fifty at once, which occasions my administering it the more frequently; and,
though I meet with many discouragements, yet I
have this satisfaction, that all my communicants
(one or two excepted) do adorn their profession by a
sober, righteous and godly life." In 1743, some
three years after Whitefield began his famous "revival of Puritanism," Mr. Beach says: "My people
are not at all shaken, but rather confirmed in their
principles by the spirit of enthusiasm that rages
among the Independents roundabout us; and many
of the Dissenters, observing how steadfast our people are . . . while those of their own denomination are easily carried away with every kind of
doctrine, have conceived a much better opinion of
our Church than they formerly had, and a considerable number in this colony have lately conformed, and
several Churches are now building where they have
no minister. . . . Were there in this country
but one of the Episcopal order, to whom young men
might apply for ordination, without the expense and
danger of a voyage to England, many of our towns
might be supplied which must now remain destitute." (This letter is dated at "*Reading*, in New
England," as all his published reports are, between
1740 and 1760.) "My people are poor, (he con-
tinues) and have but few negro slaves, but all they

8

have, I have, after instruction, baptized, and some of them are communicants." In October of the same year he says : " I beg the venerable Society's direction in an affair I am just now perplexed with. There are about twenty families . . . at New-Milford and New-Fairfield, which are about fifteen miles hence. I preach to them several times a year, but seldom on the Lord's day. They frequently come to Church at Newtown ; but by reason of the distance, they can't attend constantly, and their families very seldom, and, when they can't come to Church, they meet together in their own town, and one of their number reads some part of the common prayer and a sermon. They are now building a Church. . . . But the Independents, to suppress the design in its infancy, . . . have lately prosecuted and fined them for their meeting to worship God according to the common prayer. . . . The case of these poor people is very hard ; if, on the Lord's day, they continue at home, they must be punished ; if they meet to worship God according to the Church of England in the best manner they can, the mulct is much greater ; and if they go to the Independent meeting . . . they must endure the mortification of hearing the Church vilified."

After the death of the Rev. Joshua Honeyman missionary at Newport R. I. in 1750, the church of which he had the care, petitioned the Society that Mr. Beach might be sent to them, as their minister. The petition was granted, but Mr. Beach felt constrained, on account of feeble health to decline the appointment ; fearing, as he said, that " the people might complain that a wornout man was imposed upon them."

The first church on Redding Ridge, which was built in 1733, and was quite small, was in 1750 replaced by another on the same site, fifty feet long and thirty-six wide, surmounted by a turret, which, in 1797, was replaced by a steeple in which was placed the first bell. This church, according to the style of the period, was furnished with square, high-backed pews, with seats on their four sides ; so that some of their occupants had to sit with their backs to the minister. And though others doubtless besides Bishop Jarvis " could see no necessary connection between piety and freezing," there was no heating apparatus in the churches until considerably past the beginning of the present century. " Trinity Church, New Haven, had no means of being warmed until 1822, and none of the rural churches were supplied with stoves until a much later period." Many persons in the rural districts were in the habit of walking several miles, barefooted, to church in summer, and probably did not feel the lack of shoes a great privation. So common was it for men to go to church without their coats, that the first time Bishop Seabury preached in New Haven, a dissenting hearer reported that " he preached in his shirt-sleeves." Often the family was mounted, the parents with a child in arms to be christened, upon one horse, and the older children upon another. Sometimes the whole family were clustered together upon the ox-cart or sled, and thus they went up to the house of God.

In 1759, three years after the breaking out of the " Old French War," Mr. Beach, writing from " Reading, Connecticut, in N. England," says :

" My parish is in a flourishing condition, in all respects, excepting that we have lost some of our
young men in the army ; more, indeed by sickness
than by the sword, for this countrymen do not
bear a campaign so well as Europeans."

Dr. Johnson's playful remark to his son that,
" Mr. Beach had always these seeming inconsisten-
cies, to be always dying, and yet relishing mundane
things," would seem to indicate that his friend was
not really so near death's-door as he often imagined
himself : for example, in 1761, when he says : " My
painful and weak state of body admonishes me that,
although this may not be the last time of my writing, yet the last cannot be far off ;" and he had supposed himself a " worn out man" several years before.

Writing from " New-Town Oct. 3, 1764," he reports : " My congregation at Reading has increased
very little for some years past, by reason that many
who were wont to attend there, though living at a
distance of 6, 8, or 10 miles, have lately built [each]
a small church near them, where they can more
conveniently meet ; viz., at Danbury, Ridgbury,
North Fairfield and North Stratford ; which has
very much retarded the growth of the congregation
at Reading : which   .   .   .   now consists of about
300 hearers at one time." Under date of April,
1765, he says : " I am now engaged in a controversy
with some of the Independent Ministers about those
absurd doctrines, the sum of which is contained in a
thesis published by New Haven College last September.   .   .   .   They expressly deny that there is
any law of Grace, which promises eternal life upon

the condition of faith, repentance and sincere obedience ; and assert justification only by the law of innocence and sinless obedience. Though my health is small, and my abilities less, I make it a rule never to enter into any dispute with them unless they begin, yet now they have made the assault, and advocate such monstrous errors as do subvert the Gospel, I think myself obliged by my ordination vow, to guard the people as well as I can against such strange doctrines."

Again he writes in October of the same year, after the publication of that precursor of Revolution, the memorable " Stamp Act," of 1765 : " My parishes continue much in the same condition as in my last. I have of late, taken pains to warn my people against having any concern with seditious tumults with relation to the stamp duty enjoined upon us by the Legislature at home : and I can with truth and pleasure say, that I cannot discover the least inclination towards rebellious conduct in any of the Church people." A year later he says : " For some time past, I have not been without fear of being abused by a lawless set of men who style themselves the Sons of Liberty, for no other reason than that of endeavoring to cherish in my people a quiet submission to the civil government. . . . It is very remarkable, that in part of this Colony, in which many missions and Church people abound, there the people are vastly more peaceable and ready to render obedience to the Government of England ; but where there is no mission and few or no Church people, they are continually caballing, and will spill the last drop of blood, rather than submit to the late Act of Parliament." In 1767 he says : "It is some satisfaction to me to observe, that in this town [Newtown], of late, in our elections, the Church people make the major vote, which is the *first* instance of this kind in this Colony, if not in all New England." Again in 1769 : "There are in these two parishes about 2400 souls, of whom, a little more than half profess the Church of England. Here are about fifty negroes, most of whom after proper instruction have been baptized. . . . Here are no heathens or infidels. I commonly baptize about 100 children in one year, among them some black children. My actual communicants are 312. Here are no Papists or Deists." In 1771 he writes : " In Reading, my hearers at once are about 300. There is a meeting of Presbyterians about two and a half miles from our Church, in which the congregation is not so large as ours. In a manner, all . . . who live near the Church join with us ; scarce any go by the Church to meeting." " The Church, (he says in 1774) stands not in the centre of the town, but on one side, to accommodate the Church people, who live near, though out of the bounds of Reading."

One of the most interesting of his reports is that of May 5th, 1772 :

" It is now forty years since I have had the advantage of being the venerable Society's Missionary in this place. . . . Every Sunday I have performed divine service, and preached twice, at New Town and Reading alternately ; and in these forty years I have lost only two Sundays, through sickness ; although in all that time I have been afflicted

with a constant cholic which has not allowed me one
day's ease, or freedom from pain. The distance between the Church . . . is between eight and
nine miles, and no very good road ; yet I have never
failed . . . to attend at each place according to
custom, through the badness of the weather, but
have rode it in the severest rains and snow storms,
even when there has been no track, and my horse
near sinking down in the snow-banks ; which has
had this good effect on my parishioners, that they
are ashamed to stay from Church on account of bad
weather. . . . I have performed divine service
in many towns where the Common Prayer had never
been heard, nor the Holy Scriptures read in public,
and where now are flourishing congregations of the
Church of England ; and in some places where there
never had been any public worship at all, nor sermon preached by any teacher, of any denomination.

" In my travelling to preach the Gospel, once was
my life remarkably preserved, in passing a deep and
rapid river. The retrospect of my fatigues, lying
on straw &c, gives me pleasure ; while I flatter
myself that my labor has not been quite in vain ;
for the Church of England people are increased more
than 20 to 1, and what is infinitely more pleasing,
many of them are remarkable for piety and virtue ;
and the Independents here are more knowing in
matters of religion, than they who live at a distance
from the Church. We live in harmony and peace
with each other, and the rising generation of Independents seem to be entirely free from every pique
and prejudice against the Church." In a previous
report he said : " They who set up the worship of
God according to our Liturgy, at Lanesboro', at
Nobletown and Arlington, proceed chiefly from my
parishes. But notwithstanding these frequent emi-
grations, my congregations increase."

His last report, which was made about six months

before his death, is dated October 31st, 1781, and is as follows :

" It is a long time since I have done my duty in writing to the venerable Society, not owing to my carelessness, but to the impossibility of conveyance from here. And now I do it sparingly. A narrative of my troubles I dare not now give. My two congregations are growing : that at Reading being commonly about 300 and at New Town about 600. I baptized about 130 children in one year, and lately 2 adults. New Town and the Church of England, part of Reading are, I believe, the only parts of New England that have refused to comply with the doings of the Congress, and for that reason have been the butt of general hatred. But God has preserved us from entire destruction.

" I am now in the 82d year of my age ; yet do constantly, alternately, perform and preach at New Town and Reading. I have been 60 years a public preacher, and, after conviction, in the Church of England 50 years ; but had I been sensible of my inefficiency, I should not have undertaken it. But now I rejoice in that I think I have done more good towards men's eternal happiness, than I should have done in any other calling.

" I do most heartily thank the venerable Society for their liberal support, and beg that they will accept of this, which is, I believe, my last bill, viz : £325, which, according to former custom, is due. [Probably at £50 per annum for six years and a half, or from 1775.] At this age I cannot well hope for it, but I pray God I may have an opportunity to explain myself with safety ; but must conclude now with Job's expression : ' Have pity upon me, have pity upon me, O ye my friends ! ' "

Tradition has preserved a few incidents in his experience during the War of Independence :

"In the autumn of 1775, several officers of the militia, having collected a number of soldiers and volunteers from the different towns in Western Connecticut, undertook to subdue the tories. They went first to Newtown, where they put Mr. Beach, the Selectmen, and other principal inhabitants, under strict guard, and urged them to sign the Articles of Association, prescribed by the Congress at Philadelphia. When they could prevail upon them neither by persuasion nor by threats, they accepted a bond from them, with a large pecuniary penalty, not to take up arms against the Colonies, and not to discourage enlistments into the American forces."

Shortly after the declaration of Independence (*i.e.*, July 23d, 1776) the Episcopal clergy of the colony fearing to continue the use of the Liturgy as it then stood—praying for the king and royal family—and conscientiously scrupulous ·about violating their oaths and subscriptions, resolved to suspend the public exercise of their ministry. " All the churches were thus for a time closed, except those under the care of Mr. Beach. . . . He continued to officiate as usual" (as himself testifies) during the war. " Though gentle as a lamb in the intercourse of private life, he was bold as a lion in the discharge of public duty ; and, when warned of personal violence if he persisted, he declared that he would do his duty, preach, and pray for the King till the rebels cut out his tongue."

Whether the following were separate incidents, or are but different versions of one and the same, is uncertain : It is related that a squad of soldiers marched into his church in Newtown, and threat-

ened to shoot him if he prayed for the king ; but
when, regardless of their threats, he went on, without so much as a tremor in his voice, to offer the for-
bidden supplications, they were so struck with ad-
miration for his courage, that they stacked their
arms and remained to listen to the sermon.

A band of soldiers entered his church during service, seized him, and declared that they would kill
him.   He entreated that, if his blood must be shed,
it might not be in the house of God.   Thereupon
they took him into the street, where an axe and
block were soon prepared.   " Now, you old sinner
(said one), say your last prayer."   He knelt down
and prayed : " God bless King George, and forgive
all his enemies and mine, for Christ's sake."   One
of the mob then pleaded to " let the old fellow go,
and take some younger man instead."

The following is familiar to the people of Redding
Ridge parish.   The old church of 1750 had a single
door in the centre, and the pulpit and chancel were
at the west end, opposite the door.   A squad of soldiers, seven in number (hired, it is said, by 'Squire
Betts with a gallon of French brandy to shoot Mr.
Beach), gathered before the open door of the church,
and from one of them a bullet was fired which
lodged in one of the ribs of the sounding-board, a
foot or more above the head of the venerable preacher.   As the congregation sprang to their feet in
unfeigned consternation to rush from the church, he
quieted them by saying : " Don't be alarmed, brethren.   Fear not them that kill the body, but are not
able to kill the soul ; but rather fear him which is
able to destroy both soul and body in hell ;" and

then proceeded with his discourse as if nothing had happened.

The " History of the Episcopal Church in Connecticut" informs us that " the Redding Association of Loyalists was a strong body, whose secret influence was felt throughout the mission of the venerable pastor ;" but how or in what way that influence was exerted, does not appear. The " Sons of Liberty" have been already mentioned in Mr. Beach's reports.

After the death of Mr. Beach in 1782, the Revs. Richard Samuel Clarke and Andrew Fowler officiated here alternately for a short time. Clarke emigrated to Nova Scotia with others of the missionaries, and many of the members of their flocks, in 1784 or 1785. He returned on a visit in October, 1786. The discontinuance of the stipends of the missionaries by the S. P. G., whose charter restricted its benefactions to the British provinces and plantations, was a severe blow to the Episcopal churches, which had been already greatly weakened by the effects of the War of the Revolution. Mr. Beach's congregations were exceptions to the general rule, in that they increased while others diminished in numbers ; but whether few or many of the Redding Churchmen formed a part of the thirty thousand Loyalists who, Hawkins says, emigrated to the British provinces from New England and New York, it is impossible to ascertain. It is not probable, however, that there were half that number of Churchmen in all New England at the close of the war.

The next name on the list of ministers of this parish is that of Truman Marsh in 1785, who " visited the Parish every third Sunday ;" but, as he was not ordained till 1790, he must have been only a licensed lay-reader, though it is not improbable that he *preached*—as some of that class did, in those days when there was a dearth of ordained ministers. In 1794 the Rev. David Perry, M.D., minister of the parishes of Redding, Ridgefield, and Danbury, in consequence of some reports to his disadvantage as a clergyman, and of some errors in regard to baptism, was suspended from the ministry, and the next year, at his own request, deposed. He returned to the practice of medicine in Ridgefield.

The revenues of the Church were gathered after the Revolution much as they were before. " The Episcopal parishes were taxed to build churches and to sustain religious services, and the Diocesan Convention assessed the parishes to provide for the Bishop's Fund. Each parish was required to make an annual return of what was called the ' Grand Levy '—that is, its taxable list according to its last enrolment—and upon this return rested the right of a lay delegate to his seat in the Convention. The resolution which fixed this rule was adopted in 1803. The first published Grand Levy appeared in the Journal of 1806 ; and from that time onward for fifteen years the roll of the lay delegates was accompanied by the taxable list of the several parishes which they represented. If the list of any parish exceeded ten thousand dollars, such parish was en-titled to .   .   .   two delegates." The Grand Levy of the Redding parish in 1806 was $12,960.

" It is interesting to note the changes since that period in the relative wealth of the Church in Connecticut. In those early days, as reported, Litchfield was stronger than Waterbury or Hartford, Woodbridge was stronger than Meriden, Huntington than Derby, Redding than Bridgeport, and Newtown than New Haven."

The longest pastorate since Mr. Beach was that of his great-grandson, the Rev. Lemuel B. Hull, who resigned his charge in 1836, after twelve years' service. " In 1815, a fund of a little more than $3000 was raised."

On the second Tuesday in October, 1833—the year in which the present church edifice was built—the Annual Convention of the Diocese at Norwich failed to organize for want of two more lay delegates to form a quorum. " On the morning of that day, at three o'clock, the steamboat New England, on her passage from New York to Hartford, having on board seventy-one persons, burst both her boilers near Essex, and eight persons were immediately killed and thirteen seriously injured. Among those who were fatally injured were Mr. John M. Heron and Dr. Samuel B. Whiting, lay delegates from Christ Church, Redding ; and they were within a mile of their landing-place at the time of the accident."

In the spring of that year several members of the parish withdrew by certificate ; among these was John Meeker, clerk.

At a parish meeting, October 25th, 1834, the vestry were instructed " to take proper [legal] steps to procure the Records of the Parish from the hands of the late Clerk, without delay." At another meeting in December following, the agents of the parish (James Sanford, Jr., and Charles Beach) were authorized to "prosecute to final judgment such suits as they should deem necessary for the recovery of the books, records, funds or other property of the Society, before any Court proper to try the same."

In October, 1835, fifty dollars were appropriated from the parish treasury "to enable the agents to carry on the suit commenced against the heirs of John Meeker, deceased." Some money was thus recovered, but the records have never yet been found.

In 1847 the old parish debt of $870 (incurred in the building òf the church in 1833) was paid by subscription.

In 1850 the parish fund, about $2700, which before had been held as a loan by members of the parish, was by a considerable effort, and against the desire and judgment of the minority, collected and invested in the stock of the Fairfield County Bank. The same year the church edifice was altered and repaired, at an expense of $380.25. "On Advent Sunday" of this year, "the last Sunday of my ministry" (says the Rev. Joseph P. Taylor), "the sum of $600 was collected at the Offertory for the purpose of building a new parsonage."

"The above-named sum," says the Rev. Orsamus H. Smith, his successor, "having been put upon the plate in written pledges, there remains of them unredeemed in April, 1853, from fifty to one hundred dollars," which being "part of the money relied upon for the building, . . . the Vestry were obliged to borrow it, and it remains a debt upon the parish. The new house was finished in October, 1851, and immediately occupied by the family of Mr. Smith.

In 1858, says the Rev. W. W. Bronson : " The Glebe lot was very much improved by the purchase of a strip of land [on the west side] and the erection of a suitable fence, mainly through the exertions of the ladies of the parish."

In 1863 the organ was repaired, and the broken bell replaced by a new one of similar tone, from Meneeley's, at Troy.

In 1873 the church spire was repaired, and the old [English] weathercock, a relic of Colonial times (one of whose legs had been shot off by one of Tryon's soldiers in 1777), having persistently refused to remain upon his perch, was excused from further duty, and a gilded cross erected in his place. The venerable bird, however, is still to be seen on one of the outbuildings of the great-grandson of the Rev. John Beach, in East Redding. The parsonage was adorned in 1874 with a new and spacious veranda, in 1876 with a set of blinds.

The noticeable incidents of the present year, 1879, are the destruction of the church sheds by fire on the evening of the 12th of May, and the acquisition of a baptismal font of Italian marble, purchased with contributions of the Sunday-school and other members of the parish, collected during the rectorship of the Rev. Mr. Kelley. The number of nominal communicants is sixty-five ; of baptized persons, about one hundred and twenty.

LIST OF MINISTERS OFFICIATING IN THE PARISH OF CHRIST CHURCH, REDDING.

	FROM	TO
Rev. Henry Caner	1727	1732
" John Beach	Oct., 1732	Mar. 19, 1782
" R. S. Clarke } alt'nates. ' Andrew Fowler }	1782	
" Truman Marsh	1785	
" David Belden	1786	Officiated a short time only, on account of ill-health.
" Ambrose Hull	1789	1791
" David Perry, M.D	1791	Susp'd Nov. 1794.
" David Butler	Jan. 20, 1799	1804
" Elijah G. Plumb	Jan. 30, 1806	1811
' Reuben Hubbard	1812	1818
" Ambrose S. Todd, D.D	1820	1823
' Lemuel B. Hull	1824	Feb. 23, 1836
" Edward J. Darken, M.D	Aug., 1836	Dec. 25, 1837
" Charles Jarvis Todd	June, 1838	Easter, 1842
" William Atwill	May 8, 1842	1845
" David H. Short, D.D	Easter, 1845	1846
" Abel Nichols	1846	1847
" Joseph P. Taylor	Easter, 1847	Dec., 1850
" Orsamus H. Smith	Nov. 29, 1850	Mar. 31, 1853
" Abel Ogden	July 10, 1853	Died May 8, 1854.
·· James Adams	Autumn, 1854	Oct., 1856
" Wm. White Bronson	1857	1860
" Alfred Londerback	May 25, 1861	Aug. 5, 1862
" Henry Zell	March 12, 1863	Died Nov. 5, 1863.
" Wm. L. Bostwick	Easter, 1864	June 15, 1867
" John W. Hoffman	Dec. 6, 1868	Nov. 30, 1871
" Charles W. Kelley	Jan. 5, 1873	April 30, 1876
" Ximenus Alanson Welton	July 1, 1877	

The number of communicants belonging to Christ Church, Redding, as reported at different periods, were :

In 1809	55	In 1860	47
" 1810	63	" 1863	55
" 1811	67	" 1866	45
" 1815	61	" 1869	37
" 1817	61	" 1873	40
" 1845	42	" 1874	55
" 1851	60	" 1875	61
" 1854	56	" 1877	59
" 1856	57	" 1878	64
" 1858	58	" 1879	65
" 1859	56		

CHAPTER VII.

METHODIST EPISCOPAL CHURCH.
1789–1879.

WHEN Jesse Lee left New York on the mission which was to quicken and vitalize the New England churches, his first resting-place was at Norwalk, where he preached on the highway under a spreading elm, no house being opened to him. From Norwalk he proceeded to Fairfield and New Haven, and from the latter place to Redding. He reached this town on Wednesday, the 24th of June, 1789, and from this period we are to date the origin of the Methodist Church in Redding, although some six months elapsed before it was formally organized. In his journal under the above date, Mr. Lee thus narrates some of the incidents of this first visit :

" I travelled a stony road to Redding and according to directions called on Esquire Benedict but he was not at home ; so I got my horse and rode to Mr. Rogers to consult him about the matter. While I was talking to him Mr. Bartlett a Congregational minister came by, and being informed who I was asked me home with him. After I had been there a while he asked me some questions relative to doctrines, and I endeavored to inform him what kind of doctrines we preached. He said he could not invite me into the meeting house, because I held what he thought was contrary to the gospel. I told him I did not expect an invitation to preach in the meeting house, but if I was asked I should not refuse. However Mr. Rogers sent his son down in a little time to let me know that there was a school house that

9

I could preach in, so I made the appointment for the
people at six o'clock. Having met at that hour I
preached on Isa. 55 : 6 : ' Seek ye the Lord while he
may be found &c.' I bless God that I had some
liberty in preaching.''

The school-house where this first sermon was delivered probably stood on the common near the old
meeting-house. The few and simple doctrines that
Mr. Lee preached were the witness of the Spirit,
the entire efficacy of the Atonement, and the possi-
bility of falling from grace, and they were presented
with so much force and earnestness as to produce a
deep impression on those who heard them ; yet he
had no time to remain and note the effect produced,
but rode away the next day, carrying his tidings to
other communities. Twice again Lee visited Redding—July 8th, and September 16th of the same
year—without seeing any fruits of his efforts ; for,
although many were impressed with the truth of his
doctrines, they hesitated about coming out openly
and joining the new sect. At length on his fourth
visit, December 28th, 1789, he '' joined two in society for a beginning. A man who has lately received a witness of his being in favor with the Lord
led the way, and a woman who I hope was lately
converted, followed.'' This was the second Methodist society organized in New England, the first being at Stratford. The two first members mentioned
above were Aaron Sanford and his mother-in-law,
Mrs. William Hawley. Mr. Sanford by this act became the first male member of the Methodist Church
in New England ; he was at once appointed leader
of the class thus formed, and its meetings were held

for years at his house. After its organization the growth of the Society was very rapid, chiefly through the class-meeting, and that agency so effectively used by Methodism, the lay preachers.

It is unfortunate that, owing to the loss of the early records of the church, we can give the names of but few of its original members. From the records of the first society I copy the following certificate, dated December 15th, 1789 :

" I hereby certify that Aaron Sanford of Reading, has constantly attended the Methodist meetings in this town, and pays his part toward my support as a minister of the gospel.

" JESSE LEE."

Similar certificates were given, February 9th, 1790, to Hezekiah Sanford, and August 6th of the same year to Isaac Sherwood, and S. Samuel Smith.

From the church book of baptisms which has been preserved, we learn that prior to 1794 the early preachers had baptized children of Daniel and Anna Bartram, Silas and Huldah Merchant, Jonas and Lucy Platt, Paul and Mary Bartram, Jabez, and Sarah Gorham, Elijah and Menoma Elder, Aaron and Mary Odle, John and Sarah Sherman, Uriah and Hannah Mead, Benjamin and Elizabeth Knap, Chester and Elizabeth Meeker, Charles and Lucy Morgan, Ezekiel and Easter Bertram, Jesse and Martha Banks, Isaac and Betty Platt, and Aaron and Eunice Hunt, and we may safely reckon them as members of the church at that time.

Early in 1790 Lee organized his first circuit in New England ; it was called the " Fairfield Circuit," and embraced Norwalk, Fairfield, Stratford, Milford, Redding, Danbury, Canaan, and intermediate places. The first regularly appointed minister whose name appears on the Society records was John Bloodgood, who was here as early as January 21st, 1791, perhaps earlier. He was a native of the South, and after serving on the Fairfield Circuit one year, was transferred to the Baltimore Conference, to which his ministerial labors were chiefly confined. He died in 1810. Like most of his colleagues, he preached in the school-houses, under trees, sometimes in the barns, but always so fervently, and with such native eloquence, that multitudes flocked to hear him. He was succeeded at the May (1791) session of the Conference by Nathaniel B. Mills and Aaron Hunt.

Mr. Mills is described by his colleague, Mr. Hunt, as " a man small in stature, intelligent, sound, an able preacher, and rather inclined to dejection." He was born in New Castle County, Delaware, February 23d, 1766. He entered the Baltimore Conference in the spring of 1787, and after a laborious ministry of forty-two years, both in New England and the South, was compelled in 1835 to retire to the ranks of the superannuated, where he remained until his death in 1844. His colleague, Rev. Aaron Hunt, was born in Eastchester, Westchester County, N. Y., March 28th, 1768, and entered the Methodist ministry in 1791, making some of his first essays at preaching on the Redding Circuit.

In 1793, while preaching in Redding, he married Miss Hannah Sanford, daughter of the Mr. Aaron Sanford before mentioned, and shortly after " lo·cated" in Redding, where he continued to reside for

many years, and where most of his large family of
children were born. Mr. Hunt was prominent among
the early Methodist preachers, and was well known
throughout the State. During his pastorate the
church had been encouraged by a visit from the eminent Bishop Asbury, who passed through Redding
in June, 1791, during his hasty tour through New
England, and preached here " with much satisfaction," as he remarks in his journal. The church received another and longer visit from him in September, 1796. " The society in that village," says Mr.
Stevens, the historian of Methodism, " had been
gradually gathering strength. They assembled to
greet him at Mr. Sandford's, where he gave them an
encouraging discourse from 1 Peter 1 : 13–15."
From this time until 1811, the record of the church
is one of continued growth and prosperity ; revivals
were frequent and accessions many ; classes were
early formed at Lonetown, Redding Ridge, Sanfordtown, Boston, and at Long Ridge, the latter some
years later becoming a separate church organization.

Still the society was without a house of worship,
and the want was beginning to be severely felt.
In 1803 they first leased the town-hall for a place of
public worship, as appears by the following extract
from the town records : " At a town meeting held
December 12, 1803, it was voted, ' That the Town
House be leased to the Methodist Society for $15
per year to be used as often, and as much as they
please for public worship, and said Society to repair
all damage done to the Town House while they are
assembled therein for public worship.' " This lease
was continued from year to year at varying rates,

until the erection of the first church in 1811. Of the
building of this edifice we have no data except such
as is contained in this extract from the society
records :

"At a Society meeting of the Methodists, duly
warned and held at the house of William Sanford
in Redding, on Tuesday the 30th day of October,
1810. Voted, that Seth Andrews, William Sanford,
and John R. Hill be a committee to said society for
the ensuing year, to do and transact all temporal
business. Voted, That our said committee carry
round a subscription paper immediately to raise
money for the purpose of building a Meeting-House
in said Redding, for the purpose of Divine Worship.

"AARON SANFORD, *Clerk.*"

The church was built the succeeding summer. It
stood on the site of the present residence of Deacon
Charles Smith, on land purchased of Jonathan R.
Sanford, Esq. His deed conveying the land, dated
June 6th, 1811, was given to Seth Andrews, William
Sanford, and John R. Hill, trustees for the Methodist church and society in Redding, the consideration
being $130. No actual description of the first
church is preserved to us, except that it was built
after the usual fashion of Methodist churches in
those days. It had no steeple nor tower, no ceiling
except the roof, and there were no means of warm-
ing it, except by foot-stoves carried in by the female
worshippers. With the above exceptions, the following description of an early Methodist church would
probably apply to this in every particular :

"The building was as unpolluted by paint within
and without as when its timbers were standing in

their native forest. A gallery extended around three sides. At the extreme end of the left gallery was a small room partitioned off for class meetings. The pulpit was elevated about six feet above the floor, and in form resembled a large dry goods box, the breastworks so high as almost to conceal the preacher if small of stature from view. From the pulpit extended a staircase conducting to the class-room in the gallery, to which the preacher and the members repaired at the close of the public services."*

None of the incidents in the history of the old church are so vividly remembered and described as the quarterly meetings which were held there. The quarterly meeting to the early Methodist was the most important of all the institutions of the church, and those held in Redding were especially note-worthy ; it was a sort of home-coming to the mother church, and at such times all the Methodist homes in town were open to the brethren from abroad. The presiding elder and the two preachers on the " Circuit" were always present on these occasions, and the membership was gathered from Danbury, Ridge-field, Easton, and Newtown, as well as from places more remote. The exercises on these occasions began at 9 o'clock on Sabbath morning with the " love-feast" and the passing of bread and water, of which all partook, as a token of their brotherhood in Christ. At 10.30 a sermon was preached by the elder. At 12 M. the Sacrament of the Lord's Supper was administered. At 1 P.M. another sermon was preached, generally by one of the preachers in

* Sermon of Rev. J. L. Gilder, before the N. Y. East Conference.

charge. At the conclusion of this discourse the genial elder would proceed to designate to the guests their respective places of entertainment. The day was usually concluded by a series of prayer-meetings held in the different districts, and conducted with great warmth and fervor.

The old church seems to have been intended for a temporary structure, and was succeeded in 1837 by the present neat and commodious edifice. A brief account of the erection of the present building will be interesting and probably *new* to many, though little more than forty years have elapsed since its timbers were standing in the forest.

We find on the society records the following entries :

" The members of the Methodist Episcopal Society of Redding are hereby notified and warned, that a society's meeting for said society will be held on Tuesday the 26th day of instant January at one o'clock P.M. at the Methodist Church in said Redding for the purpose of taking into consideration the propriety of building a new church in said society, and locating the same near the intersection of the roads near the Town House, appointing a building committee to superintend and carry said object into effect, make arrangements to dispose of the old house if thought proper, and to do any other business proper to be done at said meeting.

" SHERLOCK TODD, 〕
   JESSE BANKS, 〉 *Trustees.*
   AARON MALLETT, 〕

" REDDING, Jan. 20, 1836."

A society meeting was held at the appointed time—Rev. H. Humphreys being chairman, and

Thomas B. Fanton clerk. It was then voted "To approve of the proposed plan in the caption of the subscription paper to raise subscriptions and build a new house. . . . "

It was also further provided "that the said House shall be located somewhere near the four corners that intersect at Redding Town House, But the said object not to take effect, unless the sum of Two thousand Five hundred Dollars be subscribed, and the said House be built within eighteen months from the date hereof."

Voted : "To build a House agreeable to the above caption, provided a place be obtained that is approved by the committee appointed for that purpose."

Voted : "To appoint a Building Committee of three persons to superintend, and take charge, and contract for the same House, viz. : Thomas B. Fanton, John R. Hill, and Gershom Sherwood."

Voted : "To add two more to the building Committee—Jesse Banks and David Duncomb."

Voted : "To adjourn the meeting two weeks from this day at one P.M."

THOMAS B. FANTON, *Clerk.*

No account of the adjourned meeting is to be found in the society records. The twenty-five hundred dollars needed was speedily subscribed, and the building was erected in the summer of 1837 and dedicated in December of the same year, Rev. C. K. True preaching the dedication sermon.

In 1868, during the pastorate of Rev. William T. Hill, the church was thoroughly remodelled and refurnished. The pulpit was cut down, and the antique pews exchanged for the present neat and comfortable ones. The rededication service at this time was perhaps the most interesting occasion in the history of the church. Bishop Janes was present, and preached the dedication sermon to an audience that filled every nook and corner of the building, and many old pastors and friends of the church added by their presence to the interest of the occasion.

In September, 1870, Rev. Aaron Sanford Hill gave to the church some ten acres of land lying in the northerly part of the town, the income from which was to be appropriated to the use of the church. This gift Mr. Sanford supplemented by another of $4000 in 1871, of which the interest only was to be used in meeting the expenses of the church. This fund is known as the Sanford Hill Fund. In 1877 another benefaction of $500 was given by William A. Sanford, Esq., to be applied in the same manner as the preceding.

Revivals in the church have been frequent, and attended with gratifying results: notably in 1815 under the preaching of Rev. Reuben Harris, in 1822 during the pastorate of Aaron Hunt, in 1838 under that of Rev. John Crawford, in 1855 under Rev. E. S. Hebbard, and in 1867 under Rev. William T. Hill.

According to the minutes of the Annual Conferences the following ministers were appointed to Fairfield Circuit (which included Redding), beginning with its organization in 1790 :

1790 John Bloodgood.
1791 Nathaniel B. Mills, Aaron Hunt.
1792 Joshua Taylor, Smith Weeks.
1793 James Coleman, Aaron Hunt.
1794 Zebulon Kankey, Nicholas Snethen.

Those appointed to Redding Circuit were :

1795 Daniel Dennis, Timothy Dewey.
1796 Elijah Woolsey, Robert Leeds.
1797 David Buck, Augustus Jocelyn.
1798 William Thatcher.
1799 David Brown.
1800 Augustus Jocelyn.
1801 Samuel Merwin, Isaac Candee.
1802 James Coleman, Isaac Candee.
1803 James Campbell, N. U. Tompkins.
1804 Peter Moriarty, Sylvester Foster.
1805 Peter Moriarty, Samuel Merwin.
1806 Nathan Felch, Oliver Sykes.
1807 James M. Smith, Zalmon Lyon.
1808 Noble W. Thomas, Jonathan Lyon.
1809 Billy Hibbard, Isaac Candee.
1810 Nathan Emory, John Russell.
1811 Aaron Hunt, Oliver Sykes, and John Reynolds.
1812 Seth Crowel, Gilbert Lyon, S. Beach.
1813 Aaron Hunt, Henry Eames.
1814 Ebenezer Washburne, Reuben Harris.
1815 Elijah Woolsey, Reuben Harris.
1816 Samuel Bushnell, John Boyd.
1817 Samuel Bushnell, Theodocius Clarke.
1818 James M. Smith, Theodocius Clarke.
1819 J. S. Smith, Phineas Cook.
1820 Laban Clark, Phineas Cook.
1821 Laban Clark, Aaron Hunt.
1822 Samuel Cochrane, Aaron Hunt.
1823 Samuel Cochrane, John Reynolds.
1824 Elijah Woolsey, John Reynolds.

To Redding and Bridgeport Circuit :

1825 Marvin Richardson, H. Humphreys, Frederic W. Siger.
1826 Marvin Richardson, H. Humphreys.
1827 Henry Stead, John Lovejoy, J. C. Bontecue.

To Redding Circuit :

1828 Henry Stead, Gershom Pearce.
1829 Ebenezer Washburn, Gershom Pearce.
1830 Ebenezer Washburn, Oliver V. Ammerman.
1831 James Young, Josiah Bowen.
1832 Nicholas White, Jesse Hunt.
1833 Jesse Hunt, John B. Beach.
1834 Josiah Bowen, John B. Beach.

To Redding and Newtown Circuit :

1835 Humphrey Humphries, Josiah L. Dickerson,
       John Davies.
1836 Humphrey Humphries.

March 28th, 1837, the society, "after due deliberation, existing circumstances being considered, voted to try a station the ensuing year ;" which was accordingly done, and the Rev. Humphrey Humphries became the first stated pastor.

Since then the church has enjoyed the undivided care of its pastors, and has been generally prosperous and aggressive.

The list of pastors since 1837 comprises many well-known names and will be read with interest. They are as follows :

      1838   John Crawford, 2d ; Morris Hill.
      1839–40   Paul R. Brown.
      1841–2   Daniel Smith.
      1843   Phillip L. Hoyt.
      1844–5   William F. Collins.
      1846–7   Joseph D. Marshall.
      1848–9   Jacob Shaw.
      1850–1   John L. Gilder.
      1852–3   Friend W. Smith.
      1854–5   E. S. Hibbard.
      1856–7   Hart F. Pease.

1858   George C. Crevey.
1859   William H. Gilder.
1860–1 John W. Horne.
1862–3 George Hollis.
1864–6 David Nash.
1867–8 William T. Hill.
1869   Alexander Graham.
1870–2 Theodore C. Beach.
1873   William R. Webster.
1874–6 Joseph Smith.
1877–8 John Dickinson.
1879   John Haugh.

Of the above list, but one, Rev. Jacob Shaw, died and was buried in Redding. Of the laymen who nobly aided these clergymen in their ministry many will be held in grateful remembrance by the church.

The names most familiar to the early membership perhaps were those of the lay preachers, Aaron Sanford, Hawley Sanford, Rory Starr, and Walter Sanford; the class leaders, John R. Hill, Abraham Couch, Urrai Meade, Sherlock Todd, and Bradley Burr; and the official members, Thomas B. Fanton, David S. Duncomb, Aaron Sanford, Jr., Charles Gorham, Eben Treadwell, and John Edmonds.

The present membership of the church is 149. Males, 57; females, 92.

II.

THE METHODIST EPISCOPAL CHURCH AT LONG RIDGE.

The origin of the Methodist Episcopal Church in Long Ridge, as narrated by Rev. Paul R. Brown, pastor of the church in 1842, was as follows:

" One evening as Father Coleman (a Methodist preacher) was passing through Starr's Plain, on his way to Danbury, he saw a man sitting on the fence by the wayside, and inquired the distance to town. The man told him, and added : ' Are you a Doctor ? ' ' No, sir.' ' Are you a Lawyer ? ' ' No, sir.' ' Then,' said the man, following up the question, ' what are you ? ' Father Coleman answered, ' I am a Methodist preacher.' ' Methodist preacher ! What's that ? ' replied the man. ' If you will open your house, and invite in your neighbors, I will let you hear a Methodist preacher, the next time I come this way,' was the reply. The offer was accepted, and Father Coleman preached to them on his next visit ; he soon organized a class, and among the members of that class was the man who sat upon the fence and questioned the preacher. After that the class grew into a society, and in due time a small church was built in Long Ridge, which gave way to a larger edifice, in the course of a few years."

The first church was built when the society consisted of but eleven members, under the following circumstances. They were assembled for the weekly class-meeting at the house of one of their number, and were speaking of their need of a church, when Uriah Griffin remarked, that if he had a hundred dollars in hand he would build them a church. David Osborne, the youngest member present, at once agreed to furnish the required sum, and the church was built the same year. This was in 1820–1, during the pastorate of Rev. Laban Clark. The little society at once became connected with Redding Station as an auxiliary, the preacher in charge there having the care of its temporal concerns, and filling its pulpit once in four weeks. In the interim the pulpit was supplied by the lay preachers, Aaron Sanford, Morris Hill, Aaron S. Hill, of Redding, Rory Starr, of Danbury, and others. The society's connection with Redding ceased in 1848, and the same relation was formed with the church in Bethel. For several years past it has been a separate station. The pastors of the church from 1820 to 1848 were the same as those of Redding, and are given in the history of the Redding Church. The pastors since 1848 have been as follows :

1848–9 Morris Hill.
1850   Elias Gilbert.
1851–2 Charles Bartlett.
1853–4 George Stillman.
1855–6 Samuel H. Smith.
1857–8 John Crawford.
1859   David Osborn.
1860–1 Sherman D. Barnes, local preacher.
1862–3 Elias Gilbert.
1864   William H. Adams.
1865   J. W. Bramblee.
1866–7 G. W. Polley, local.
1868   Stephen J. Stebbins.
1869   James H. Crofut, local.
1870   Frank F. Jorden, local.
1871   William P. Armstrong, local.
1872   Frank F. Jorden, local.
1873   Joseph W. Pattison, local.
1874–5 William Cogswell, local.
1876   Joseph W. Pattison, local.
1877–8 Charles A. Wilson, local.
1879   Henry A. Van Dalsem.

The membership at present is sixty.*

* The present church edifice is situated in Danbury, a few yards from the Redding line, but as the church was so long identified with Redding, it was thought proper to preserve its history here.

III.

A few yards from Redding Station, on the banks of the Saugatuck River, is situated the old campground, noted for being the place where the first camp-meeting of the Methodists in New England was held. Just when this event occurred we are unable to state, but it was about 1810, probably under the leadership of Nathan Bangs. The tents of this first assemblage were of the most primitive kind, many of them being constructed of the branches of trees, and others of blankets stretched over a framework of poles. Meetings continued to be held in this grove every year for over sixty years.

About 1860, owing to some difficulty in leasing the grounds, and from other causes, the meetings here were discontinued, and another camp-ground opened at Milford, Conn., on the line of the Naugatuck Railroad.

This grove was, however, soon abandoned, never having been popular with the Methodist public. In 1878, after the lapse of nearly twenty years, the old camp-ground at Redding was reopened, and that year a very successful and well-attended meeting was held there.

It was supposed, then, that the grove would be purchased and continue to be used for camp-meeting purposes, but this desirable consummation was not effected.

CHAPTER VIII.

THE BAPTIST CHURCH IN GEORGETOWN (NOW EXTINCT).

THAT there was a society of Baptists in Redding as early as 1785, appears from an entry in the records of the First Society, dated December 9th, 1785, wherein Michael Wood has a certificate given him by John Lee, Deacon, as a member of the Baptist church in Redding.

Similar certificates were given to John Couch, Micayah Starr, and Jabez Wakeman; but we have no evidence of the existence of a church here until 1833. On the 28th of January of that year an ecclesiastical council was held at the house of Timothy Wakeman, in Redding, and a church formally organized. The record of the proceedings of this meeting constitutes the first entry in the Church Book of Records, and is as follows:

"Chose Elder Thomas Lascombe Moderator, and Elder Nathan Wildman, Clerk. Invited Brethren present to a seat with the Council. Proceeded to hear the Articles and Covenant, also reasons why they wished to be constituted into a Church. The Council unanimously voted to proceed to the constitution. Repaired to the meeting house. Introductory prayer and sermon by Elder Nathan Wildman. Right hand of fellowship in behalf of the Council, and closing prayer by Elder Thomas Lascombe. "NATHAN WILDMAN, *Clerk.*"

There were but 18 original members—4 males and 14 females. For some years there was no settled pas-

10

tor, and the pulpit was supplied alternately, once in four weeks, by Elders S. Ambler, of Danbury, and Stephen B. Bray, a licentiate from Southbury, Conn. Elders N. Wildman, of Weston ; Erastus Doty, of Colebrook, Conn., and Chandler Curtis also preached occasionally. June 3d, 1837, the church extended a unanimous call to Rev. William Bowen, of Mansfield, Conn., which was accepted, and he became the first pastor of the church. He continued to sustain this relation to the church until November, 1838, when he was dismissed, owing to the inability of the society to meet his salary. The same month the church edifice was nearly destroyed by mob violence—the only instance of the kind that ever occurred in this staid and conservative town.

It was 1838, the period of the slavery excitement, when abolitionist and pro-slavery man engaged in almost daily conflict, and men thought to stifle with shot-gun and bludgeon the first faint stirrings of the national conscience. A few pithy entries in the church records thus refer to the affair :

" Nov. 26th. Rev. Nathaniel Colver lectured on slavery in our meeting house—was disturbed by unruly persons."

" 27th. Another lecture on Slavery molested as night before."

" 28th. Meeting house blown up by a mob, but not entirely destroyed."

This is all the information the church records give us on the subject, but from the files of the Norwalk *Gazette* for that year we glean a full account of the affair. This article is interesting, as showing

the manner in which even the Whigs handled the
question of slavery at that time.

"HIGH-HANDED OUTRAGE.—We learn that Judge
Lynch has been exercising his summary proceedings
in this vicinity within the week past. Colver, the
abolitionist lecturer, has been holding forth, as we
understand, for a number of evenings, on the subject
of immediate emancipation, in the Baptist church in
Redding, and in the course of his lectures had taken
occasion to exhibit before his audience the *practical amalgamationism* of the Vice-President of the
United States, the Hon. Richard M. Johnson. We
are informed that he accused this distinguished per-
sonage of making merchandise of the offspring of
his own loins, of selling his own sons and daughters
into slavery. This so enraged some of his political
partisans, that they determined to *abolish* the walls
which had echoed the nefarious libel upon ' Dick,
the Tecumseh Killer.' So, after the lecture was concluded, a keg of gunpowder was deposited under
the church which had been profaned by these abo-
lition orgies—and about two o'clock on the morning
of the 29th ult. the church was blown ' sky-high,' as
John Randolph used to say. It was a small building of one story, and not worth more than $500.
But notwithstanding the provocation, and notwithstanding the comparatively trifling amount of damage
occasioned by this wanton outrage, we most sin-
cerely deprecate the prevalence of a spirit which
does violence to the dearest rights of every freeman
in the land—the freedom of speech and of opinion.
We are no apologists for the intemperate and fanatic
zeal of the abolitionists ; but we deem it the duty
of every press in the land to cry out against such
violations of the Constitution and laws. And though
we would denounce in the severest terms the exas-
perating conduct of the abolitionists, we would at the
same time do our utmost to bring the trespassers

upon the rights which the Constitution guarantees to every citizen and the violators of the public peace, to condign punishment."*

This action of the mob, with the dissensions engendered by it, proved a sad blow to the church, and from which it never fully recovered, although it continued in existence for several years. Elder John H. Waterbury served the church as pastor for some months in 1839, and was succeeded in 1841 by Elder John Noyes, of North Haven.

Mr. Noyes' letter of dismission from the Baptist church in North Haven is as follows :

"*The Baptist Church in North Haven to the Baptist Church in Reading.*

" DEAR BRETHREN, This certifies that Rev. John Noyes and his wife Ann are members of this church in good standing, and as such we commend them to your Christian affection and fellowship. We have voted that when they are received by you, we shall consider their connection with us dissolved.

" In behalf of the church in North Haven.
                "M. F. ROBINSON, *Clerk.*
" May 1, 1841."

April 2d, 1842, Mr. Noyes was dismissed to Phillipstown, N. Y. Rev. George Crocker, of Danbury, supplied the pulpit for the succeeding twelve

---

* A resident of Georgetown at the time gives the following additional particulars : About two o'clock on the morning following Mr. Colver's lecture, the inhabitants of Georgetown were startled by a tremendous report and rumbling noise, which jarred the houses and broke the windows in the immediate neighborhood. In the morning, this unusual disturbance was found to have been caused by the explosion of a keg of powder which had been placed directly under the pulpit, a portion of the underpinning of the church having been removed for that purpose. The pulpit was demolished, the front of the building displaced several feet, the windows broken out, and the walls destroyed.

months. Elder David Pease was the next preacher, he being called February 11th, 1844. His connection with the church was short and uneventful. There is no record of any other preacher being called ; in fact, the society was becoming too weak to support an organization, and shortly after, in October, 1847, was dissolved by the unanimous vote of its members.

CHAPTER IX.

THE METHODIST PROTESTANT CHURCH IN GEORGE-
TOWN (NOW THE CONGREGATIONAL CHURCH).

THE Methodist Protestant Church in Georgetown had its origin in a small schism in the Methodist Episcopal Church, commencing about 1818, in the New York Conference.

Among the ministers who seceded from the church at this time was the Rev. William M. Stillwell, who, in 1820, organized a small class of persons in Georgetown, sharers in his peculiar ideas of church polity, but who still retained the name of Methodist, though called by their opponents Stillwellites. In 1829 a convention was held and adopted the name of Methodist Protestant, and in 1839 the church at Georgetown was formally organized as the Methodist Protestant Church and Society, of Wilton Circuit. The first members of the class, so far as can be ascertained, were Ebenezer Hill, Banks Sherwood, David Nichols, Isaac Osborne, and Benjamin Gilbert and wife. The first minister was Rev. William M. Stillwell.   The first entry in the church records is as follows :

" The first Methodist Protestant church in Redding was organized in the year of our Lord 1839, on the 15th of the 9th month, at a regular warned meeting held at the house of Sturges Bennett.   The following officers were chosen.   David Nichols chairman, John O. St. John, secretary.   John O. St. John was duly elected clerk of said society, and the oath was administered by Walker Bates, Esq.   John O. St. John was also elected Treasurer of said society."

Aaron Osborne was the first sexton.   (He was to open the church thirty minutes before service, sweep the house, make the fires, and attend to the lights, for a yearly salary of $6.00.)

The present house of worship had been built in 1839, prior to the organization of the church, by John O. St. John and Charles Scribner.   For a number of years the church records show only the ordinary routine of business.   In 1851, March 10th, a society's meeting passed the following resolutions :

" *Resolved*, 1st : That we take into consideration the amount of Damage sustained by the society, by the Danbury and Norwalk R. R. crossing the society's grounds near this house of worship.   2nd : That the assessment of damages by crossing the society's grounds be left to three men—one chosen by the trustees, one by the Rail Road contractors, and those two to choose a third.   3rd : That the trustees be instructed to hold the contractors or Rail Road Company responsible for all damage to the society's house of worship."

To these resolutions a meeting held December 27th, 1851, added the following :

" *Resolved*, by vote of this meeting that the society's committee be authorized to give by deed to the Danbury and Norwalk Railroad Company a right of way across said Society's ground, for the consideration of one hundred and fifty Dollars." At a meeting held February 19th, 1853 : " On motion S. M. Main and Hiram St. John, were appointed a committee to circulate a subscription to raise money to build a parsonage house." A meeting held November 17th, 1853, voted : " that the society's committee be authorized to circulate a subscription paper, to raise money to the amount of six hundred dollars for the purpose of purchasing Mr. Weed's house for a parsonage ; and at a subsequent meeting held November 26th, the committee were authorized to purchase Mr. Weed's house so soon as six hundred dollars is pledged for that purpose." It was also voted that the " horse sheds be located 40 feet south of the butternut tree in the yard, provided the ground can be obtained for one dollar."

At a meeting held December 7th, 1867, Messrs. John R. Sturges, J. O. St. John, and Sturges Bennett were appointed a committee to ascertain the denominational preferences of all the members of the church, " with a view to a change of name to that of Congregational, or that of letting it be the Methodist Protestant Meeting."

This committee reported to an adjourned meeting, held December 14th, in favor of a change of name, and by a unanimous vote the name of the church was changed from Methodist Protestant to Congregational. It was also voted to petition the next legislature to change the name of the society in accordance with the above vote, and to secure to the Congregational Society the property now held by the Methodist Protestant Society. The committee appointed for this purpose were Messrs. David E. Smith, Hiram St. John, and E. G. Bennett. From October, 1865, to May, 1875, the church was supplied by Rev. Samuel St. John, of Georgetown. He was succeeded by Rev. Albert H. Thompson, of Yale Theological Seminary, who supplied the pulpit until November, 1876. Mr. Thompson's successor was Rev. C. B. Strong, of Hartford Seminary, who remained until the close of 1877. The present pastor, Rev. C. A. Northrop, began his labors with the church January 6th, 1878, and was ordained and installed as pastor October 2d, 1878.

The present membership of the church is 79. Males, 30 ; females, 49.

The records of the Methodist Protestant Church give no data of the settlement or dismissal of pastors. From old members of the church, however, I gain the following names of those who served the church in this capacity. The list is probably complete, though the names are not given in the order of succession. They were : William M. Stillwell, Stephen Treadwell, Abram Glasgow, Stephen Remington, —— Shemeall, —— Vredenburgh, James Summerbell, Aaron G. Brewer, Richard K. Diossy, James Rolliston, William McCutcheon, William H. Bosely, William Cliff, Samuel M. Henderson, Jacob Timberman,—— Wade, Elizur W. Griswold, Merwin Lent, William H. Johnson, John L. Ambler, Joseph J. Smith, Joshua Hudson, Thomas K. Witsel, John H. Painter, M. E. Rude, William C. Clarke.

CHAPTER X.

HISTORY OF SCHOOLS.

WE have before spoken of the care of our Puritan
ancestors to provide for the church and the ministry
in their infant settlements. They were equally careful to furnish them with the school and the teacher.
If piety was one of the pillars of Democracy, so
also was intelligence ; and church and school were
alike deemed indispensable to the growth and
security of the state : hence we find the pioneers of
Redding making early provision for the establishment of schools among them. The first *recorded*
movement of the parish in the matter was in 1737,
when, at a parish meeting held December 26th, 1737,
it was voted to have a parish school, and to maintain
said school by a parish rate. John Read, Joseph
Lee, Joseph Sanford, John Hull, Nathan Lion, Stephen Morehouse, and Daniel Lion were the first
school committee. The meeting also voted : " that
said school be divided into three parts, that is to
say, five months in that quarter called the Ridge,
and five months on the west side of the parish near
the mill, and two months at Lonetown, understanding that the centre of division is the meeting-house,
and that Stephen Burr belongs to the west side."

These were the original school districts of the
town : in them the first rude school-houses were
erected, and from the one to the other went the
peripatetic school-master as his duties called him.
These school-houses were built of logs : their furni-

ture was of the most meagre description, consisting
of a·sloping desk of boards affixed to the wall and
extending around three sides of the building,
benches of rough-hewn plank, and a planed pine
board whereon the student "figgered" with bits of
charcoal. Nor was the curriculum of the schools
much more extensive. Reading, writing, and arith-
metic were all that was then thought necessary for
the country boy to know ; further knowledge was
to be acquired in schools of a higher grade.

As years passed on, and new families moved into
the place, the districts became strong enough each
to support its own school.

Hence we find a parish meeting held December
10th, 1742, voting : " that the interest of the school
money belonging to the parish shall be divided into
three equal parts for the year ensuing, for the maintaining of three separate schools (each to be kept by
a master,) one third part of the money for that part
of the Parish east of Little River, one third part for
that part of the Parish between Little River and the
Saugatuck River, and one third for that part west
of the Saugatuck. Provided, that each part of the
Parish as above divided, keep a school as abovesaid
three months in the year ensuing, but if any part of
the Parish fail in keeping a school as abovesaid, the
other two parts that keep said school, shall equally
divide the said money between them, and if two
parts of the Parish fail in keeping a school as abovesaid, that part of the Parish that shall keep said
school the three months, shall draw the whole of the
school money." The same districts are defined in
the appropriation of the school money in 1743 as

being " the school on the West side of Aspetuck
River, the school by Mill River (Saugatuck) and the
school by the Church."

In 1745 the appropriation was made to the same
districts, with the provision that each should " keep
a school with a school master sufficiently capable to
learn children to Wright and Reade."

There seems to have been no change in this respect until 1764, when it was voted : " that the
school money should be subdivided according to
the lists within such subdivisions." In 1768 the
bounds of the districts were first set out by a committee appointed at town meeting for the purpose.
This first committee consisted of Stephen Mead,
Daniel Hill, and Daniel Sanford. The school committee for this year, appointed at town meeting, consisted of seven, and it is probable that each represented a district—which would give us seven districts in the town at that time.

December 19th, 1792, the following important vote
was taken : " that the School money shall be lodged
with the Treasurer, and he to collect the interest
arising on the School bonds annually by the first
day of April, the Interest already arisen and unpaid
to be collected forthwith, and in failure of pay-
ment of back interest, he to send the bond, or
bonds, and collect principal and interest, and to conduct in the same manner on neglect of annual pay-
ment of interest on said Bonds, and to pay said Interest and School Money to the School Committee
as it may be appropriated by the committee of the
Districts annually."

As to the source or origin of these school bonds.
or by whom taken, I am unable to give a positive
answer. The town of Redding has a school fund of
$400, distinct from the State fund, and which dates
back to a period beyond the reach of memory or
tradition ; it is more than probable, however, that it
was the sum realized from the sale of lands in Litchfield County in 1733, called western lands, and
which was divided among the several towns in proportion to their poll list and ratable estate for that
year and to be secured and forever improved for the
use of the schools kept in said towns according to
law. Redding, unlike most of her sister towns, has
preserved this fund inviolate, and still uses its pro-
ceeds in support of her schools. In 1795 came the
sale of the Western Reserve, and Connecticut's munificent grant to her common schools, which has put
them in the front rank of educational forces, and
contributed so much to the material prosperity of
the State. In October of that year the inhabitants
of Redding met, and formed themselves into a
school society, in order that they " might have the
advantage of the monies arising from the sale of
western lands." Peter Sanford, James Rogers, and
Simeon Munger were the first committee chosen by
this society. Prior to 1870, the cost of supporting
the schools above that derived from the school
funds was borne by the parents or guardians of the
scholars, but in that year the legislature passed a
law compelling the towns to maintain free schools,
and this plan has since been pursued. The town
appropriation for schools this year, 1879, is $2500 ;

before 1879, it was $3000. The income from the School Fund is $936.40.

There are at present ten school districts in the town, and three half districts, named and numbered as follows :

			Name.	No. of Children enumerated in 1879.
District No.	1		Centre	30
"	"	2	Ridge	48
"	"	3	Couch's Hill	15
"	"	4	Diamond Hill	17
"	"	5	Boston	54
"	"	6	Hull	20
"	"	7	Umpawaug	51
"	"	8	Lonetown	29
"	"	9	Pickett's Ridge	9
"	"	10	Foundry	23
"	"	11	half district, Georgetown	40
"	"	12	" Florida	46
"	"	13	" Rock House	5

The total number of children enumerated was 387. The whole number who attended school was 406.

Messrs. Arthur Hill, William R. Duncomb, and Rev. X. A. Welton comprise the present Board of Education for the town. William E. Duncomb and Rev. X. A. Welton are the acting School Visitors.

From an early period Redding has been favorably known for the number and excellence of her select schools ; some of these were conducted by the pastors of the different churches, and others by professional teachers. One of the earliest of these schools was that kept by S. Samuel Smith, Esq., in the centre. The Rev. Jonathan Bartlett opened a school for boys and young men about 1795, that at-tained a high reputation and flourished for a term of years ; his school was kept in his dwelling-house—now the residence of Mr. Lemuel Sanford. The first boarding-school in town was opened by Mr. Walker Bates about 1825. Mr. Bates was a pupil of Mr. Bartlett's, and a very successful teacher. A few years after, Mr. Eli Gilbert opened a select school at the centre, which continued in successful operation for a term of years ; and in 1836 two schools were established on Redding Ridge—one by Mr. John Osborne, the other by Mr. Aaron B. Wilson.

One of the most noteworthy schools of the town was the Redding Institute, founded by Daniel San-ford, A.M., in the fall of 1847. Mr. Sanford, after receiving a thorough education, and spending some years as a teacher at White Plains, N. Y., returned to Redding and built the large and well-appointed school-house adjoining his dwelling. His school from a small and feeble beginning grew to be large and flourishing, containing at one time forty schol-ars, most of them sons of prominent New York and Brooklyn families. In 1851 he secured the services of Mr. Edward P. Shaw, a graduate of Wesleyan University, who continued with him as a teacher un-til 1867, when Mr. Sanford retired, and Mr. Shaw became principal and conducted the school success-fully until 1873, when, owing to a family bereave-ment, he was obliged to discontinue it.

The boarding-school opened by Mr. Burton Brad-ley about 1850, and Miss Polly Sellick's boarding-school for young ladies, founded in 1844, were successful and well-conducted institutions. The only select school at present existing in the town is the Misses Sanford's school for young children.

In 1878 Rev. Aaron S. Sanford, of New Haven, donated the sum of five thousand dollars for the endowment of a High School. This munificent gift was accepted by the people of the town, and the Hill Academy was incorporated under the laws of the State. The trustees of the institution are seven in number, viz., Francis A. Sanford, Aaron Treadwell, John Todd, X. Alanson Welton, Stephen Sanford, Thaddeus M. Abbott, and Arthur B. Hill.

The officers of the corporation are : President, Francis A. Sanford ; Vice-President, T. M. Abbott ; Secretary, Arthur B. Hill ; Treasurer, Aaron Treadwell ; Auditor, Stephen Sanford. The first principal of the academy was Mr. T. M. W. George, of Hartford, who closed his first year's labor July 1st, 1879.

CHAPTER XI.

MANUFACTURES.

In 1793, under a State law, a specific tax was laid on the various trades and professions, and from the grand list of that year we may gather accurate knowledge of the number of tradesmen, artisans, and professional men in the town at that time.

The following table is prepared from this list :

Trade or Profession.	Tax.	Trade or Profession.	Tax.
ATTORNEYS.		**BLACKSMITHS.**	
Thaddeus Benedict.	$60	Aaron Barlow...............	$5
S. Sam. Smith.............	50	Thaddeus Abbott............	5
		Enoch Merchant.............	5
PHYSICIANS.		**WEAVERS.**	
Thomas Davies............	10	Chauncey Merchant.........	5
Thomas Peck..............	10		
TRADERS.		**SADDLER.**	
James Rogers........... ...	25	Edward Starr..............	5
Benj. Sanford & Co........	25	**TANNERS AND SHOEMAKERS.**	
Stephen Betts & Co........	25		
William Heron............	25	Asahel Salmon.............	5
Ezekiel Jackson & Co......	25		
Abijah Parsons...........	25	**TAVERN-KEEPERS.**	
TAILORS.		Stephen Betts..............	15
		Ezekiel Sanford............	15
Justus Whitlow..........	5	Ezekiel Jackson............	15
Joel Byington............	5	Abel Burr.................	15
CLOTHIER.		**GRIST-MILLS.**	
Elisha Bradley....	5	Ephraim Wheeler..........	3
		Stephen Burr and Daniel	
WHEELWRIGHT.		Perry....................	6
		Seth Meeker & Co..........	4
Joel Gray.....	5	Crawford & Sanford........	5
COOPER.		**SAW-MILLS.**	
Stephen Gray....	5	Stephen & John Fairchild.....	4
		Oliver Sanford ....·........	4
JOINERS.		Barlow & Sanford..........	6
		Enos & Seth Wheeler.......	4
Eli Lyon.................	5	**IRON-WORKS.**	
Stephen Lyon.............	5		
Daniel Perry........	5	Oliver Sanford.............	10

From this date down to 1850 the town made a

very creditable advance in manufactures. The iron smelting works of Oliver Sanford in Sanfordtown were one of its earliest and most prominent industries. Ore was brought from Brookfield and Roxbury in great wagons and smelted at the mills, and after smelting was conveyed in the same manner to Westport or Norwalk, and shipped to various points. This enterprise was the pioneer of its kind in America, and proved quite profitable to its projector. The works were entirely destroyed in the great freshet of 1805, and never afterward rebuilt, the business being removed to Valley Forge. Fulling-mills were early erected, the first, probably, by Abraham Fairchild about 1742, near Nobb's Crook, on the Saugatuck River. The first woollen-mill was erected in 1812, near the site of the old fulling-mill, by Comstock, Foster & Co. It did a prosperous business through the war and for some years afterward. It was later bought by Mr. Joel Foster, one of the members of the old company, who continued the business until the burning of the factory in 1843, or 1844. Carriages began to be built in Sanfordtown as early as 1800, and the business soon became one of the leading industries of the town. Ephraim Sanford built the first carriage factory in the rear of the house on the corner now owned by Mr. Bradley Treadwell. He was succeeded in 1820 by his two sons David and Enoch A. Sanford. David Sanford died in 1834, and the business was continued by Enoch A. Sanford, the surviving partner. A few years after, Daniel Sanford was admitted a partner, and the firm entered largely into the Southern trade. In this they proved unfortu-

11

nate, and failed. Subsequently Mr. E. A. Sanford formed a partnership with Charles Duncomb, and later with G. A. Sanford, by whom the business was conducted with varying success. In its palmiest days this firm did a large business, employing from twenty-five to thirty men, and maintaining a depot for their goods in New York. Mr. Aaron Bartram built a carriage factory in 1840 (now standing), and in company with Mr. Eben Wilson did a large business for a term of years. Mr. Bradley Sanford began the manufacture of carriage axles in Sanfordtown in 1833, and continued it until 1838, when he was succeeded by Mr. G. A. Sanford.

Hat-making was at one time a prominent industry in Redding. To Mr. Billy Comstock is due the credit of erecting the first hat manufactory, which stood near his house in the Boston district. Mr. Daniel Gould had a large hat shop in Lonetown, and later Mr. Jesse Banks carried on the business somewhat extensively in Sanfordtown. He employed at one time from twenty-five to thirty men, and supplied the Southern and West India market. Mr. Milo Lee also carried on the business for a number of years, first with Mr. Banks, and afterward in a factory near his house. Bricks were made at one time by Mr. Alanson Lyon, on Redding Ridge ; and in the same district a large shirt manufactory was once in successful operation, under the management of Mr. Curtis Fanton, and his son, Henry Fanton. In 1856 the Redding Manufacturing Company was organized in Sanfordtown for the manufacture of pins, and other small articles in brass. The large building in Sanfordtown still known as the pin factory was built by this company ; for a time its prospects for a successful career were excellent, but owing to some mismanagement on the part of the directors, it soon proved a failure.

The Hill Limekiln in Lonetown is perhaps the oldest lime-burning establishment in the State. It was probably opened at an early day by Colonel John Read, who was the owner of the tract of land in which the quarry is situated.

In 1810 it came into the possession of John R. Hill, a grandson of Colonel Read, who conducted an extensive business and acquired a fortune. Mr. Hill retired in 1823, and was succeeded at different period by his sons Aaron S. Hill, Moses Hill, William Hill, and John L. Hill. These gentlemen conducted the business with the same energy and success that had characterized their father's management. Since Mr. John L. Hill's retirement, the business has been conducted, successively, by Messrs. Ames & Osborne, Barnes, Smith, and Philo Wood.

In 1842 Squire James Sanford built a foundry on the Aspetuck River in the Foundry district, and entered largely into the manufacture of agricultural implements. He had before invented an improved hay-cutting machine, in which the cutting was done by revolving cylinders furnished with knives, which he manufactured here, and which had an extensive sale throughout the country. This foundry is almost the only one of the old-time industries of Redding that remains in successful operation to this day.

The Aspetuck River, dashing through a gorge in this district, furnishes abundant water-power, and this the skill and energy of the Sanford brothers has utilized in the manufacture of buttons. Their three button factories have a capacity of between three and four hundred gross of buttons per day, employ twenty-eight hands, and have made this district one of the busiest and most prosperous localities in the town.

The pleasant village of Georgetown, in the western part of Redding, owes its existence largely to the establishment in its midst of the Gilbert & Bennett Manufacturing Company's works. This firm is largely engaged in the manufacture of sieves, iron wire, wire cloth, galvanized wire netting, ash sieves, and cheese and meat safes. They have a warehouse in New York, and at present employ a force of one hundred men. Until 1877 they were also engaged in the manufacture of glue and curled hair, but at that time this part of their business was purchased by the J. P. Gage Manufacturing Company, of New York, who still continue the business, having added to it the manufacture of sand paper. The origin of the Gilbert & Bennett Manf. Co. dates from the year 1818, when Benjamin Gilbert commenced the manufacture of sieves and curled hair. Afterward, his sons, Sturges Bennett, and E. O. Hurlbut formed a co-partnership under the name of Gilbert, Bennett & Co., for the manufacture of the above-named articles, including glue. In 1874 a fire destroyed the main factory, together with a large amount of manufactured stock and machinery, causing a loss of over $100,000.

After the fire the concern was incorporated under the name of the Gilbert & Bennett Manufacturing Co., with Sturges Bennett as president, David H.

Miller, secretary, and W. W. Beers as treasurer. The works before the fire employed a force of 125 men, and its manufactured•products amounted to $500,000 annually.

CHAPTER XII.

MISCELLANEOUS.

A FAVORITE dish with the Latin nations is the olla podrida—a thing of shreds and patches, composed of odds and ends of the larder that could be utilized in no other way. This chapter is intended as a sort of mental olla podrida, and we have no doubt will prove as varied, if not as savory, as the dish above described. For our first ingredients we insert some quaint and curious extracts from the town records as follows :

January 2d, 1778. It was voted, "that the selectmen provide a Spade, Pick Axe, and Hoe to be kept for the use of digging graves." August 11, 1783, "Voted, that the town will set up a singing meeting. Voted to lay a tax of 1d. on a pound to pay the Singing Master." March 13, 1787, "Voted not to admit Small Pox by innoculation : Voted to admit Small Pox by Innoculation next fall." October 19th, 1795 : " Voted that the select men prosecute those persons that cut timber on the highways." September 19th, 1798 : " Voted that the district to which Silas Merchant belongs, shall pay him $2 for his dragg." In 1801 the town voted to relinquish to Enoch Merchant the fine imposed on him by William Heron, Esq., for " admitting puppet shows into his house contrary to law." December 20th, 1802, John Read, Jr., was "excused" for admitting puppet shows into his house, "on said Read's paying the costs." In 1804 it was voted, "that this town will not remit to Ebenezer Robinson of Danbury, the fine imposed on him by William Heron Esq. for breaking the Sabbath, which fine is now uncollected." The same year Aaron Read was appointed "Keeper of the Key to the Town House." In 1807, it was voted to remit the fines—$1.67 in amount—of Peter Bradley, and Nancy his wife, for Sabbath-breaking : also voted, that William Heron Esq. be paid $11.08, amount of costs in defending a suit brought by William P. Jones against him, for a fine collected and paid into the treasury of the town. In 1808, voted that the town will remit the fines of all those persons who labored on the Sabbath the 31st of July last past, in this town, on payment of costs. In 1817, Daniel Sanford and Aaron Burr were appointed a committee to procure the fish called pike, and put in Umpawaug Pond. In 1840 it was voted, that if any non-resident should kill birds within the limits of the town he should be fined and if he killed robins, except in case of sickness, he should be fined $5.

In the records of a town meeting held December 8th, 1806, occurs the following curious entry : " Voted, that S. Samuel Smith, Lemuel Sanford, and Benjamin Meeker be a committee to write to William Crawford requesting him to name the person belonging to Redding to whom he delivered Mrs. Sarah Fleming's letter in May last, notifying him that in case of refusal, the Inhabitants of this town, will feel themselves authorized to declare to the world, that he never did deliver such a letter to any person belonging to Redding.''

Conversing with an aged citizen of Redding on the generous and confiding nature of our towns-people, he substantiated the fact by a list of the public enterprises which they had aided at different times, with the amount contributed to each, as follows :

Eagle Bank, New Haven	$6,000
Virginia Land Company	8,000
Michigan Land Company	20,000
Bethel Bank	40,000
Midland Railroad	20,000
Making a total of	$94,000

The above in round numbers. He is quite sure that there have been enough minor enterprises aided to swell the grand total to $100,000.

Isaac Hilliard was a poet of considerable local celebrity whom Redding had the honor of producing, but at this late day I am able to collect but few facts and anecdotes concerning him, and most of these are gathered from the Federal journals, who were his traducers, owing to the fact that Mr. Hilliard, like a true poet, had espoused the cause of the people and was a Whig. The *New England Republican* of August 29th, 1804, has this to say concerning him :

"Forlorn Hope.

"Isaac Hilliard, a wretched vagabond, originally of Reading, in Fairfield County, has lately published a large pamphlet, in which he warmly advocates the cause of democracy. To criticise such a work, one must sink himself to a level with the author ; that is, he must become an idiot, or a lunatic, or a brute. The composition is just about on a level with Peter St. John's poetry. The pitiable but wrong-headed writer is now busied in hawking his pamphlets about the streets. He presents them to every man whom he is not afraid to insult, and tells those to whom he delivers them, to pay him twenty-five cents each, if they like the work ; otherwise to return it. Never was a man better fitted to any cause than Hilliard to democracy ; and never was a cause better adapted to the man engaged in it than democracy to Hilliard."

The pamphlet referred to above, entitled the "Rights of Suffrage," and also Mr. Hilliard's chief poem, "The Federal Pye," the writer has been so fortunate as to procure. They are included in a pamphlet of some seventy pages, printed at Danbury in 1804.

A brief examination of the first-named work would force one to conclude that, however brilliant a poet Mr. Hilliard may have been, he was not a master of prose. His nouns, adjectives, nominatives, and verbs are so commingled, that it is difficult to separate them ; but in his preface Mr. Hilliard observes that he has written for persons of limited education, and had not therefore adopted a lofty and flourishing style—a fact which explains, perhaps, the somewhat ungrammatical construction of his sentences. An extract from his poem " The Federal Pye" we will submit for the criticism of the reader. At a Federal " caucus" one Holdfast, a Federalist, arises and opens the proceedings with the following speech :

" BRETHREN, I know you see my tears,
  The strong expression of my fears.
There's no one here that is a stranger—
  Then every one must know our danger.
Poor people all begin to see
  Their rights are gone, they are not free ;
Some wicked men espouse their cause,
  And say they're lost by cruel laws.
They have found out, as sure as death,
  That they are taxed for their breath.
I am very sorry that our youth
  Should ever find out so much truth :
The poor old men now make a noise
  And say we tax all their poor boys.
Somehow or other, those poor souls
  Find other States don't tax their polls.
They say 'tis cruel, and a sin
  To pay for breath which they breathe in—
And now they all set up this note,
  If they pay taxes they will vote :
They say they've found what we're about—
  We taxed their polls and left ours out.
That faculties, and the poll tax,
  They wish were under the French axe,
Together with all those that like 'em,
  And let it have one chance to strike 'em.
Why, they might just as well have said
  They wished all Federal rulers dead.
The poor will rise in every nation
  When they are drove to desperation."
             Etc., etc.

Redding is now much sought after by invalids for its health-giving properties, but it has been occasionally visited by epidemics of a fearful character. Small-pox, before Dr. Jenner's discovery of inoculation, was a fearful scourge, and news of its appearance in town always excited the wildest apprehension. The roads near the infected spot were at once fenced up, and no one save the physician and nurse was permitted to have any communication with the stricken family. If the disease became epidemic, pest-houses were erected in secluded localities, whither the patients were removed. Those dying of this disease were placed in a rude coffin, and buried at midnight, the clergyman standing at a safe distance and reading in a loud voice the service for the dead. An epidemic called the "camp distemper" raged in the town in 1780—the year succeeding the encampment here of Putnam's division. It seems to have been of the same general character as the dysentery, but from the fact of its raging more violently in the neighborhood of the camps was called the camp distemper.

A severer scourge was an epidemic that visited the town about 1810, and which displayed many of the characteristics of Asiatic cholera. Strong men were stricken down by it in a day, and there was scarcely a house where there was not mourning for the dead. In one school district alone, Lonetown, it is said that twenty died of this disease. The victims of this scourge were interred in the old cemetery near the Congregational Church. They were buried hastily, at midnight, and the Rev. Nathaniel Bartlett, who officiated on the occasion, stood on the ledge, a few yards south of the church, and there read the burial service, in tones so stentorian, that they were heard by residents on Umpawaug Hill, fully two miles distant.

An old account-book mildewed and mouldy, its leaves discolored by time, and its writing half illegible from the same cause, may not be supposed to furnish very interesting reading ; yet if one will go through its pages carefully, he may cull much that is both instructive and entertaining.

A book of this character, 130 years old, the day-book and ledger of a former merchant of the town, furnishes the following extracts :

Jan. 24, 1751. *Jeams Hull Dr.*

		£.	s.	d.
	To 1 ink horn 3/6, reckning 3/	0	6	6
July 2.	To 2 qts. rum 16/6, 1 do. 11/6	1	7	0
" 13.	To 2 qts. rum 22/, the sugar 6/, rubston 3/6	1	11	6
" 22.	To 2 qts. rum 22/	1	2	0
Sept. 24.	To 2 hanks har. 8/ rum, 2/6	0	10	6
Dec. 3.	To 1 ax 55/, 1 pint rum 2/6	3	1	0
1752.	To licker 4/9, licker 1/6	0	6	3

1750. *Daniel Gould, Dr.*

		£.	s.	d.
Dec. 2.	To making clock	0	9	0
1751.	To punch 2/	0	2	0
May 16.	To 17ᵈ buckram 16/, 24ᵈ woding 16/	1	12	0
Aug. 22.	To punch 6/, rum 2/6	0	8	8
Sept. 11.	To 1 qt. wine 12/	0	12	0

There is also credited to Mr. Gold :

1 cow waid 389 lb., @ 1/9 . . . . .25 18 8

Robert Sedley, Dr.

July 3, 1753. To Testament 25/, 2 trays 12/,
Oct. 22. To 2 lb. nails 14/, 1 comb 14/,
To parshon 15/, to 10 lbs. hogs fat 20/,
To 1 brom 6/, to bunit paper 3/, silk 6/.

Other entries at this period are :

1 gal. molasses at 19/, ½ bush. salt 17/, almonek 1/9, Philip 6/, 1 pail 12/, 1 skimmer 3/6, 1 basket 9/, 14 yds. Calocho 13/9, 1 tray of pins 4/, 2 lbs. brimstone 12/, To paid the pedler 34/, to sundrys training day 25/6, 1 cake soap 8/, by 3 dear skins £28, 0s. 0d., 4 bbls. £3, ¼ bush. ots 8/, 1 doz. butins 6/, To poundeg. of sheep 8/, 1 hogshed 80/, 1 hankerchief 25/, 6 pipes 2/6, To writing note 2/, 1 sickle 23/, ½ bl. powder 11/, 1 botle 3/, 8 sqr. glass 40/, 90 lbs. pork £9, 10s. 9d., 1 pr. cards 45/, 1 lb. Tobacco 4/, 17 bush. rye in Boston cleaned £11, 12s. 9d., 1 oz. Indigo 15/, To charge of writ 16/, 2 qts. Methegling 20/, 1 beaver hat £13, 1 caster hat $8, 1 frying pan 78/, ¼ lb. allam 4/, 1 Spanish dollar 64/, 1 pr. gloves 23/, 1 cartwhip 5/, 1 pr. nee-buckles 6/6, 4 lb. 11 oz. Tobacco 20/10, 3½ lbs. hay sead 54/6, 1 pr. cart wheels £7, 10s., 1 grindston 50/, 1 lb. shot 3/6, 2 vinegar cruses 20/, 1 mustard pot 10/, ½ quire paper 7/, 1 lb. lead 4/, poundeg of 14 hogs £9/4, 2 qt. basons 42/, By poundeg of Barlow's hors 8/, 6 tacks 1/6, To interest, and fall of money 6/, flints 3/, 2 doz. pewter buttons 7/, 35 bush. wheat in Boston cleaned £55, 18s., 3d., 1 bbl. pork in Boston £20, 1 hat band 2/.

This list might be extended indefinitely, but enough has been given to show the prices of articles in general use at that day.

A Lodge of Free Masons was once in active operation on Redding Ridge, as is shown by the following extract from the records of the Grand Lodge :

"Oct. 19th, 1796. A petition from sundry Freemasons residing in the towns of Redding and Weston, was presented to the Grand Lodge of Freemasons then in session at New Haven, praying to be formed into a new Lodge, which petition was laid over until the next session of the Grand Lodge. At the next session of the Grand Lodge of F. & A. M. held at New Haven on the 17th May, 1797, the prayer of the petitioners was granted, and a Lodge formed under the name of Ark Lodge No. 39, F. & A. M. and William Heron was appointed Master."

At the October session 1804, of the Grand Lodge, Lemuel Sanford represented Ark Lodge, also at the May Session 1808, the October session 1808, and the May Session, 1813.

In 1823, a Lodge was built by the Members of Ark Lodge No. 39, on Redding Ridge. This Lodge continued its labors until May 12th, 1839, when it surrendered its charter to the Grand Lodge.

On the 23d of December, 1869, the charter was again taken up by the following members : David H. Miller, Chas. A. Jennings, Chas. H. Canfield, Lewis Northrop, Chas. O. Olmsted, David E. Smith, H. R. Osborn, E. Thompson, Aaron H. Davis, Luzon Jelliff, Seth P. Beers and Waterman Bates, and is still working, its present Lodge Room being situated in Georgetown.

A Lodge of Odd Fellows succeeded that of the Free Masons on Redding Ridge, but only continued in active operation for a few years.

One of the earliest antislavery societies in the State was organized in Georgetown, in December, 1838. Dr. Erasmus Hudson and Rev. Nathaniel Colver were appointed by the Connecticut Anti-slavery Society agents for the evangelization of the State, and in October, 1838, entered Fairfield County in the furtherance of their mission. They lectured at Sherman, Danbury, Redding, Georgetown, and Norwalk, being driven from each place in succession by mobs who abused and threatened, and in some cases stoned them. At Norwalk they were burnt in effigy, and assailed with brickbats and all manner of missiles. At Weston they organized the first society in the county. In November a call was issued for a convention to be held in Redding (Georgetown) December 12th, 1838. On the 29th November, Messrs. Colver and Hudson went to Georgetown to hold meetings. They met on Monday night in the Baptist church, but the mob was so violent that the meeting was adjourned until Tuesday evening. All through Tuesday there was great commotion among the enemies of the cause, and this culminated in the evening, when a mob composed of men and boys, some with painted faces and some wearing masks, surrounded the church, and assailed it with stones, clubs, and hideous outcries. Being dispersed by the citizens the band betook itself to quieter forms of mischief. Dr. Hudson drove to the meeting a beautiful milk-white horse, and on that night his tail was sheared so closely that it resembled a corn-cob ; and other outrages were committed. At this meeting a society was organized, called the Georgetown Anti-slavery Society. The constitution of this society bears date December 4th, 1838 ; its officers were : President, Eben Hill ; Secretary, William Wakeman ; Treasurer, John O. St. John.

From the lofty ridges which form a distinguishing feature of our landscape, fine views of the' Sound, the shipping, and of a pleasant country of farms may be obtained. The " Glen" in the valley of the Saugatuck is widely famed for its beautiful and picturesque scenery. The valley of the Aspetuck, in the eastern part of the town, also offers many attractions to the tourist. Little River, in the upper part of its course, flows through a wild and picturesque region, and near its western bank may be seen the well-defined limits of Putnam's camp. Near the camp is Phillip's Cave, so called, according to tradition, because in colonial times it afforded shelter to a runaway slave of that name, who lived here for a term of years, and levied on the fields and poultry yards of the settlers for subsistence.

Gallows Hill, in the western part of the town, near Redding Station, was the scene of the execution of a spy and a deserter in the war of the Revolution.

CHAPTER XIII.

REDDING IN THE CIVIL WAR.

THE news flashed over the wires in 1861 that the old flag had been fired upon at Sumter, and that war was imminent, was received by the citizens of Redding with the same courage and decision that had been displayed by their ancestors at the opening of the Revolution, nearly a hundred years before.

The old flag had been dishonored, and the Union, the inalienable birthright bequeathed by the fathers, had been declared to be at an end.

It was felt to be a time for action, for the burying of party differences, and for uniting in support of the measures which were at once adopted for overcoming the threatened evil. Public meetings were held, at which sentiments of the purest patriotism were expressed, and volunteers hastened to enroll themselves for the defence of the flag. These acts of loyalty were supplemented by certain practical measures adopted at special town meetings, and which can be best exhibited by extracts from the town records of the period. On the 23d of April, ten days after Sumter fell, the following " Notice" was issued :

" The legal voters of the town of Redding are hereby notified and warned to attend a special town meeting to be held at the Town House in said Town on Monday Apr. 29, 1861, at 2 o'clock P.M., to consider the expediency of appropriating funds to defray the expenses of the families of those who enlist in the service of the U. S. army under the present call of the President for troops.

" JOHN EDMOND,   ) *Selectmen*
BURR MEEKER,   }   *of*
FRANCIS A. SANFORD,) *Redding.*

" REDDING, April 23, 1861."

" At a special Town Meeting legally warned and held in Redding on the 29th day of April, 1861, Walker Bates, Esq., chosen Moderator.

" *Voted*, unanimously, that an appropriation be made from the treasury of the Town, for the families of those who have enlisted, or may enlist from the town in the service of the U. S. Government under the present call of the President for troops, the same being a call for 75,000 volunteers for the space of three months.

" *Voted*, unanimously, that such appropriation be as follows, to wit, three dollars per week for each of the wives, and one dollar per week for each of the children of the several persons enlisting as aforesaid, during the time of service of such person under said call.

" *Voted*, that a committee of three be appointed for each grand division of the town, to disburse the foregoing appropriation—such committee to receive no pecuniary compensation for their services. Sturges Bennett, Thaddeus M. Abbott, and James Sanford chosen such disbursing committee.

" *Voted*, that the selectmen be instructed to draw

orders on the Treasurer of the Town on application
of either of the foregoing named committee, in favor
of such as are entitled to an appropriation as aforesaid, under the foregoing vote.

" *Voted,* that the selectmen be instructed to call a
special town meeting as soon as practicable, for the
purpose of making an appropriation for those who
enlist from this town in the service of the U. S. Government.

" The above and foregoing is a true record.

" Attest,   LEMUEL SANFORD,
                              " *Town Clerk.*"

A call for additional troops was issued by the
President early in the summer of 1862, and a draft to
fill it seemed imminent. Under these circumstances
a special town meeting was held July 26th, 1862, at
which it was voted, " that the selectmen be a committee to correspond with the Adjutant-General, to
ascertain whether if the town furnished its quota
under the recent call for additional troops, it would
exempt the town from a draft under said call," and
the meeting was adjourned to July 31st, 1862, to await
the action of the Adjutant-General. His answer being in the affirmative, the meeting on reassembling,
July 31st, passed this resolution : " Resolved, That a
bounty of fifty dollars be offered to every volunteer
from this town, who shall enlist into the service of
the United States between the present time and the
20th of August next, under the present call for additional troops, such bounty to be paid to each volunteer enlisting as aforesaid, on certificate of his ac-
ceptance from the proper authority when presented
to the selectmen." A subsequent meeting held
August 23d extended the time in which the bounty

12

would be paid to September 1st. September 1st, a meeting was held for the equalization of bounties, and the bounty of $50 was voted to all who had enlisted prior to the vote of July 31st, 1862, as well as to all who should enlist hereafter, except those enlisting under the first call of the President for troops.

The selectmen were also authorized " to borrow such sum of money as might be needed to carry out such vote. Mr. John Edmond was also appointed an agent for the town to ascertain the full numbers of those who had enlisted from the town. Six days after, September 6th, another town meeting was held and voted an additional bounty of $50 to all who had previously enlisted (except under the first call), and an additional bounty of $100 to all who should thereafter " volunteer to fill up the quota under the present call," thus making the bounty paid each volunteer $200. Throughout the war the town was anxious to avoid a draft, and made strenuous efforts to fill its quota by volunteering. July 13th, 1863, when a fourth call for troops was daily expected, a town meeting was held, and the selectmen authorized to draw from the treasury of the town and pay over as a bounty " to each person who shall or may be drafted under the next call of the United States Government for troops, and who shall not be able to get excused for physical inability, or any other cause, the sum of $300, or such less sum as the Secretary of War shall fix upon for the procuration of a substitute ;" and George Osborn, David S. Johnson, and Daniel Rider were appointed a committee to procure recruits. Substantially the same plan was pursued by the town for filling its quota under the various calls of the President for troops, and so successfully, that no draft ever occurred within her limits. The sum total of the war expenses of the town is variously estimated at from twenty-two to twenty-five thousand dollars.

The war record of Redding, so far as it relates to the number of men furnished the General Government, is, it is believed, exceeded by but few towns in the State. From official returns in the Adjutant-General's office, it appears that Redding furnished one hundred and eight men to the land forces of the United States—more than one fifteenth of the entire population of the town, and fully one third of all its able-bodied male inhabitants. To this number must be added many of her sons who enlisted in other towns and States. The names of these one hundred and eight soldiers constitute a roll of honor whose lustre time will not dim, but brighten, and which all good citizens will be glad to see preserved in this enduring form. They are given with as full details as can be gathered from the somewhat meagre returns in the Adjutant-General's office.

SECOND REGIMENT (ARTILLERY).

1. Andrew H. Sanford, volunteered Jan. 5, 1864, was taken sick through fatigue and exposure while in Virginia, and died in hospital in Philadelphia, June 5, 1864.

2. Morris H. Sanford, volunteered July 21, 1862 ; was made 2d Lieutenant, Co. C.; promoted to be 1st Lieutenant Aug. 1, 1863. Again promoted to be Captain. Was wounded in the shoulder at the battle of Fisher's Creek.

THIRD REGIMENT (THREE MONTHS). MUSTERED IN,
MAY 14, 1861.

3. George W. Gould, Co. G. Honorably discharged Aug. 12, 1861.

FIFTH REGIMENT. MUSTERED IN JULY 12, 1861.

4. John H. Bennett, Company A. Transferred to Invalid Corps Sept. 1, 1863.

5. Rufus Mead, Jr., Co. A. Re-enlisted as a veteran Dec. 21, 1863.

6. Hezekiah Sturges, Co. A. Died Oct. 14, 1861, and is buried in the Hull Cemetery, Sanfordtown.

7. Arthur M. Thorp, Co. A. Transferred to the Invalid Corps Sept. 1, 1863.

8. Benjamin F. Squires, Co. A. Served three years, and was honorably discharged.

SIXTH REGIMENT. MUSTERED IN OCTOBER 28, 1863.

9. John Foster, Co. B.

10. Francis De Four, Co. C.

11. John Murphy, Co. G.

SEVENTH REGIMENT. MUSTERED IN SEPTEMBER 5, 1861.

12. Andrew B. Nichols, Co. D. Re-enlisted as a veteran. Killed at the battle of Drury's Bluff, Va., May 16, 1864.

13. Oscar Byington, Co. D.

14. William Nichols, Co. D. Discharged for disability Jan. 3, 1863.

15. George W. Peck, Co. I. Enlisted in United States Army Nov. 4, 1862.

16. Henry Clark, Co. I., recruit. Enlisted Oct. 30, 1863.

17. Jerome Dufoy, recruit. Enlisted Nov. 6, 1863. Killed at Olustee, Fla., Feb. 20, 1864.

18. Emil Durand, recruit. Enlisted Nov. 2, 1863.

19. H. R. Chamberlain, recruit. Enlisted Nov. 4, 1863.

20. Henry D. Harris, recruit. Enlisted Oct. 29, 1863.

21. Peter Hill, recruit. Enlisted Oct. 31, 1863. Transferred to U. S. Navy Apr. 28, 1864.

22. Robert Hoch, recruit. Enlisted Nov. 3, 1863.

23. John Miller, recruit. Enlisted Nov. 4, 1863.

24. John H. Thomas, recruit. Enlisted Nov. 3, 1863.

25. Antoine Vallori, recruit. Enlisted Oct. 29, 1863.

26. William Wilson, recruit. Enlisted Nov. 6, 1863.

27. William Watson, recruit. Enlisted Nov. 2, 1863. Transferred to U. S. Navy Apr. 28, 1864.

EIGHTH REGIMENT. MUSTERED IN SEPT. 25, 1861.

28. Aaron A. Byington, Corporal, Co. H.

29. Lewis Bedient, Co. H.

30. Thomas Bigelow, Co. H. Re-enlisted as a veteran Dec. 24, 1863.

31. William Hamilton, Co. H. Re-enlisted as a veteran Dec. 24, 1863.

32. William H. Nichols, Co. H. Re-enlisted Jan. 5, 1864.

33. Franklin Paine, Co. I. Died March 8, 1862.

34. Albert Woodruff, Co. I. Discharged for disability May 11, 1862.

35. Charles M. Platt, recruit. Enlisted Feb. 24, 1864.

NINTH REGIMENT.

36. Michael Dillon, recruit. Enlisted Feb. 17, 1864.

TENTH REGIMENT. MUSTERED IN SEPT. 21, 1861.

37. Francis H. Grumman, Co. D. Died Apr. 1, 1864.

ELEVENTH REGIMENT. MUSTERED IN OCT. 24, 1861.

38. Nathan Cornwall, Sergeant, Co. A. Re-enlisted Jan. 1, 1864, and promoted to First Lieutenant. A prisoner at Andersonville.

39. Samuel B. Baxter, Co. A. Discharged for disability Dec. 4, 1862.

40. Charles O. Morgan, Co. A. Wounded by the fragment of a shell, and discharged for disability June 3, 1864.

41. George Sherman, Co. K, recruit. Enlisted Feb. 16, 1864.

TWELFTH REGIMENT. DATE OF MUSTER FROM NOV. 20, 1861, TO JAN. 1, 1862.

42. George Green, Co. B. Died June 11, 1863, of wounds received at Port Hudson.

FOURTEENTH REGIMENT.

43. George Lover, Co. A. Mustered in June 16, 1862.

44. Wesley Banks, Co. E. Mustered in Oct. 1, 1863. Died Feb. 12, 1864, of wounds received at Morton's Ford, Va.

SEVENTEENTH REGIMENT. DATE OF MUSTER FROM JULY 14 TO AUG. 14, 1862.

45. Waterman Bates, Co. A. Discharged for disability Dec. 18, 1863.

46. Edmund Treadwell, Co. D. Taken prisoner in Florida.

47. George W. Banks, Sergeant, Co. G. Discharged Sept. 15, 1862.

48. David S. Bartram. Enlisted as a private in Co. G., Aug. 16, 1862. Promoted to 2d Lieutenant May 8, 1863. Participated in the battle of Chancellorsville ; and was taken prisoner at Gettysburg, July 3, 1863. Was an inmate of rebel prisons for twenty-two months, experiencing in succession the horrors of the Libby Prison at Richmond, and of the prison pens at Danville, Macon, Savannah, Charleston, Columbia, and Goldsboro. He was paroled March 1, 1865, near Wilmington, N. C., and succeeded in reaching the Union lines at the latter place.

49. Morris Jennings, Co. G. Discharged for disability March 26, 1863.

50. James M. Burr, Co. G. Discharged for disability March 9, 1863.

51. Martin Costello, Co. G. Taken prisoner.

52. Andrew D. Couch, Co. G. Killed at Chancellorsville May 2, 1863.

53. John W. De Forrest, Co. G. Discharged for disability Apr. 4, 1863.

54. Edmund Godfrey, Co. G. Discharged for disability March 9, 1863.
55. George Hull, Co. G.
56. Burr Lockwood, Co. G.
57. John Lockwood, Co. G.
58. Aaron Peck, Co. G.
59. John M. Sherman, Co. G. Discharged for disability Dec. 10, 1862.
60. George Whalen, Co. G.

TWENTY-THIRD REGIMENT.   DATE OF MUSTER FROM
AUG. 15 TO SEPT. 20, 1862.

61. David H. Miller, Major of the regiment. Discharged Aug. 31, 1863.
62. Obadiah R. Coleman, Co. D. Discharged Aug. 31, 1863.
63. Charles A. Gregory. Discharged same date.
64. George W. Gould, Corporal, Co. E. Discharged Aug. 31, 1863.
65. Azariah E. Meeker, Co. E. Discharged Aug. 31, 1863.
66. Frederic D. Chapman, Co. E. Discharged Aug. 31, 1863.
67. Henry H. Lee, Co. E. Discharged Aug. 31, 1863.
68. Charles Albin, Co. E. Discharged Aug. 31, 1863.
69. Edward Banks, Co. E. Discharged Aug. 31, 1863.
70. Henry W. Bates, Co. E. Discharged Aug. 31, 1863.

71. Charles H. Bates, Co E.   Discharged Aug. 31, 1863.

72. Smith Bates, Co. E.   Discharged Aug. 31, 1863.

73. Lemuel B. Benedict, Co. E.   Discharged Aug. 31, 1863.

74. Peter W. Birdsall, Co. E.   Discharged Aug. 31, 1863.

75. William F. Brown, Co. E.   Discharged Aug. 31, 1863.

76. Henry F. Burr, Co. E.   Discharged Aug. 31, 1863.

77. Martin V. B. Burr, Co. E.   Discharged Aug. 31, 1863.

78. Aaron Burr, Co. E.   Discharged Aug. 31, 1863.

79. Ammi Carter, Co. E.   Died Aug. 12, 1863.

80. William Coley, Co. E.   Discharged Aug. 31, 1863.

81. Cyrus B. Eastford, Co. E.   Discharged Aug. 31, 1863.

82. William Fanton, Co. E.   Discharged Aug. 31, 1863.

83. Charles A. Field, Co. E.   Discharged Aug. 31, 1863.

84. Samuel S. Gray, Co. E.   Discharged Aug. 31, 1863.

85. James F. Jelliff, Co. E.   Discharged Aug. 31, 1863.

86. Charles Lockwood, Co. E.   Discharged Aug. 31, 1863.

87. Elihu Osborne, Co. E.   Discharged Aug. 31, 1863.

88. John Osborne, Co. E.   Discharged Aug. 31, 1863.

89. Henry Parsons, Co. E.   Discharged Aug. 31, 1863.

90. Henry Platt, Co. E.   Discharged Aug. 31, 1863.

91. Sanford J. Platt, Co. E.   Discharged Aug. 31, 1863.

92. James J. Ryder, Co. E.   Discharged Aug. 31, 1863.

93. George E. Smith, Co. E.   Discharged Aug. 31, 1863.

94. Anton Stommel, Co. E.   Discharged Aug. 31, 1863.

95. Jacob B. St. John, Co. E.   Discharged Aug. 31, 1863.

96. Ralph S. Meade, Co. G.   Discharged Aug. 31, 1863.

97. Henry Wheelock, Co. G.   Discharged Aug. 31, 1863.

98. George S. Tarbell, Co. G.   Discharged Aug. 31, 1863.

99. Almon S. Merwin, Co. G.   Discharged Aug. 31, 1863.

100. Lyman Whitehead, Co. K.   Discharged Aug. 31, 1863.

101. Seth P. Bates, Sergeant, Co. E.   Promoted to 1st Lieutenant.   Discharged Aug. 31, 1863.

TWENTY-NINTH REGIMENT (COLORED).   MUSTERED IN MARCH 8, 1864.

102. John H. Hall, Co. A.
103. John M. Coley, Co. E.
104. Theodore Nelson, Co. E.   Died Apr. 6, 1864.

105. Lafayette S. Williams, Co. E.
106. Edward Voorhies, Co. E.
107. Joseph F. Butler, Corp., Co. G.
108. Henry B. Pease, Co. G.
109. Cato Johnson, Co. G.

On February 4, 1862, a meeting was held in Georgetown for the purpose of electing officers for Co. E.,
8th Regt., 2d Brigade, Conn. State Militia, the
Company being known as Co. E., National Guard.

David H. Miller was elected	Captain	...........Redding.
Hiram St. John " "	1st Lieut	.........Wilton.
Geo. M. Godfrey " "	2d Lieut	.... "
John N. Main " "	1st Sergt	.........Redding.
Jas. Corcoran " "	2d "	.........Wilton.
Lewis Northrop " "	3d "	.........Weston.
David S. Bartram " · "	4th "	.........Redding.
Aaron O. Scribner " "	5th "	.........Wilton.
Wm. D. Gilbert " "	1st Corpl	.... "
Aaron H. Davis " "	2d "	.........Redding.
Alonzo Dickson " "	3d "	.... "
Jerem'h R. Miller " "	4th "	.........Wilton.
Edw'd Thompson " "	5th "	.........Redding.
Seth P. Bates " "	6th "	.... "
Geo. W. Gould " " ·	7th "	.... "
Albert D. Sturges " "	8th "	.........Wilton.

PRIVATES.

John W. Mead................................Ridgefield.
Moses Comstock..............................Wilton.
James Lobdell................................ "
James F. Jelliff..............................Weston.
Hezekiah B. Osborn..........................Redding.
Joseph R. Lockwood..........................Wilton.
Henry Parsons...............................Redding.
Wm. H. Canfield.............................. "
Minot S. Patrick.............................. "
Charles A. Jennings..........................Wilton.
Edwin Gilbert...............................Redding.
David E. Smith.............................. "
Hiram Cobleigh.............................. "
Samuel A. Main.............................. "
Anton Stommel .... "
George L. Dann.............................Wilton.
Jonathan Betts...............................Weston.

Charles Olmsted...........................Wilton.
Charles Albin...............................Redding.
Fred. D. Chapman........................... "
Henry Hohman. .... "
Wm. B. Smith............................... "
Wm. E. Brothwell...........................Wilton.
Azariah E. Meeker..........................Redding.
Charles S. Gregory.......................... "
Charles S. Meeker........................... "
Charles H. Downs........................... "
Wm. Coley................................. "
Lorenzo Jones.............................. "
Henry F. Burr.............................. "
Obadiah P. Coleman......................... "
Charles H. Canfield......................... "
John L. Godfrey.............................Wilton.
Sylvester Albin....... ....Redding.

The Company uniformed itself and drilled until
August, 1862. When Governor Buckingham called
for troops to serve for nine months, the entire command volunteered its services, and was accepted.
The company was immediately recruited up to 108
men, and reported for duty at Camp Terry, New
Haven, where it was mustered into the U. S. service
as Co. E., 23d Regt. Conn. Vols. On the formation of the 23d Regt., Capt. Miller was promoted
to be Major of the regiment. Geo. M. Godfrey was
elected Captain of Co. E., to fill the vacancy caused
by the promotion of Capt. Miller ; and John N. Main
promoted to 2d Lieutenant, to fill vacancy caused by
the promotion of Lieut. Godfrey.

The company was sent with the regiment from
New Haven to Camp Buckingham, on Long Island,
and from thence by steamer Che Kiang to New Or-
leans, where it was embodied in the 19th Army Corps,
under Gen. Banks. It was engaged at Lafourche
Crossing, La., on June 21, 1863, with a superior force
of the rebels, but came out victorious.

The company was mustered out of the U. S. service at New Haven, Sept. 3, 1863, after a service of nearly thirteen months.

CHAPTER XIV.

THE EARLY FAMILIES OF REDDING.*

ADAMS.

JOSEPH ADAMS removed when a young man from Boston to Fairfield, and married, soon after, Joanna Disbrow, of Fairfield. About 1760 he removed to Redding, and settled in Lonetown, on the farm now owned by his grandson Stephen. His children were : Stephen, baptized August 15, 1762. Hezekiah, baptized September 30, 1764. Ellen, baptized November 10, 1765. Abigail, baptized March 6, 1768. Joseph, baptized April 28, 1771. Israel, baptized January 10, 1773. Aaron, baptized July 16, 1775. Nathan, baptized September 6, 1778. Of these children, Stephen enlisted in the Continental Army and never returned. Hezekiah married Betty Parsons, and had children :—Betsey, who married John Gray, and settled in Norwalk ; Stephen, now living in Redding, at the age of eighty-nine ; Lemuel, now living in Redding, aged eighty-six ; Aaron, who re-

* These notes, arranged alphabetically, are not intended as complete histories of the families mentioned, but rather as sketches of the early settlers of the town, and as aids to the genealogist in his researches. For complete histories, the inquirer should consult the ancient records of Norwalk, Stratford, Fairfield, and Danbury, as well as those of Redding.

moved to the West ; and Elinor, who married Hawley Judd. It is related of Hezekiah Adams, that, too young to enlist as a soldier in the Revolutionary Army, he entered the service as a teamster, and on one occasion drove a wagon, loaded with Spanish milled dollars, to Baltimore.

Abraham Adams, brother of Joseph, was contemporary with him in Redding. His wife was Sarah ——. Their children were : Ann, baptized March 6, 1768. Deborah, baptized April 28, 1771. Sarah, baptized July 31, 1774 ; died in infancy. Sarah, baptized October 20, 1776. Eli, baptized January 30, 1780. Family record mentions a son Abraham.

BANKS.

JESSE BANKS, son of Joseph Banks, of Fairfield, removed to Redding at an early day ; married, June 11, 1763, Mabel Wheeler (town record says *Mehitable* Wheeler). Their children were : Hyatt, born December 9, 1764. Jesse, born October 29, 1766. Joanna, born July 27, 1768. Mabel, born October 2, 1772 ; died in infancy. Mary, born June 23, 1774. Mabel, born November 17, 1776.

Jesse married, December 15, 1787, Martha Summers. Mabel married Ebenezer Foot, August 29, 1797. Seth Banks also appears in Redding contemporary with Jesse ; married Sarah Pickett November 20, 1766, and had children : Mehitable, born January 15,.1768, and Thomas ; and perhaps others.

BARLOW.

THE Barlow family in Redding is descended from John Barlow, who appears in Fairfield as early as

1668, and died in 1674. Samuel Barlow, son of Samuel Barlow, of Fairfield, grandson of John Barlow, he a son of the first settler of that name, removed to Redding about 1740, and settled in what is now Boston district, near the present residence of Bradley Hill. He married, first, Eunice, daughter of Daniel Bradley, of Fairfield, August 2, 1731. Their children were : Daniel, born November 24, 1734. Ruhamah, born January 22, 1737. James, born January 29, 1739. Jabez, born March, 21, 1742. After the death of his first wife, Samuel Barlow married Esther, daughter of Nathaniel Hull, of Redding, August 7, 1774. She died August 28, 1775, aged fifty-four years. Their children were : Nathaniel, born May 13, 1745. Aaron, born February 11, 1750. Samuel, born April 3, 1752. Joel, the poet, born March 24, 1754. Huldah, born ———. Mr. Samuel Barlow purchased his farm of James Bradley for £2500. It consisted of 170 acres, with "buildings thereon," and was bounded on the north by the first cross highway from the rear of the long lots— without doubt the road before mentioned leading from Boston through the centre to Redding Ridge. " This northern boundary," says Mr. Hill, " together with the familiar names of the old owners of property on the other ' side of the farm, and also the names of such familiar localities on the farm as ' the boggs,' and the ' flat ridge,' and the ' up and down road, leading to each from the main road, mark this farm purchased by Samuel Barlow as being unmistakably the present property of Bradley Hill, and the heirs of Gershom Hill. There was on it at the time a good substantial dwelling-house of respectable size, erected by a previous owner, and which stood about four hundred feet west of the present residence of Bradley Hill, on the same side of the street. The house was demolished in 1823. Having purchased this property January 2, 1749, he undoubtedly located his family on it the following spring, as in subsequent deeds he is recognized as a resident of the " Parish of Reading." It was here that Aaron, Samuel, Joel, and Huldah were born. It was here he lived and died, and from here he was buried in the old cemetery west of the Congregational Church in Redding Centre."

Of the children of Samuel Barlow, Daniel and Ruhamah died early. James settled in Ridgefield, on a farm of 130 acres conveyed to him by his father March 30, 1770. He had four children : Samuel, who removed to the South ; Lewis, Abigail, and James, who settled in Vermont. Jabez, the youngest son by the first wife, settled in Ohio.

Nathaniel Barlow married Jane Bradley, who was born May, 1744. Their children were : Gershom, born October 21, 1765 ; died of consumption September 24, 1794. Esther, born September 30, 1767 ; a deaf mute ; died May 10, 1783. Sarah, born January 16, 1770 ; died April 11, 1845. Jonathan, born April 14, 1772 ; died August 28, 1775. Betsey, born August 2, 1778 ; died September 9, 1864. Huldah, born April 3, 1780 ; a deaf mute, died August 29, 1787. Mr. Nathaniel Barlow died December 26, 1782.

Aaron Barlow settled in Redding, on Umpawaug Hill, on a farm purchased by his father several years before. He was a man of ability, tall, and of imposing bearing, and served in the capacity of a colonel in the Revolution. He removed to Norfolk, Va., and died there of yellow-fever. His children were : Elnathan, who died young. Elnathan, died in the war of 1812. Samuel, removed to Ohio. Stephen was a lawyer in Ohio. Daniel, lived and died in Redding. Aaron, died at sea. Esther, died at Norfolk, of yellow-fever. Joel, died in Redding. Rebecca, lived and died in Redding ; and Thomas, called after Thomas Paine by his uncle Joel.

Thomas was educated and adopted by his uncle, the poet, and accompanied him to France as his private secretary. He was also his companion on the fatal journey to Wilna. After the death of his uncle, Thomas returned to America and established himself as a lawyer in Pittsburg, Pa., and died there.

Samuel Barlow, the third son by the second wife, was a soldier in the Revolutionary Army, and died at Rhinebeck, N. Y., on his return from the expedition against Ticonderoga. A stone to his memory was erected in the old cemetery in Redding, near the Congregational Church, and which is still standing.

Of Joel Barlow, the poet, a full account is given elsewhere.

BARTLETT.

REV. NATHANIEL BARTLETT, second pastor of the Congregational Church in Redding, became a resident in 1753, and so remained until his death in 1810. He married, June 13, 1753, Mrs. Eunice Russell, of Branford, Conn. Their children were : Russell, baptized June 9, 1754. Daniel C., baptized January 16, 1757. Anne, February 25, 1759. Eunice, April 26, 1761. Jonathan, October 14, 1764.

13

Lucretia, March 27, 1768. Russell married, February 28, 1776, Rachel Taylor, and had children : Clare, baptized March 30, 1777, and Flora, baptized August 29, 1779. Daniel C. married Esther Read January 7, 1778, and settled in Amenia, N. Y., where some of his descendants now reside. Rev. Jonathan married, first, Roda, daughter of Lemuel Sanford ; second, Betsey Marvin, of Wilton ; and, third, Abigail, daughter of Lemuel Sanford. He had no children.

Sketches of Rev. Jonathan Bartlett, and of his father, Rev. Nathaniel Bartlett, are given in the history of the Congregational church.

BARTRAM.

DAVID BARTRAM removed from Fairfield to Redding as early as 1733, in which year he appears as surveyor of highways. He was a farmer, and settled in Lonetown. He had five sons and three daughters born in Fairfield, viz., David, Paul, James ; Daniel, born October 23, 1745 ; John, Mabel, Hannah, and Betsey. All the sons settled in Redding. David married, April 30, 1762, Phebe Morehouse, by whom he had Joel, David, John, Jonathan, Hulda, Hepsy, and Phebe. (Family record.) Paul married, September 19, 1756, Mary Hawley. Their children were : Joseph, born January 28, 1758 ; died in infancy. Mary, born May 12, 1760. Sarah, born August 6, 1762. Eunice, born January 3, 1765. Eli, born March 30, 1767. Ruth, born January 7, 1769. Ezekiel, born July 9, 1770. (Town record.) Ezra, baptized May 9, 1773. Joseph, baptized March 10, 1776. (Family record mentions a daughter

Olive.) Of these children, Mary married Jabez Burr, and removed to Clarendon, Vt. Sarah married Milo Palmer, and removed to the same place. Eunice married Daniel Parsons, of Redding. Eli married Dolly Lyon, of Redding; and about 1804 removed to Delaware Co., N. Y. His children were William, Belinda, Phebe, and Lodema. Ezekiel married Esther, daughter of Jonathan Parsons, of Redding. Their children were : Mary, Jared, Milo, Clarissa, Elizabeth, Jehu, Sarah, Elias, Ezra, Phebe, and Noah. One of his sons, Jehu, studied law and rose to eminence in the profession ; was judge, representative, and senator. Ezekiel moved to Ohio at an early day, and settled in Marion, where he resided until his death, March 15, 1845. Ezra was a sailor ; married Elinor, daughter of Chauncey Merchant, of Redding, and quitting the sea, removed to Delaware Co., N. Y., where he died shortly after, leaving children—Joel M., Ezra, Uriah, and Lucy. Joseph removed first to Vermont, and afterward to Tioga Co., N. Y. Olive married Justus Stillson, of Redding, and removed to Groton, N. Y.

James Bartram, son of David, settled in Redding. Was a private in the Revolution. Married Hannah Morehouse, who became the mother of twenty-one children, ten only of whom survived. These were : Isaac, born April 15, 1758. Noah, born 1760. James, born 1770. Aaron, born February 21, 1784. Lucy, Hannah, Betsey, Irena, and Anna.

Of these children, Isaac settled in Redding ; married Molly Hamilton, by whom he had seven children—Isaac, Harry, David, Willis, Chasie, Lucy, Polly, and Huldah. Aaron also settled in Redding, married Eunice Jenkins, and raised a large family of children.

Daniel, fourth son of David, also settled in Redding, was a tanner and currier by trade, and built the first works of the kind in the town, on the ground now occupied by Walter M. Edmonds for the same purpose. He married, October 10, 1768, Ann Merchant, of Redding. Their children were : Esther, born April 16, 1770. Gurdon, born October 25, 1771 ; died in infancy. Anna, born January 23, 1773 ; died in infancy. Elinor, born March 1, 1774 ; died in infancy. Gurdon, born September 21, 1776. Anna, born August 10, 1778 ; married —— Mead ; settled in Ridgefield. Elinor, born February 4, 1780 ; died in infancy. Uriah, born January 9, 1782. Elinor, born October 28, 1783 ; married —— Nash ; settled in Marion. Julilla, born November 12, 1785 ; married —— Bangs ; settled in Central N. Y. Levi, born November 26, 1787. Phebe, born September 19, 1790 ; married —— Curtin. David, born June 5, 1795. At the time of Tryon's invasion, with nearly every other man in the town capable of bearing arms, Daniel Bartram joined the militia and marched to the defence of Danbury. Being absent several days, he sent word to his wife that she must get some one to take the hides from the vats or they would spoil. There was not a man to be found ; and so the brave woman, leaving her four small children to amuse one another, caught her horse, hitched him to the bark mill, ground the bark, took the hides out, turned and repacked them and had just seated herself at the dinner-table when her husband rode up, having gained leave of absence for the purpose of attending to the matter. On the 3d of May, 1810, Daniel Bartram left Redding, accompanied by his wife, his four children, Uriah, Levi, Phebe, and David, and several of his neighbors, for what was then the wilderness of Ohio. They arrived in Madison, Lake Co., Ohio, on the 10th of June, where they settled, and where many of their descendants now reside. Daniel Bartram died in Madison, May 17, 1817. His widow died August 3, 1835. Gurdon Bartram, the eldest son of Daniel, remained in Redding. He married, January 1, 1804, Lorraine, daughter of Oliver Sanford, of Redding. Their children were : Aaron R., Lucy A., Barney, Coley, Betsey, Oliver, Daniel S., Ephraim, Levi, Frederick, Mary, and Julia. Gurdon Bartram died April 12, 1845, at the old homestead now occupied by his grandson David. Uriah, second son of Daniel, settled in Madison, Ohio, where he died quite suddenly of heart-disease, June 28, 1830, leaving a wife and six children. Levi, third son of Daniel, settled in Madison, Ohio ; married, June 17, 1813, Betsey Nott Walker, who was born in Ashford, Conn., April 29, 1790. Mr. Bartram died of heart-disease May 12, 1857, leaving a family of five children. His widow died June 13, 1863. David, fourth son of Daniel, also settled in Madison, and subsequently removed to Trumbull, Ashtabula Co., Ohio. He married, March 12, 1818, Elizabeth Gregory, formerly of Harpersfield, N. Y. They had six children. Mr. Bartram died of heart-disease September 2, 1875.

John Bartram, son of David the first, married, September 19, 1756, Charity Bulkley. Family record mentions two children, Sally and Samuel.

BATES.

ELIAS BATES was received to church-membership in Redding January 19, 1745. His wife, Sarah, March 4, 1748. There is no hint of his previous residence, and he probably came here direct from England. His children recorded in Redding were : Justus, baptized, July 26, 1747 ; and Sarah, baptized February 2, 1752 : by a second wife, Tabitha ——, Walker, baptized January 6, 1760. Elias, baptized February 16, 1761, died in infancy.

John Bates, probably son of Elias, married Esther ——. Their children were : Ezra, baptized March 23, 1760, died in infancy. John, baptized July 25, 1762. Sarah, baptized May 5, 1764. Esther, baptized August 23, 1767. Nathan, baptized March 25, 1770. Aaron, July 1, 1772. Martha and Slawson, January 26, 1778.

Justus Bates, son of Elias, married Hannah Coley, May 23, 1770. They had one child, Elias, baptized October 4, 1772, who married, November 9, 1793, Lydia Andrews, of Redding, and was the father of three children—Walker, born June 4, 1796 ; Amaziah, born May 17, 1801 ; and Harriet, born May 21, 1804.

BEACH.

JOHN BEACH, missionary of the Church of England in Redding, was born in Stratford, Conn., October 6, 1700. His father was Isaac Beach, son of John Beach who came from England in 1643. He graduated from Yale College in 1721. He married, first, Sarah ——, who died in 1756 ; and, second,

Abigail Holbrook, who after his death returned to Derby. He had in all nine children. Those who had families were : Joseph, born September 26, 1727. Phebe, born 1729 ; married Daniel Hill of Redding ; died 1751, leaving a son Abel. John, born 1734 ; married Phebe Curtis ; died in 1791. Lazarus, born 1736 ; had two children, viz., Lazarus, born 1760, and Isaac, born 1773.

Lazarus inherited his father's land in Redding, at Hopewell, near which he built his house. Lazarus Beach, Jr., was of a literary turn, and edited a paper at Bridgeport, and afterward at Washington, D. C. On his journey to the latter place he lost his trunk or valise, containing the Beach manuscripts, and all his materials gathered for the purpose of writing a memoir of his distinguished grandfather. He built the house now standing near Mr. Godfrey's. Isaac Beach built the house now occupied by Hull B. Bradley. The Rev. John Beach lived about thirty to forty rods south of the church, probably on the site of the old Captain Munger house, which has long since disappeared. The *well* is still used by Mr. E. P. Shaw. Lucy, daughter of the Rev. John Beach, married Rev. Mr. Townsend, and was lost at sea on her passage to Nova Scotia, probably at the time of the great exodus of Loyalists after the Revolution. The mother of James Sanford, Sen., was the daughter of Lazarus and grand-daughter of Rev. John Beach.

BENEDICT.

The Benedicts were a Norwalk family and settled quite largely in Ridgefield. The first of the name whom I find in Redding was Thaddeus Benedict, who was a lawyer and town-clerk for a term of years. His house stood in the lot adjoining the Congregational parsonage, near the site of the present residence of Joseph Squire. His law office was under the great elm in front of his house. He married Deborah Read, July 12, 1775, daughter of Colonel John Read, who bore him several children.

BETTS.

LIEUTENANT STEPHEN BETTS, a prominent character in the Revolution, lived on Redding Ridge, in a house that stood on the corner, nearly opposite the former residence of Francis A. Sanford. He was an active Whig, and was taken prisoner by the British on their march to Danbury in 1777. He had a son Daniel, and two or three daughters, of whom I have no record. His son Daniel was a merchant for a while on Redding Ridge and then removed to New Haven, where some of his children are now living.

BURR.

AMONG the earliest settlers of Redding were Jehu, Stephen, and Peter Burr, sons of Daniel Burr, of Fairfield, and brothers of the Rev. Aaron Burr, President of Princeton College. They all appear at about the same time, viz., 1730. In October of that year Stephen Burr was elected a member of the first Society Committee of the parish. He married Elizabeth Hull June 8th, 1721. Children : Grace, born December 12th, 1724. Elizabeth, born January 17th, 1728. Hezekiah, born September 1st, 1730. Sarah, born November 9th, 1732. Martha, born

March 24th, 1735. Esther, born February 5th, 1743. Rebecca. He married, second, Abigail Hall, of New Jersey. He lived in a house that stood where Dr. Gorham later built his residence. His only son, Hezekiah, died December, 1785, unmarried. Of the daughters, Grace married Daniel Gold, Elizabeth married Reuben Squire, Sarah married Joseph Jackson, Martha married Zacariah Summers. Esther married Antony Angevine, and Rebecca, Seth Sanford. Deacon Stephen Burr died in 1779. Of him Colonel Aaron Burr wrote in his journal in Paris : " My uncle Stephen lived on milk punch, and at the age of eighty-six mounted by the stirrup a very gay horse, and galloped off with me twelve miles without stopping, and was I thought less fatigued than I."

Peter Burr first appears in Redding as clerk of a society meeting held October 11th, 1730. His children were : Ellen, baptized September 19, 1734. Sarah, baptized February 21st, 1736. Ezra, baptized January 2d, 1737. Edmund, baptized September 28th, 1761. Peter Burr died in August, 1779. His children shortly after removed to Virginia.

Jehu Burr and wife were admitted to church-membership in Redding December 24th, 1738. None of his children were recorded in Redding, and none, so far as known, settled there. He owned property in Fairfield, and probably spent the last years of his life there.

Jabez Burr, son of Joseph Burr, of Fairfield, and his wife Elizabeth, appear in Redding as early as 1743. Their children were Elijah, baptized May 15th, 1743. Nathan, born January 1st, 1745. Jabez, —— Ezekiel, born March 23d, 1755. Stephen, born January 16th, 1757. Joel, born September 9th, 1759. Eunice, Huldah, and Hannah. Jabez Burr died in 1770. He is said to have settled in the Saugatuck Valley, near the present residence of Stephen Burr, and to have built there the first grist-mill in the town. Of his children, Elijah married Roda Sanford, April 2d, 1767, and had children—Lemuel and Elizabeth ; and by a second wife—Eunice Hawley, married April 27th, 1773—Joseph, Roda, John (who died of yellow-fever in the West Indies), and Lucy, who married Jonathan Knapp, of Redding. Nathan, the second son, removed to Pawlings, Dutchess Co., N. Y., in 1792, and there founded a numerous and wealthy family. Jabez, the third son, married Mary, daughter of Paul Bartram, and removed to Clarendon, Vt., in 1786. He had one son, Aaron. Ezekiel, married Huldah Merchant, of Redding, who bore him three children : Aaron, who lived and died in the house now owned by Captain Davis ; William, who removed to Kentucky in 1816 ; and Huldah, who married Daniel Mallory in 1806, and removed to the West.

A son of William Burr is now President of the St. Louis National Bank. Another son, George, a teller in the same institution, was the companion of Prof. Wise in his late fatal balloon expedition, and shared the fate of the aëronaut. Stephen Burr married Mary Griffin, of Redding. His children were : Clara, Mary, Stephen, and Ezekiel. Joel Burr married Elizabeth Gold and settled in Ballston Springs, N. Y.

BURRITT.

WILLIAM BURRITT and wife were admitted members of the church December 9th, 1739. No hint of their previous residence is given. Their children recorded at Redding were : Mary, baptized December 16th, 1739. Abijah, January 18th, 1741. Roda, October 24, 1742. Sybil, February 19, 1744. Gershom Burritt appears at the same time. His son Solomon was baptized August 5th, 1739. Noah, January 31st, 1742. Nathaniel, October 17th, 1743. Isaac, July 21st, 1745.

BURTON.

BENJAMIN, son of Solomon Burton, baptized December 19th, 1742. Ruth, daughter, baptized October 7th, 1744. Solomon Burton and wife, church members July 5th, 1741.

CHATFIELD.

SAMUEL CHATFIELD and wife were admitted church members July 29th, 1733. Their children recorded were : Samuel, baptized July 29th, 1733. Daniel, baptized August 31st, 1735. Sarah, April 17th, 1737. Martha, baptized May 20th, 1739.

COUCH.

CAPTAIN SAMUEL COUCH, of Fairfield, was one of the largest landholders in Redding at one time, and was largely instrumental in its settlement. He was, however, never resident here. Ebenezer Couch appears here as early as 1739. His children recorded were : Daniel, baptized July 29th, 1739. Adea, bap-

tized September 19th, 1742. Elijah, baptized July
26th, 1747. Thesde, January 26th, 1755.

The following children of John Couch and his
wife Elizabeth are recorded : John, baptized March
20th, 1748. Stephen, January 21st, 1753. Adria,
baptized April 20th, 1755. Elizabeth, baptized July
17th, 1757. Samuel, baptized August 30th, 1758.

At an early day, nearly the entire district of Couch's
Hill was purchased by Mr. Simon Couch, of Fair-
field, who gave his name to the district purchased.
His wife was Abigail Hall, a member of a notable
Fairfield family. His will, dated March 2d, 1712–13,
is still in the possession of Mr. Nash Couch, of
Couch's Hill, who is a lineal descendant. In this will
he gives his "Negro man Jack" and "negro maid
Jinne" to his wife, in addition to other bequests.
His children mentioned in the will were : Simon, Jr.,
Thomas, Abigail, Hannah, Sarah, Isabel, and Deborah.
Thomas was lost at sea while on a voyage to England. Simon settled on his father's estate in Redding ; married, January 27th, 1753, Rebecca, daughter of Captain Thomas Nash, of Fairfield. Their
children, as given in the genealogy of the Nash family, were : Abigail, baptized February 10th, 1754 :
died young. Simon, born May 18th, 1755 ; settled
at Green's Farms. Thomas Nash, born April 18th,
1758 ; settled in Redding. Rebecca, born January
31st, 1761. Abigail, baptized January 27th, 1765.
Lydia, born October 20th, 1767. Deacon Simon
Couch died April 25th, 1809.

Thomas Couch, of Fairfield, removed to Redding
prior to the Revolution, and settled on Umpawaug

Hill. He married, April 2d, 1772, Sarah, daughter of Jonathan Nash, of Fairfield. Their children were : Sarah, born August 9th, 1773 ; died young. Thomas, born September 23d, 1774. Jonathan, born February 13th, 1777, who was the father of Major-General Couch, distinguished in the War of the Rebellion. Sarah, born September 18th, 1779. Nathan, born September 25th, 1781. Esther, born December 14th, 1783. Moses, born October 2d, 1786. Edward, born March 7th, 1789. Hezekiah, born March 14th, 1791. Mary, born April 21st, 1793. John, born July 28th, 1795. Mr. Thomas Couch died in Redding in 1817.

At the outbreak of the Revolution Thomas Couch enlisted in the patriot army, and was one of the band of heroes who were present with Montgomery at the siege of Quebec. He left his wife with their young children in Fairfield. When Tryon moved on that town, Mrs. Couch had what furniture and grain she could gather put into an ox cart drawn by two yoke of oxen, and started for Redding, where she owned land in her own right. She followed on horseback, carrying her two children in her arms. At the close of the war, Thomas joined his wife in Redding, where they continued to reside until death.

Simon Couch, brother of Thomas, settled in Redding, on Umpawaug Hill, about the same time. He married, January 7th, 1776, Eleanor, daughter of Jonathan Nash, of Fairfield. Their children were : Elizabeth, born October 9th, 1776. Jessup, born August 3d, 1778. Seth, born August 31st, 1780. Eleanor, born August 26th, 1782. Simon, born December 1st, 1784. Nash, born April 23d, 1787.

Priscilla, born June 27th, 1790. Edward, born July 14th, 1792. Simon A., born December 6th, 1794. Caroline, born June 23d, 1801. Simon Couch died April 16th, 1829. Of the children, Simon and Jessup graduated at Yale College. Jessup graduated in 1802, and in 1804 removed to Chillicothe, Ohio, where he practised law until his appointment as Judge of the Superior Court of Ohio in 1815. This office he continued to hold until his death in 1821. In the War of 1812 he was also aide-de-camp to Governor Meigs, of Ohio, and bearer of dispatches to General Hull.

Simon Couch, his brother, settled at Marion, Ohio, where he practised medicine until his death in 1826.

DARLING.

EUNICE, daughter of Joseph Darling, baptized January 25th, 1736. Benjamin, baptized April 13th, 1738. Martha, January 11th, 1741. Joseph, baptized November, 1743.

FAIRCHILD.

THOMAS FAIRCHILD removed to Redding from Norwalk in 1733 ; was one of the original members of the church. His wife Mary was admitted January 29th, 1738. Their children recorded were : Timothy and William, baptized October 22d, 1738. Sarah, April 12th, 1741. Abijah, May 27th, 1744. Mary, October 27th, 1745.

Abraham Fairchild, probably brother of above, came from Norwalk in 1746, and built the first fulling-mill in the town, near the site later occupied by

Deacon Foster's woollen-mill. His wife was Sarah Scribner, of Norwalk. Their children were: Abraham, born January 1st, 1745; died aged 17 years. Ezekiel, born October 26th, 1746. Daniel, born December 26th, 1748. Isaac, born March 4th, 1751. David, born June 5th, 1753. Samuel, born July 9th, 1755. Stephen, born March 7th, 1758. Rachel, born February 2d, 1761. John, born March 15th, 1764. Ellen, born October 16th, 1767. Six of these brothers were in the Revolutionary army at one time. David was captured by the British, and confined in Trinity Church, New York. The small-pox was communicated to the prisoners—it is said with design, and he with many others died of the disease. Stephen was wounded at Ridgefield, but recovered : married Lizzie Fitch, of Wilton. Their children were : Daniel, Kier, Isaac, Ellen, and Stephen. Ezekiel married Eunice Andrews ; had four children, Abraham, Sarah, Abigail, and Burr. Daniel married Betsey Mead, and removed to the West. Isaac married Rachel Banks, and removed to Liberty, N. Y. Samuel married Nabbie Platt, of Redding, and had two children, Aaron and Betsey. John married Abigail Wakeman, of Weston. Their children were : Eli, David, Rachel, Moses, Henry, and Eliza. David married Charlotte Guyer, of Weston. Their children were : Eli, William, David, Mary, and John. Rachel married Seth Andrews, of Redding. Ellen married Minott Thomas, a Baptist clergyman.

Stephen, Samuel, and John built a grist mill at an early day on the site of the one later known as Treadwell's mill. It was carried off by the great freshet of 1807, and the large stock of grain it contained was scattered over the meadows below. They also owned a saw-mill just below, and sawed plank for the soldiers' huts in the Revolution.

REGINALD FOSTER, the founder of the family in America, came to this country in 1638 with his five sons, Abraham, Reginald, William, Isaac, and Jacob, and settled at Ipswich, Essex Co., Mass. Jacob Foster was the ancestor of the Redding family. Jonah Foster settled in Redding about 1775; married Hannah Benedict, of Ridgefield, and shortly after removed to that town, and there resided until his death in 1815. His son, Joel Foster, was born in Redding November 8th, 1780, and lived in Ridgefield with his parents until his marriage with Esther Seymour in 1802. In 1803 he removed to Redding, and bought of Moses Fox a small place, on which was a fulling-mill and other conveniences for cheapening cloths. This mill stood a little below the present bridge over Nobb's Crook brook, and the ruins of its dam are still to be seen. In 1804, Mr. Foster built an addition to his fulling-mill building, which was leased to Zalmon Toucey, of Newtown, and in which Toucey erected a carding machine, paying a yearly rent of twenty dollars.

How long Mr. Toucey's lease continued is not known, but he probably soon relinquished it to Joel Foster, as the latter continued the business until about the time of the opening of the War of 1812, when a company was formed, styled Comstock, Foster & Co., who built a woollen factory a few rods below the old fulling-mill, and continued the manufacture of woollen goods during the entire period of the war, being very successful. The company, a few years after the war, was bought out by Joel Foster, who continued the business until the burning of his factory in 1843 or 1844, when he retired. Mr. Foster died in 1854, aged seventy-four years. He had four children, all born in Redding : Daniel, Betsey, Eliza, and Charles F.

GOLD.

DANIEL, SAMUEL, and STEPHEN GOLD (now written Gould), brothers, members of a Fairfield family that had been prominent in church and state for several generations, were among the early settlers of the town, though none of their descendants are now found among us. Daniel appears first : he married Grace, daughter of Deacon Stephen Burr, and lived where James Lord now lives. His children, as named in the will of Deacon Burr, were : Abigail, who married Richard Nichols. Esther, who married Nathaniel Northrop. Sarah, who married David Turney. Mary, who married Seth Price ; and Elizabeth.

Samuel Gold settled in Lonetown, and built the house now owned by Seth Todd. He was a soldier in the Revolution, and was wounded at the skirmish in Ridgefield. Some of the officers of Putnam's command had their quarters at Mr. Gold's during their encampment in Redding. He married Sarah Platt, of Redding. Their children were : Hezekiah, Daniel, Burr, Aaron, Sarah, Polly, and Grace. Stephen Gold settled on the farm later owned by Timothy Platt in Lonetown. He is called captain in the

14

records. He did not long remain a resident of Redding, but returned, it is said, to Greenfield.

GORHAM.

ISAAC GORHAM and his wife Ann first appear on the parish records January 25th, 1762, when their son Isaac was baptized. There is no hint of their former residence, but they were probably from Fairfield. I find no further record of children.

GRAY.

DANIEL GRAY and wife were admitted church-members December 5th, 1742. John Gray and wife February 9th, 1744, on the recommendation of Rev. Mr. Dickinson, of Norwalk.

The only child of Daniel Gray recorded was James, baptized May 8th, 1743. The children of John Gray were : Hannah, baptized July 1st, 1744. Joseph, July 15th, 1753. Eunice, January 2d, 1755, and (by a second wife, Ruamah), Eunice, baptized April 13th, 1760 ; and Joel, September 11th, 1763.

Stephen, son of Stephen and Sarah Gray, was baptized May 10th, 1747. Also Huldah, a daughter, December 14th, 1760. Hannah, October 3d, 1762 ; and Sarah, June 17th, 1764. James Gray, only son of Daniel, married Mabel Phinney February 9th, 1764. Their children were : Jesse, baptized April 14th, 1765 ; perhaps others.

GRIFFIN.

JOHN GRIFFIN appears in Redding as early as 1736. His children were : Sarah, baptized May 9th, 1736. Annie, baptized October 22d, 1738 ; and Jon-

athan, baptized November 23d, 1746. He settled in
West Redding, near the Danbury line.

HALL.

THE Halls were among the earliest settlers in Redding, the name appearing on the earliest petitions
from the parish. In 1730, at the distribution of the
estate of Samuel Hall, he is said to be of Chestnut
Ridge, in Reading. His children as given were:
Ebenezer, Johanna, Jemima, and Rebecca. Isaac
Hall, whose farm lay contiguous to Samuel's, was
one of the original church-members, and was recommended by Rev. Mr. Chapman. He died in 1741.
Asa Hall and Rachel his wife were admitted March
23d, 1736, on the same recommendation. I find no
mention of children.

HAWLEY.

JOSEPH HAWLEY and wife were admitted church-
members in December, 1740, on recommendation of
Rev. Mr. Gold, of Stratford. Their children recorded
were: Mary, baptized February 7th, 1742. Ruth,
November 5th, 1746. Eunice, October 25th, 1750.
Joseph Hawley died December 12th, 1771, aged sixty-
six years. William Hawley, who appears in Redding as early as 1762, was probably his son. He lived
where James Miller now lives ; married Lydia, daughter of Captain Thomas Nash, of Fairfield, July
12th, 1758. Their children were : Lydia, died in infancy. Joseph, born June 23d, 1762 ; settled in Redding. Lydia, born December 13th, 1763 ; married
Aaron Sanford, of Redding. William, died in infancy.
Bille, born February 9th, 1767, removed to the

West. Hezekiah, died in infancy. Hezekiah, born March 10th, 1772. Lemuel, died young, of small-pox. William Hawley, died February 16th, 1797. Mrs. Lydia Hawley died April 26th, 1812.

HILL.

THE founder in America of this family was William Hill, who on his arrival here about 1632 settled first at Dorchester, Mass., and shortly after removed to Windsor, on the Connecticut River, where he bought land and set out an orchard. At an early day he removed to Fairfield, and was among the early settlers of that town. He died in 1650. His children were : Sarah, *William*, Joseph, Ignatius, James, and Elizabeth. *William*, the second child, married Elizabeth ——. Their children were : Sarah, *William*, Joseph, John, Eliphalet, Ignatius, and James. *William*, the third, married ——, and had children, Sarah, *William*, Joseph, and David. *William* Hill, the fourth, married Sarah ——. Their children were : *Joseph*, William, and David. Deacon Joseph Hill, born April 1, 1699 ; married Abigail Dimon March 30th, 1731. The children of this marriage were : Abigail, born March 21st, 1732. Sarah, born August 21st, 1733. David, born April 22d, 1737. Ebenezer, born February 26th, 1742. Jabez, born June 17th, 1744, and Moses, born January 11th, 1748. Of the sons, only *Ebenezer*, *Jabez*, and *Moses* married. *Ebenezer* married Mabel Sherwood January 17th, 1765. Their children were : David, *Ebenezer*, Seth, Dimon, Joseph, Mabel, Eleanor, Jabez, and Esther. *Ebenezer*, his second son, married Sarah, daughter of Nathaniel

Barlow, brother of the poet, in May, 1791. He removed to Redding early in life, and settled in Boston
district. His children were: Mabel, Nathaniel B.,
Gershom, Ebenezer, Moses, and Jabez. *Jabez Hill*,
son of Deacon Joseph Hill, settled in Weston ; was a
major in the army of the Revolution ; married Sarah,
daughter of Colonel John Read, of Redding. The
children of this marriage were : Sarah, John Read,
and Moses. Sarah married Timothy Platt, of Redding. John Read settled in Redding at an early
day, and became one of its wealthiest and best known
residents. He began his business career by engag-
ing in the manufacture of lime as before narrated,
and on his retirement in 1823 purchased the
" manor" of his grandfather, Colonel John Read,
where he continued to reside until his death in 1851.
He married, March 23d, 1799, Betsy, daughter of
Aaron Sanford, of Redding. Their children were :
Aaron Sanford, Moses, William Hawley, Betsy,
John Lee, Morris, Lydia, and Joseph.

Moses Hill, son of Deacon Joseph Hill, married
Esther, daughter of Ebenezer Burr, of Fairfield, June
17th, 1773. The children by this marriage were :
William, Abigail, and Esther. *William* married
Betsey, daughter of Nathaniel Barlow, brother of
the poet, and had children, Bradley, Abigail, Horace, Burr, and William.

HERON.

IN Revolutionary days and before, Squire Heron
lived in the now ancient house on Redding Ridge,
just south of the Episcopal church. He was a native of Cork, Ireland ; a graduate of Trinity College,

Dublin ; and a man of much ability and force of character. It is said that he had taught the Academy in Greenfield Hill before coming to Redding, and had also surveyed the old stage route from New York to Boston. I cannot determine the precise date of his arrival here, but it was some time prior to the Revolution. In that memorable struggle he sided with the king, and was the recognized leader of the company of Tories on Redding Ridge. At the time of Tryon's invasion he openly gave aid and comfort to the enemy. After the war he became a prominent character in the town, and although somewhat bigoted, and imbued with the Old World notions of caste and social distinctions, is said to have exercised a great deal of influence in public affairs, especially at town meetings. "We must keep down the underbrush" was a favorite remark of his in speaking of the common people. The following story, illustrating in a marked manner the customs of the day, is related of him :

At one of the annual town meetings Mr. Hezekiah Morgan, a somewhat illiterate man, was nominated for grand juror. Squire Heron, in laced waistcoat, ruffles, and velvet breeches, and aiding himself with his gold-headed cane, arose to oppose the motion. "Mr. Moderator," said he, "who is this Kier Morgan ? Why, a man brought up in Hopewell woods : he fears neither God, man, nor the devil. If elected, who will be responsible for his acts ? Will you, Mr. Moderator ? or I ? Why, sir, he can arrest anybody : he can arrest your Honor, or even myself ;" and with like cogent reasons succeeded in defeating the obnoxious candidate.

Squire Heron died January 8th, 1819, aged seventy-seven years, and is buried in the old Episcopal churchyard on Redding Ridge. ª His children were : William, Maurice, Elizabeth, Lucy, Elosia, Margaret, and Susan. William never married. He lived on the old homestead in Redding all his days, and was a man much respected in the community. His brother Maurice graduated at Yale College, and shortly after was killed by a steamboat explosion on the Connecticut River, near Essex.

HULL.

THE Hull family are recorded in the Herald's Distinction of Devon as a very ancient family of Devonshire, but the original name, De La Hulle, in Shropshire, in the reign of Edward II., indicates that they went from the Continent to England, probably from Normandy. Shortly after the Pilgrims landed in Plymouth, five brothers named Hull came to Massachusetts from England, viz., John, George, Richard, Joseph, and Robert.

George, who was the ancestor of the Hulls of Redding, appears in Dorchester, Mass., in 1630 ; removed to Windsor, Conn., and afterward to Fairfield ; died in August, 1659. His will, dated August 25, 1659, mentions sons Josias and Cornelius, and several daughters. His son Cornelius married Rebecca, daughter of Rev. John Joanes, the first minister of Fairfield, who was of Welsh origin. His will, of the date September 16, 1695, mentions three sons, Samuel, Cornelius, and Theophilus ; and three daughters, Rebecca, Sarah, the wife of Robert Silliman, and Martha, wife of Cornelius Stratton. The children of

Cornelius were : George, Sarah, Rebecca, Nathaniel, Ebenezer, Elizabeth, John, Martha, Eleanor, and Cornelius. Deacon George Hull was one of the fathers of the infant settlement. He was moderator of the first parish meeting, a member of the first parish committee, and first deacon of the church in Redding. He also appears on numerous committees. He and his wife, Ebenezer and wife, and Theophilus and wife were among the original church members in 1733. John Hull was admitted April 18, 1736. All of them removed here from Greenfield Hill. George, Ebenezer, and Cornelius must have come to Redding prior to 1733, for their names appear in a petition to fix upon a site for a meeting-house in 1725. By a deed dated Danbury, May 19, 1729, a tract of land lying in Chestnut Ridge, between Danbury and Fairfield, is conveyed to George Hull and heirs by Jonathan Squires.

George Hull's children recorded in Redding are : Seth, baptized July 29, 1733 ; and Rebecca, May 25, 1735. He died February 9, 1769, aged 83. Seth Hull married Elizabeth Mallory, his neice. Children recorded in Redding are : Abagail, born January 28, 1762 ; Jonathan, October 25, 1763, Eliphalet, December 18, 1765 ; Walter, November 21, 1767 ; Lazarus, January 16, 1770 ; Hezekiah, March 24, 1792 ; and Martha, April 28, 1794. Besides these were Elizabeth and Sarah ; Martha married David Belden, an Episcopal clergyman ; Jonathan married Eunice Beach, and was the father of Rev. Lemuel B. Hull, former rector of Christ Church in Redding. Seth Hull died April 5, 1795.

Nathaniel Hull was born in 1695, and reared

Sarah, Elizabeth, Esther, Stephen, Nathaniel, Peter, Ezekiel, David, Aaron, Silas, and Hannah.

The children of *Silas* Hull were : Hannah, Huldah, and *Bradley*. Bradley's children were : Burr, Pamelia, Charry, Silas, Aaron B., Charles, Mary, Bradley H., Chapman, Le Grand, and Cornelia.

The children of Ebenezer were : Daniel, Ebenezer, Nehemiah, and Abagail. Daniel married Mary Betts, and removed from Redding to Berlin, Rensselaer County, N. Y., in 1770, and was one of the first settlers of that town. He died August 26, 1811, aged 89 years. He had ten children, viz., Martha, Hezekiah, Justus, Abagail, Peter, Esther, Daniel, Stephen, Harry, and Ebenezer.

Of these children all but the two last named were born in Redding. Justus was one of the first ministers of the Second Baptist Church in Danbury, and is reputed to have been a preacher of more than ordinary ability. He was in the ministry fifty-six years, and died at Berlin, N. Y., May 29, 1833, at the age of 78. His children were, Justus P. Emmerson, Polly Ann, and Alonzo Grandison. The last named is a physician, and resides in New York. He was a successful practitioner in London twelve years. Ebenezer married and emigrated to the West. His descendants reside in Iowa, Nebraska, and other Western States. Nehemiah died a bachelor.

John Hull removed to Redding when in middle life. He went with the Provincial troops in the expedition against Cuba in 1641, and fell a victim to the yellow-fever with nearly a thousand others of the sturdy sons of New England. He directed that his musket, carried in the wars, should be sent home to

his eldest son Timothy ; he to leave it to his eldest
son, and that it should descend in this manner to
the eldest son as long as it existed.   Thus it has fal-
len in regular descent to Mr. Aaron B. Hull, of
Danbury, the great grandson of the original owner.
Before enlisting, Mr. Hull made his will, dated September 16, 1740, in which he mentions sons Timothy,
James, and John, and daughters Anna, Abagail, and
Esther.   Timothy was born September 4, 1726, and
married Anna, daughter of John Gray, December
14, 1749. He died April 29, 1800. His children were
Hannah, born July 27, 1751, married Samuel Mallory, and died in Danbury, September 4, 1836.
Sarah, born February 5, 1754, married John Fairchild and emigrated west.   Ezra, born April 5, 1756,
and died in Redding, March 5, 1837.   He settled
in Boston school district. He married Elizabeth,
daughter of Onesimus Coley.   His children were :
Eunice, born July 6, 1785, married Hiram Jackson ;
died in Kingston, N. Y., May 3, 1862.   Laura, born
August 4, 1788, married John Eckert, and died in
Springfield, Otsego County, N. Y., November 17,
1865. Polly, born November 29, 1798, died in Kingston, N. Y., September 28, 1876.   Elizabeth, the wife
of Ezra Hull, died February 28, 1809 ; he married
Widow Mary Bradley, daughter of Gershom Banks,
of Fairfield, June 20, 1810 ; she died in Wilton,
April 17, 1854.   The children of this marriage were :
Ezra Bradley and Charles, who both died young,
and Aaron B.   Ezra Hull served in the Revolutionary
War, and participated in those events which transpired during Governor Tryon's expedition to and
the burning of Danbury.   Eunice, fourth child of

Timothy Hull, was born August 26, 1757, married
George Perry and removed to Kentucky. John,
born June 26, 1759, married Sarah Fairchild ; died
April 7, 1838. (His children were Aaron, Ezekiel,
Hezekiah, Abraham, and Polly.) Abraham, born
March 30, 1761, died in Danbury, October 29,
1831. David, born March 22, 1763, died in Redding, March 19, 1847 ; he married Chloe Lee, and
had children, Daniel, Harry, and Lucy. Samuel,
born June 22, 1766. (He married Anna Wakeman,
and had a daughter Eliza, who married Horace Sta-
ples, President of the Westport National Bank.
Samuel Hull died in Redding July 19, 1846.) Hezekiah, born October 22, 1769, died in Danbury, July
26, 1852. Anna, born December 7, 1771, married
Lemuel Burr ; died in Redding, December 20, 1840.
Abagail, born November 17, 1775, married Timothy
Perry ; died in Miamisburg, Ohio, March 16, 1844.

The will of James, the second son of John Hull,
of the date of April 26, 1799, mentions no children.
He died February 20, 1805, in the seventy-seventh
year of his age. John married Mollie Andrews,
February 3, 1763. His children recorded are Eleanor and Mollie. His will, bearing date June 24,
1815, mentions no children, but names his " grandson John Goodyear, and the son of his grandson
Hull Goodyear ;" also two other names not given,
but which were undoubtedly Munson Goodyear and
Ellen, wife of Harry Meeker. ⌄

Cornelius, the youngest son of Cornelius Hull, 2d,
and Abagail, daughter of Robert Rumsey, were
married August 24, 1731. Their children were : *Jedediah*, Eunice, Grace, Eliphalet, Abigail, Sarah,

and Ruey. *Jedediah* Hull was second lieuten-
ant under Colonel David Wooster in the army
which invaded Canada in 1758. His children were :
Denny, Eunice, Chapman, Molly, Cornelius, and
Jedediah. Denny and Chapman settled in Redding.
The children of the first named were : Mary, Denny,
Isaac Platt, and Eunice. Chapman's were : Morris,
Henry C., and George.

The will of Theophilus Hull, of Fairfield, the
youngest son of Cornelius, 1st, dated June 4, 1710,
gives the names of sons Theophilus, Eliphalet, John,
and Jabesh, and two, daughters, Mary and Ann.
Theophilus, his oldest son, married Widow Martha
Betts, of Redding, January 25, 1759. His will, of
the date December 1, 1785, names son Zalmon, and
daughters Sarah and Lydia. Zalmon's sons were :
Hezekiah, Theophilus B., Henry L., and his daughters, Lydia and Sally.

The Redding records contain the marriage of
Nehemiah Hull and Grizzle Perry, February 5,
1767. Nehemiah, probably a son of the above,
married Sarah Jackson. Twin children were born
to them, December 7, 1792, and were named Sally
Betsey, and Betsey Sally. The first named married
Theophilus B., son of Zalmon Hull, and the other
Morris, son of Chapman Hull.

JACKSON.

EPHRAIM JACKSON and his wife Martha removed
to Redding from Green's Farms, Fairfield, in 1748,
and were admitted church-members the same year.
He died April 28th, 1765, aged sixty-five years. The
children of his son, Ephraim Jackson, were as fol-

lows : Aaron, baptized November 12th, 1767. Mollie, baptized July 23d, 1769. Peter, September 8th, 1771. Hezekiah, February 27th, 1774. David Jackson appears in Redding as early as 1763 ; was probably son of Ephraim ; married November 18th, 1762, Anna Sanford. Their children were : Ezekiel, baptized October 23d, 1763. David, February 2d, 1766. Anna, September 30th, 1770 ; died in infancy. Anna, September 14th, 1772 ; and by a second wife, Esther, Moses, baptized December 11th, 1774 ; perhaps others. Ezekiel, son of David, married Hannah Gray, April 30th, 1786 (Town record). Their children were : Anna, born December 21st, 1786. Hiram, born April 22d, 1788. Samuel, born December 29th, 1789. Clarissa, born December 25th, 1792. Laura, born February 28th, 1794. Harriet, born December 18th, 1795. Harriet married Gideon H. Hollister, of Woodbury, and became the mother of Judge Gideon H. Hollister, the historian of Connecticut.

LEE.

WILLIAM LEE and wife were admitted church members May 23d, 1742. Their children recorded were : Daniel, baptized January 8th, 1744. Abijah, baptized September 21st, 1745. Abigail, baptized May 5th, 1748. William, baptized April 5th, 1753. Seth, baptized March 23d, 1755.

Joseph Lee and wife admitted May 8th, 1737. Their daughter Mary was baptized May 8th, 1743.

LYON.

AMONG the original members of the church at its organization in 1733 appear the names of Daniel

Lion and wife, of Benjamin Lion and wife—recommended by Rev. Mr. Gay—and Richard Lion and wife. All settled in the south-eastern part of the town, near what is now the Easton line. The record of their families is as follows. Children of Daniel were : Jonathan, baptized April 12th, 1741. Children of Benjamin were : Bethel, baptized May 29th, 1733. John, baptized August 22d, 1736. Samuel, baptized August 20th, 1738. Phebe, baptized February 24th, 1740. Richard Lion died in January 1740, aged eighty-seven years.

LORD.

DAVID LORD was admitted church-member in 1744, recommended by Rev. Mr. Parsons, of Lyme. His children were : David, baptized July 8th, 1744. Elizabeth, baptized March 5th, 1749 ; perhaps others.

MALLORY.

JONATHAN MALLORY and wife were admitted church-members December 22d, 1735, on recommendation of Rev. Mr. Chapman. She was Elizabeth Adams. They were married April 10th, 1735. Their children were : Jonathan, baptized January 11th, 1736. Eliza, baptized December 17th, 1738. perhaps others. Peter Mallory married Joanna Hall February 28th, 1737. Children : Rebecca, baptized February 5th, 1738 ; died in infancy. Rebecca, baptized January 13th, 1739. Ebenezer Mallory and Hannah Keys were married February 6th, 1744. No children found. Daniel Mallory and Sarah Lee were married November 30th, 1748. Their children were : Daniel, baptized October 25th, 1750.

Nathan, August 25th, 1754. Abigail, April 24th, 1757. Sarah, May 15th, 1763. Joseph, baptized February 12th, 1767. Eunice, daughter of Daniel Mallory, Jr., and his wife Rachel, was baptized September 5th, 1779. Samuel and Charles Mallory were born April 6th, 1780. The names of the parents are not given. Charles Mallory was the father of Stephen Mallory, United States Senator from Florida, and later Secretary of the Confederate Navy.

MEADE.

STEPHEN MEADE, the first of the name in Redding, appears as early as 1755. He married Rachel Sanford, daughter of Ephraim Sanford. Their children were : Jeremiah, born March 22d, 1752. Ezra, baptized January 19th, 1755. Hannah, baptized May 9th, 1756. Esther, baptized August 17th, 1760. Thaddeus, baptized October 25th, 1761. Stephen, baptized January 24th, 1768. Stephen Meade is called lieutenant and captain in the records. He was a man quite prominent in town affairs ; was elected the first clerk of the town at its organization in 1767, and held other important offices. He lived in the centre, on the site of the present residence of Thomas Sanford.

MEEKER.

BENJAMIN MEEKER and wife were admitted church-members June 4th, 1747. She was Catherine Burr. They were married July 20th, 1745. Their children were : Witely, baptized June 7th, 1747. Esther and Eunice, baptized August 13th, 1755. Azariah, baptized February 5th, 1769. Daniel Meeker married Sarah Johnson, July 10th, 1744.

Their children were: Elnathan baptized July 26th, 1747. Jared, baptized January 29th, 1749. Rebecca, baptized January 20th, 1751. Lois, baptized March 28th, 1753. Josiah, baptized July 17th, 1757.

About the same time appear David Meeker and Robert Meeker. The former married Hannah Hill October 31st, 1744. The latter Rebecca Morehouse, September 19th, 1746. I find no record of children. Joseph Meeker appears as early as May 4th, 1735, when his son Isaac was baptized.

MERCHANT.

GURDON MERCHANT married Elinor Chauncey (probably of Fairfield), December 9th, 1747. Their children were: Amelia, baptized February 5th, 1749. Chauncey, February 25th, 1753. John, baptized August 31st, 1755. Elinor, January 8th, 1758. Gurdon, March 16th, 1760. Joel, June 6th, 1762. Phebe, May 20th, 1764. Silas, May 8th, 1766. Gurdon Merchant was the first town treasurer, and held other offices of trust. The family figures quite prominently in the later history of the town.

MOREHOUSE.

GERSHOM MOREHOUSE and wife were admitted members of the church May 8th, 1737, on recommendation of Rev. Mr. Hobart, of Fairfield. Also, Jonathan Morehouse, July 5th, 1741. I find no children of Gershom Morehouse recorded in Redding. The Gershom Morehouse who married Anna Sanford January 18th, 1748, was probably his son. The children of the second Gershom Morehouse were:

Ezra, baptized April 28th, 1754. Bille, baptized
July 18th, 1756. Aaron, baptized June 4th, 1758.
Jane, baptized November 4th, 1760. Ann, baptized
June 19th, 1764. Hill, baptized May 5th, 1765.
Lucy, baptized July 12th, 1767. Betty, baptized
August 6th, 1769. Elizabeth Ruth, baptized No-
vember 10th, 1771. Polly, baptized May 15th, 1774.
Polly, baptized May 4th, 1777. The children of
Jonathan Morehouse were : Joanna and Mary, bap-
tized April 13th, 1738. Hannah, baptized June 3d,
1739. Elijah, baptized March 11th, 1742. Phebe,
baptized May 27th, 1744. Ruth, baptized June
14th, 1747.

PERRY.

EBENEZER PERRY removed to Redding, probably
from Stratford, in 1735, in which year he was admitted church-member. His children were : John,
baptized May 10th, 1741. Ebenezer, June 12th,
1743 ; probably others.

Daniel Perry, son of Joseph Perry and Deborah
Burr, of Fairfield, removed to Redding about 1770,
and settled in the south-western part of the town.
He married, first, Mary, daughter of Peter Sturgis, of
Fairfield, and, second, Sarah Wilson. His children, all
by the second wife, were : Grissel, born February
10th, 1745–6. Daniel, born April 15th, 1747. John,
born December 30th, 1748. Deborah, born October
8th, 1750. George, born November 26th, 1752.
Isaac, born November 3d, 1754. Thomas, born
February 21st, 1757. Of the sons, two at least, Daniel and John, settled in Redding. Daniel married,
February 19th, 1772, Elizabeth Gorham, of Green-

15

field. His children were : ˌTimothy, baptized January 10th, 1773. Isaac, baptized August 23d, 1778 ; perhaps others.

TIMOTHY PLATT was admitted a church-member May 10th, 1741, on recommendation of Rev. Mr. Chapman. But one child is found—Abigail, baptized April 8th, 1736 ; married Nathaniel Hill May 28th, 1754. He was probably father of the Timothy Platt who married the sister of John R. Hill, and settled in Lonetown, on the farm now owned by Henry Adams. Obadiah Platt, who appears in Redding as early as 1737, and Jonas Platt, who with his wife Elizabeth were admitted church-members February 5th, 1749, were probably his brothers. Timothy Platt died December 5th, 1769, aged sixty-two years. The children of Obadiah Platt were : Mary, baptized February 20th, 1737. Elizabeth, May 15th, 1739. Jonas Platt married Elizabeth Sanford, October 17th, 1747. Their children were : John, baptized February 5th, 1752. Daniel, August 11th, 1754. Eunice, May 30th, 1756. He removed to New York.

Hezekiah ˌPlatt appears in Redding as early as April 4th, 1762, when his son Justus was baptized. His other children recorded were : Hezekiah, January 16th, 1764. ˥ William, May 18th, 1766. Griswold, December 1st, 1767. Robert, September 1st, 1771.

MR. JOHN READ, perhaps the earliest settler of Redding, was one of the most eminent men of his

day. He was born in Connecticut in 1680, graduated from Harvard College in 1697, studied for the
ministry, and preached for some time at Waterbury,
Hartford, and Stratford. He afterward studied law,
and was admitted an attorney at the bar in 1708, and
in 1712 was appointed Queen's attorney for the colony. In 1714 he bought of the Indians a large tract
of land in Lonetown and settled there. He continued to reside in Redding until 1722, when he removed to Boston, and soon became known as the
most eminent lawyer in the colonies. He was Attorney-General of Massachusetts for several years,
and also a member of the Governor and Council.
He died in February, 1749, leaving a large estate.
His wife was Ruth Talcott, daughter of Lieutenant-
Colonel John Talcott, of Hartford, and sister of
Governor Joseph Talcott. They had six children :
Ruth, born (probably) in Hartford in 1700 ; died in
Redding, August 8th, 1766. She was the wife of
Rev. Nathaniel Hunn, first pastor of the church in
Redding. They were married September 14th, 1737.
John, born in Hartford in 1701 ; lived in Redding at
the " Lonetown Manor," and was a leading man in
his day in the colony ; was much in public life, both
civil and military, and was noted for his public spirit,
patriotism, and piety. He married twice. His first
wife was Mary ——, a Milford lady. His second
wife was Sarah Bradley, of Greenfield Hill. His
children were : *William*, who married Sarah Hawley,
of Redding. *Zalmon*, who married Hulda Bradley,
of Greenfield. *Hezekiah*, who married Anna Gorham. *John*, who married Zoa Hillard. *Mary*, wife of
John Harpin. *Sarah*, wife of Jabez Hill, and after-

ward of Theodore Monson. *Ruth*, wife of Jeremiah Mead. *Deborah*, wife of Thomas Benedict, a lawyer. *Mabel*, wife of Levi Starr ; and *Esther*, wife of Daniel C. Bartlett, son of Rev. Nathaniel Bartlett. One of his children, a lad of four years, fell into a burning coal-pit in 1739, and was so badly burned that he survived but a few hours. His father wrote a letter to his father in Boston, informing him of the melancholy event, and his father sent back a letter in reply. Both of the letters are yet preserved, after a period of one hundred and forty years, and are both remarkable for the piety and Christian resignation manifested in them. *William*, born in Connecticut about 1710, was a lawyer in Boston, and afterward a judge in several of the courts there. He lived a bachelor, and died in 1780, aged seventy years. *Mary*, born (probably) in Reading, Conn., April 14th, 1716 ; married Captain Charles Morris, of Boston, afterward of Halifax, Nova Scotia, where he was for many years chief-justice of the courts. They had nine sons and two daughters. *Abigail* married Joseph Miller, of Boston. *Deborah* married a Mr. Willstead, and afterward Henry Paget, of Smithfield, Rhode Island.

To the above sketch by Mr. George Read, of Boston, I will add that Colonel John Read, son of the Mr. John Read mentioned, appears as one of the original members of the first society in 1729, and was the Colonel John Read so often referred to in the town records. His " manour" comprised nearly all of what is now Lonetown, and his manor-house stood on the exact site of Mr. Aaron Treadwell's present residence. He had a fenced park, in which he kept deer, nearly opposite the present residence of William Sherwood.

Mr. George Read, of Redding Centre, has a very interesting collection of old papers belonging to the colonel, such as wills, deeds, account-books, etc. In one of them directions are given his men about feeding the deer, letting the cattle into the long meadow, etc. Another is Mr. Read's commission as colonel, and is of sufficient interest to warrant its insertion here. It is as follows :

THOMAS FITCH Esq., Governor and Commander in chief of his Majesty's Colony of Connecticut in New England,

To JOHN READ ESQ., GREETING.

Whereas you are appointed by the General Assembly of said Colony to be Colonel of the Fourth Regiment of Horse in said Colony. Reposing special trust and confidence in your Loyalty, courage, and good conduct, I do by these presents constitute and appoint you to be Coionel of said Regiment. You are therefore to take the said Regiment into your Care and charge as their Colonel, and carefully and diligently to discharge that Care and Trust in Ordering and Exercising of them, both Officers and Soldiers in Arms according to the Rules and Discipline of War, keeping them in good Order and Government, and commanding them to obey you as their Colonel for his Majesty's service, and they are commanded to obey you accordingly, and you are to conduct and lead forth the said Regiment, or such part of them as you shall from time to time receive orders for from me, or from the Governor of this Colony for the time being, to Encounter, Repel, Pursue, and Destroy by force of Arms, and by all fitting ways and means, all his Majesty's Enemies who shall at any time hereafter in a Hostile manner, attempt or enterprise the Invasion, Detriment, or Annoyance of this Colony. And you are to observe and obey such Orders and Instructions as from time to time you from Me, or other your Superior Officers, pursuant to the trust hereby Reposed in you and the laws of this Colony. Given under my hand and the seal of this Colony, in New Haven, the 3d Day of November, in the 31st year of the Reign of our Sovereign Lord George the Second, King of Great Britain &c. Annoque Doms. 1757. By His Honor's Command.

THOS. FITCH.

GEORGE WYLLYS, *Secty.*

ROGERS.

JAMES ROGERS was a prominent man in his day, and filled many responsible offices in town. He appears as early as 1762. His children were : Joseph, born October 31st, 1762. Chloe, born October 24th, 1766. James, born April 28th, 1768. Haron, born August 22d, 1770. (Town record.)

RUMSEY.

JOSEPH RUMSEY appears in Redding as early as 1747. His will, dated December 27th, 1754, mentions his wife, Sarah ——, and children, Isaac, Sarah, Joseph, Daniel, William, and Ephraim.

The will of Daniel Rumsey, of Reading, probated March 10th, 1761, mentions his father Robert, brothers John Rumsey and Seth Hull.

John Rumsey settled in Redding. His children by wife Esther were : Abigail, baptized February 19th, 1751. Rachel, baptized February 25th, 1753. Mary, June 5th, 1755. Nathan, August 8th, 1756. David, January 28th, 1759. Mary, June 15th, 1761. Esther, May 13th, 1764. Eben, February 4th, 1768.

Isaac Rumsey married Abigail St. John, May 23d, 1761. Children : Abigail, born December 25th, 1761. Jeremiah, born May 23d, 1762. Ruth, December 29th, 1763. Noah, born March 28th, 1768.

SANFORD.

THE Sanford family is one of the oldest and most numerous in the town, having been founded by four persons of the name, who removed here from Fairfield when the country was first opened to settlers. The names of these four settlers were : Nathaniel, Lemuel, Samuel, and Ephraim.

The first two were original members of the church ; the last two joined it during the first year of its existence, viz., in 1734. According to Savage, Ephraim Sanford, who settled in Milford, and married Mary Powell, of New Haven, in 1669, had children, Mary, Samuel, Ephraim, Thomas, Nathaniel and Zacariah. Samuel, Ephraim, and Nathaniel, are no doubt identical with those who settled in Redding, as they were elderly men with families when they removed here.

According to the above-named authority, Ezekiel, eldest son of the above Thomas Sanford, was freeman in 1669 and died in 1683, leaving a widow, Rebecca and children, Ezekiel, Thomas, Sarah, Mary, Rebecca, Martha, and Elizabeth. Ezekiel,* eldest son, settled in Fairfield, and in his will, dated Janu-

---

* Mr. E. J. Sandford, of Knoxville, Tenn., sends me the following account of Ezekiel Sandford, which he derived from Rev. Thomas F. Davies : Ezekiel Sandford was an English engineer, and had charge of the erection of the stockade fort at Saybrook, at the mouth of the Connecticut River, for protection against Indians. He afterward removed to Fairfield, and built the first mill in the county, at Mill River, for which he received a large grant of land from the English Government

ary 29th, 1729, mentions two sons, Lemuel and Ezekiel.   Lemuel settled in Redding, as above stated.
Thomas Sanford, father of Ezekiel and Ephraim,
was the first of the name in America.

We shall trace the families of these ancestors in
Redding in the order of their arrival here.   Nathan-
iel Sanford settled in Umpawaug.   His children re-
corded were : Abel H., baptized March 25th, 1733.
Ruth, baptized May 12th, 1737.   Esther, baptized
May 27th, 1744.

I have no further record of this family.

Lemuel Sanford settled in the centre.   He was one
of the first committee-men of the society, and prominent in public affairs.   He married —— Squire, of
Fairfield.   Their children were : *Hezekiah*, probably
born in Fairfield.   Sarah, baptized September 19th,
1734.   Anne, baptized November 1st, 1736.   Lydia,
baptized June 4th, 1738.   *Lemuel*, baptized April
20th, 1740.   *Ezekiel*, baptized July 4th, 1742.
Anne, baptized October 7th, 1744.   Roda, baptized
February 26th, 1749.

Hezekiah married Hannah ——, and settled in the
centre, on the farm now owned by Mr. Delavan.   His
children were : Aaron, baptized May 29th, 1757.
Hannah, baptized August 26th, 1759.   William, baptized October 14th, 1764.   Eunice, baptized June
7th, 1772.   Huldah, baptized May 18th, 1777.

Aaron, his eldest son, settled in the centre, and lived
in the house now owned by Mrs. Connors.   He was
the first male member of the Methodist Church in
New England, and was the leader of the little class
organized in Redding in 1790.

The Methodist preachers in their rounds always

found a home with him, and often held their meetings in his house. Later in life he became an acceptable local preacher in that church. He married Lydia Hawley, daughter of William Hawley, November 2d, 1780. Their children were : Betsey, born October 5th, 1781. Hannah, born May 31st, 1784. *Aaron*, born July 8th, 1786. *Hawley*, born July 16th, 1789. Jesse Lee, born July 27th, 1791. Eunice, born August 10th, 1793. *Walter*, born February 18th, 1796. Charlotte, born January 8th, 1800. Lydia, born September 23d, 1803. William A., born January 15th, 1807.

Aaron Sanford, Jr., settled, on Redding Ridge, in the eastern part of the town. He married, December 19th, 1813, Fanny Hill, daughter of Andrew L. Hill. Their children were eleven in number : Andrew H., Daniel, Mary, Clara, Henry, Aaron, Fanny, Jesse L., Mary, Elizabeth, John, and Julia H. *Hawley*, the second son, married Betsey Stow November 2d, 1814, by whom he had two children, Russell and Betsey. On the death of his wife he married, second, Sarah Ketchum November 20th, 1823. The children of this marriage were : Francis A., Aaron K., (now presiding elder on the Poughkeepsie District), Hawley, Lydia, David, Morris, and Mary. *Walter*, the third son, married, December 6th, 1821, Harriet M. Booth. They had one son, Charles. Walter Sanford married, second, Emily Gorham. William Sanford, the fourth son, married Harriet Tuttle May 2d, 1832. Of the daughters, Betsey married John R. Hill. Hannah married the Rev. Aaron Hunt, a Methodist clergyman, celebrated in his day as being the first to successfully contest the old co-

lonial law which forbade all ministers except those
of the " Standing Order" to perform the marriage
ceremony. Mr. Hunt was at one time located and
resided for several years in Redding. Charlotte
married Thomas B. Fanton. Lydia married Aaron
Sanford Hyatt.

Lemuel Sanford, second son of Lemuel Sanford,
settled in the centre, near his father. He married,
September 20th, 1768, Mary Russell, of North Branford, Conn. The circumstances attending his marriage are thus narrated : He left Redding on horseback, early on the morning of his wedding-day, but
was delayed on the road and did not reach Branford
until midnight. By that time the wedding guests
had dispersed and the family had retired ; but he
roused them up, collected the guests, and the ceremony was performed. The next day bride and
groom returned to Redding, travelling on horseback. The children of Lemuel and Mary Sanford
were : Lemuel, born July 18th, 1769. Roda, born
March 4th, 1773. Mary, born May 18th, 1776 ; married Dr. Thomas Peck. Abigail, born 1779 ; died in
infancy. Jonathan R., born February 11th, 1782.
Abigail, born April 18th, 1784. Lucretia, born May
4th, 1786.

Mr. Lemuel Sanford died March 12th, 1803, at
Danbury, in the performance of his duties as Judge
of the County Court, leaving a most honorable record. He had filled all the positions of honor and
trust in his native town, and during the Revolution
had been a member of the Committee of Supply, the
duties of which kept him absent in Danbury and
Fairfield nearly the whole period of the war. He

several times represented the town in the General Assembly, and also held the office of Associate Judge of the County Court.

Lemuel Sanford, eldest son of Judge Sanford, after being educated at President Dwight's famous academy on Greenfield Hill, returned to Redding, married Mary Heron, daughter of Squire Heron, and settled in the centre, on the farm now owned by Albert Gorham. He was a man of much ability, and quite prominent in town affairs. He had but two children, Mary and Abigail.

Jonathan R., the second son, married Maria, daughter of Dr. Thomas Davies, October 17th, 1808. Their children were : Amanda, Maria, (who died in infancy), Lemuel, Jonathan R., and Thomas. Mr. Jonathan Sanford died August 20th, 1858. In 1808 Mr. Sanford was appointed town-clerk and treasurer, and held those offices until his death, a period of half a century. He also filled the office of Judge of Probate for several years, besides representing his native town at different periods in the State legislature.

Ezekiel, third son of Lemuel Sanford the first, married Abigail Starr November 21st, 1773, and settled in Boston district, in the western part of the town. His children were : Mollie, baptized December 18th, 1774. Rebecca, baptized April 24th, 1777. Ezekiel, baptized November 1st, 1778. Abigail, baptized March 19th, 1780 ; perhaps others. He is called captain in the old records. Some of his descendants are now living in Amenia, N. Y.

Samuel Sanford the first, settled in Umpawaug. He is called captain in the records. His children were : Daniel, baptized April 22d, 1734. Seth, baptized August 23d, 1735. Mary, March 19th, 1738. David, December 2d, 1739. Abigail, January 30th, 1743. Samuel, May 5th, 1745. Sarah, May 10th, 1747. Esther, April 16th, 1749. Ezra, March 25th, 1751. Rachel, February 25th, 1753. Peter, May 23d, 1756. Captain Samuel Sanford died November 6th, 1768, aged sixty-two years.

Daniel married Esther Hull April 18th, 1758. Children : Eli, baptized August 16th, 1761. Chloe, July 5th, 1767 ; and others. Seth married Rebecca, daughter of Deacon Stephen Burr, April 25th, 1759. Her children, as named in Deacon Burr's will, 1776, were : Elias, Ebenezer, Joel, Elijah, Samuel, and Seth. Mary married Timothy Sanford, son of Joseph. Abigail married John Hawley December 21st, 1762. Samuel, Jr., married Sarah Olmsted July 23d, 1767. (Town record.) His children recorded were : Uriah, baptized February 14th, 1768. Thomas, December 17th, 1769. Peter married Abigail Keeler June 1st, 1780.

Ephraim Sanford the first, settled in Sanfordtown, and was a large land owner there, as is shown by several deeds now in the possession of his descendants, some of which date back as far as 1733. His children by his wife Elizabeth Mix, according to the parish record, were : Rachel, baptized July 29th, 1733. Abigail, baptized May 18th, 1735. John, April 29th, 1739. Oliver, September 20th, 1741. Lois, September 17th, 1743. Huldah, May 5th, 1748. Augustus, July 15th, 1753. Esther, April 27th, 1755. His will, dated January 30th, 1761, mentions also Ephraim, Elizabeth, and Tabitha. Ephraim

Sanford, according to the family tradition, was the first man having a store of goods in Redding. His goods were brought from Boston. Of his children, Abigail married Daniel Jackson October 2d, 1755. John married —— ——, and settled in the Foundry district, in Redding. His children were : James, Stephen, Ephraim, John, Eli, Huldah, Lois, Betty, Elizabeth, and Annie. James, the eldest son, settled in the Foundry district, near his father. He was a teamster in the Revolutionary army, and was present at the execution of Jones and Smith on Gallows Hill. He married Sarah, daughter of John Beach, and grand-daughter of Rev. John Beach, the faithful missionary of the Church of England. He was the father of Squire James Sanford. John, Jr., the fourth son of John Sanford, settled in Redding, and was the father of John W. Sanford, a well-known citizen.

Oliver Sanford, son of Ephraim, married, in April, 1767, Rachel, daughter of Deacon David Coley, of Weston. Their children were : Mary, baptized July 31st, 1768. David, August 20th, 1769. Ephraim, September 15th, 1771. Abigail, May 29th, 1774. Enoch A., April 28th, 1776. Levi, December 14th, 1777. Oliver C., Abigail, Mary, Betsey, and Lorraine.

SMITH.

ANNA, daughter of Samuel Smith, of Redding, was baptized July 6th, 1740 ; and Seth Samuel, son of Samuel and Lydia Smith, September 28th, 1760. The latter was the first lawyer who located in Redding. He had an office in the centre, where also he kept a select school. He was town-clerk for a term of years, and wrote a most elegant hand, as will be remembered by those familiar with the records of his times. He also filled many other important positions in the town. He married Huldah ——. Their children were : Zalmon, baptized February 3d, 1780 ; and probably others.

STOWE.

ROBERT STOW, the first of the name in Redding, settled in Lonetown, on the farm now owned by his grandson, Sumner Stowe. He married Anne Darrow January 26th, 1775. Their children were : Daniel, born July 4th, 1779. Abigail, born April 11th, 1776 ; married Israel Adams. Sarah, born October 4th, 1777. Sarah, born August 11th, 1781. Sumner, born September 17th, 1783. Huldah, born February 6th, 1787 ; married Andrew An drus, of Danbury. Abraham, born March 4th, 1792. Polly, born September 20th, 1794 ; married Moses Parsons, of Newtown. Robert Stow died November 5th, 1795. Daniel Stow married Lucy Hoyt, of Bethel, and settled in Redding, near his father. His children were : Robert, Almira, Sarah, Harriet, Lucy, Sumner, Mary, and Polly. Abraham settled in Bethel. Sumner died when a young man.

Other settlers in the town at an early date, but who do not appear to have been permanent residents, were : Daniel Bradley, Thomas Williams, Thomas and William Squire (of Fairfield), Ebenezer Ferry, George Cowden, Nathaniel Booth, Edmund Sherman, Jonathan Squire, John Whitlock, John

Truesdale, Frederick Dikeman, and John Nott. The families of Byington, Chapman, Hamilton, Knapp, Osborne, Dennison, Bennett, St. John, Gilbert, Johnson, Abbott, Duncomb, Edmonds, Olmstead, Rider, Treadwell, and Todd figure in the later records of the town.

CHAPTER XV.

BIOGRAPHICAL.

JOEL BARLOW, the poet and statesman, was born in Redding March 24th, 1754. He received his early education first from the Rev. Mr. Bartlett, pastor of the Congregational church in Redding, and second at Moor's preparatory school for boys, near Hanover, N. H. He entered Dartmouth College in 1774, at the age of twenty, and shortly after removed to New Haven and was entered at Yale. His college course was a highly creditable one in many respects. During the college terms he was a faithful student, especially winning distinction for literary attainments ; and during the long summer vacations he joined the Continental army as a volunteer, and aided in fighting the battles of his country. He graduated in 1778. From 1779 to 1783, he was chaplain of one of the Connecticut regiments in the Revolutionary army. Shortly after leaving the army in 1783, he married Miss Ruth Baldwin, daughter of Michael Baldwin, Esq., of New Haven, and in 1785 settled as a lawyer in Hartford, Conn. In Hartford Mr. Barlow appears as lawyer, journalist (editor of

the *American Mercury*), bookseller, and poet. In
the latter capacity he produced a revision of Dr.
Watts's "Imitation" of the Psalms, and also, in 1787,
his famous poem, "The Vision of Columbus." In
1789 he accepted from the Sciota Land Company the
position of foreign agent for the sale of their lands
in Europe, and went to England and later to France
for this purpose ; but shortly after his arrival the
company made a disgraceful failure, and he was
again thrown on his own resources. Fortunately,
his literary reputation had made him quite a lion in
the French capital, and he easily succeeded in ob-
taining work on the French journals. Later he em-
barked in some mercantile ventures, which proved
successful and brought him a competence. He at
first participated actively in the French Revolution,
which broke out soon after his arrival in France,
but becoming disgusted with the atrocities of the
Jacobins, he withdrew and went over to England.
In London, in 1791, he published his "Advice to the
Privileged Orders," a work which drew out a formal
eulogium from Fox in the House of Commons.
This was succeeded in 1792 by his "Conspiracy of
Kings," a poem so bitterly hostile to royalty, that
he found it prudent to leave England for France im-
mediately on its publication. On his return to
France, at this time, the privileges of French citi-
zenship were conferred on him, only before accorded
to but two Americans, Washington and Hamilton.
In 1793 he accompanied Gregorie, former Bishop of
Blois, and other dignitaries to Savoy, and aided in
organizing that country into a department of the
Republic. While here he wrote his "Hasty Pud-

ding," the mock-heroic, half-didactic poem, which has chiefly endeared him to his countrymen. In 1795 President Washington appointed him consul to Algiers, with instructions to ratify the long pending treaty with the Dey, and to liberate the American prisoners there. Colonel Humphreys, American Minister to Portugal, an old friend of Mr. Barlow, himself came to Paris to urge him to accept; and proving successful, the two friends left Paris on the 12th of September, 1795, for Lisbon. From Lisbon Mr. Barlow proceeded to Algiers *via* Alicant, and after a year and a half of effort, succeeded in ratifying the treaty and in liberating the captives. He then returned to France. During the succeeding eight years he resided in an elegant villa near Paris, formerly the property of the Count Clermont Tonnere, enjoying the friendship of the chief men of the nation, as well as that of all Americans of eminence who visited the capital.

But in 1805 the desire to once more revisit the land he had left seventeen years before, became too strong to be resisted longer, and disposing of his estates in France, he returned in July of this year to America. He was warmly received in his native land, and after an extensive tour, extending into the western country, he returned to Washington, where he built an elegant mansion called Kalorama, and which was widely famed in its day for its beauty and elegance, and as being the resort of all the famous men of the times. At Kalorama, Barlow gave his chief attention to the cultivation of the Muses, and to philosophical studies. Here, in 1808, he finished his great poem, "The Columbiad," which was

16

printed at Philadelphia, and was one of the most elegant volumes ever issued from the American press. He also busied himself with collecting materials for a general history of the United States. In 1811 President Madison offered him the responsible position of Minister to France, in the hope that his reputation and his influence with the French Government might secure for us a treaty giving indemnity for past spoliations on our commerce and security from further depredations. Barlow accepted the position from motives of the purest patriotism, in the belief that his talents and position might be made useful to his country. He sailed from Annapolis in July, 1811, in the historic frigate Constitution, Captain Hull, which had been placed at his disposal by the Government. His negotiations with Napoleon, while on this mission, were conducted through the Duke de Bassano, Minister of Foreign Affairs, and covered a space of nearly a year and a half. Napoleon acknowledged the justice of the claims of the United States, and expressed a willingness to ratify a treaty of indemnity; but he was so absorbed in directing the campaign against Russia, and in his other operations on the European field, that it was very difficult to bring the matter to a satisfactory conclusion.

At length, on the 25th of October, 1812, Mr. Barlow received a letter from the Duke de Bassano, written at Wilna, Poland, saying that the emperor had deputed the business of the treaty to him, and that if Mr. Barlow would come to Wilna, he had no doubt but that the treaty might be speedily ratified. Barlow, on receipt of the note, at once set out, and trav-

elling night and day, reached Wilna about the first
of December, only to find the village filled with fugi-
tives from Napoleon's retreating army, while the
duke was out on the frontiers hurrying forward re-
inforcements to cover the emperor's retreat. Dis-
appointed in his mission, he hastened to retrace
his steps ; but at Zarniwica, an obscure village in
Poland, he was seized with an acute attack of pneu-
monia, the result of privations and exposure, which
terminated his life December 26th, 1812. He was
buried in the little village where he died, and a marble pillar was erected by Mrs. Barlow to his memory. No friendly pen has ever written the poet's
biography, and his memory has pretty much faded
from the minds of his countrymen ; but there were
few men of his day more widely known, or who did
deeds more worthy of grateful recognition by the
American people.

"STEPHEN RUSSELL MALLORY, second son of
Charles Mallory, of Redding, Conn., was born in the
West Indies in 1814, and came to the United States
when but three months old. In 1819 he accompanied his father to Florida, and was placed at an
' old field school' near Mobile, from whence he was
removed to the academy at Nazareth, Pa., where
he spent several years. He returned to Florida in
1830, and established his residence at Key West,
where he embraced the profession of law. Mr. Mallory has filled many important trusts under the
State and General Governments, and was collector
of the customs and superintendent of the revenue
at Key West, under Mr. Polk. In 1850 he was

elected to the United States Senate for the term of six years." The above is from Gleason's " Pictorial Companion" for 1853. Mr. Mallory's subsequent career as Secretary of the Confederate Navy is familiar to the reader.

DUDLEY SANFORD GREGORY, Mayor of Jersey City, N. J., and prominently identified with the early history of that city, was a native of Redding.

MAJOR-GENERAL DARIUS COUCH was born of Redding parents, in South-East, New York, July 25th, 1822. The following sketch of his career, taken largely from Cullum's History of the Officers and Graduates of the United States Military Academy, will be read with interest :

" Darius N. Couch, born in New York, appointed from New York, cadet at United States Military Academy from July 1st, 1842, to July 1st, 1846, when he was graduated and promoted in the army to Brevet Second Lieutenant 4th Artillery. Served in the war with Mexico in 1846–47–48, being engaged in the battle of Buena Vista, Mex., as Second Lieutenant in Captain Washington's Battery, Light Artillery, for which he was brevetted First Lieutenant for gallant and meritorious conduct. Participating in the occupation of the Seminole country in 1852–3, he planned and executed at his own expense a scientific expedition into Central and Northern Mexico, the results of which were very creditable to his enterprise. He married, in 1854, a daughter of Hon. S. L. Crocker, of Taunton, Mass., and grand-daughter of Isaiah Thomas, founder of the Antiquarian Society of Worcester, Mass., and author of the ' History of Printing.' The next year he resigned from the army. At the breaking out of the Rebel-

lion, being settled in Taunton, Mass., he raised the
7th Reg. Mass. Vols., and proceeded to Washington
in July, 1861. Was made Brigadier-General in
August, and assigned to the command of a brigade
in the defence of that city. In McClellan's Campaign on the Peninsula, General Couch commanded
the 1st Division, 4th Army Corps, holding the left
of the line at the siege of Yorktown. At the battle
of Fair Oaks, his brave Division held their ground
for more than two hours against the combined attack of the Confederate troops. With part of his
Division he reinforced Hooker in the hot action of
Oak Grove, June 25th, 1862, and was in various
skirmishes during the seven days until July 1st, on
which morning General McClellan posted him on the
main road leading to Richmond, where was fought
the successful battle of Malvern Hill.

" Being promoted to the rank of Major-General,
July 4th, 1862, he joined Pope with his Division on
the retreat from Manassas, in the Northern Virginia
Campaign. October, 1862, in command of the 2d
Army Corps, Campaign of the Rappahannock. At
Fredericksburg December 12th, 13th, 14th, and
15th, it fell upon General Couch to assault Mary's
Heights, in which desperate work that brave, mag-
nificent 2d Army Corps lost more than 4000 men.
The loss of his Corps at the disastrous battle of
Chancellorsville, where he was second in command,
was very heavy. In November, 1864, he joined
Thomas, who was besieged at Nashville, and was
assigned by that commander to the command of an
Army Corps. In the battle which followed he commanded a division, turned Hood's left, and captured several pieces of artillery and many prisoners. In North Carolina, March, April, and May,
aiding Sherman in closing the war. Resigned in
June, 1865, the Great Rebellion having been crushed
out.

" The General has for several years resided at

Norwalk, Conn., having been Quartermaster-General at Hartford during the years 1877–78.''

HON. GIDEON H. HOLLISTER, of Litchfield, is a descendant of two of our Redding families, as will be seen by reference to the notes on the Gray and Jackson families. He was born December 14th, 1818, in Washington, Conn., and graduated at Yale College in 1840. Studied law in Litchfield, and was admitted to the bar in April, 1842. He practised law in Litchfield until 1859, when he opened an office in New York. He went as United States Chargé d'Affaires to Hayti when that country was under the administration of Salnave. In 1855 he published a History of Connecticut in two volumes, of which two editions, of two thousand copies each, have been exhausted. He is the author of three historical dramas, one of them bearing the title of '' Thomas à Becket.'' He has also written a legal treatise on the Law of Eminent Domain. Mr. Hollister is now engaged in writing a history of Hayti.

Attorney-General Bates, of Missouri, was of Redding ancestry.

Judge Strong, of the United States Supreme Court, spent his childhood and youth in Redding, and made his maiden plea here before a justice court.

Mrs. Dora Goodale, a writer for *Scribner's*, is a native of Redding, being a descendant of Colonel John Read, one of the earliest settlers. She is the mother of Elaine and Dora Goodale, the child poets, whose charming verses have been so warmly welcomed by the American public.

In the several professions Redding has been well

represented. " Dr. Asahel Fitch, the first physician who settled in the town, is remembered in Fairfield County as a worthy man, and one of its most respectable practitioners of medicine. He was among the principal pioneers in the formation of the County Society, but died soon after its organization. His death occurred in 1792, or about that period. I understand that he was the grandfather of Professor Knight, of Yale College.

Among the physicians of Fairfield County who enjoyed a long and successful practice was Dr. Thomas Davies, of Redding. He removed to Redding in 1793, on the decease of Dr. Fitch, and there continued in the duties of his profession until his death, which occurred in 1831. Dr. Daveis possessed the reputation of being among the first of the physicians of the county who assumed regularly obstetrical duties, and so successful were his labors, that he became particularly eminent in that department.

The doctor was once summoned as an important wtiness to appear before the Court in Fairfield, and not appearing, the sheriff was sent to compel his attendance. Being absent, and learning on his return that the officer was awaiting at a public-house in the vicinity, he without notice to the official rode to Fairfield, and appeared before the Court. On the question occurring with the Court regarding the costs attending the *capias*, he requested one or two of his legal friends to excuse the delinquency. The judge decided, notwithstanding, that the law must be observed and that the doctor must bear the expenses. Dr. D. then requested a hearing in his own behalf, which being granted, remarked : " May it please the

Court : I am a good citizen of the State, and since I was summoned to attend this Court I have introduced three other good citizens into it."

The Court replied, that for so good a plea, he would leave the parties to pay the expenses.

Rev. Thomas F. Davies, of Philadelphia, is the only male descendant of Dr. Davies.*

Among the later practitioners of the town, Dr. Charles Gorham was very widely known and respected. He was the son of Meeker Gorham and Elizabeth Hubbell, of Greenfield Hill, in the town of Fairfield. He began the study of medicine with Dr. Jehiel Williams, of New Milford, and afterward pursued his studies at the College of Physicians and Surgeons in New York. He settled in Redding in 1816, at the age of twenty-one years, and practised as a physician and surgeon in Fairfield County forty-two years. He married Mary, daughter of William King Comstock, of Danbury. Dr. Gorham is described as a man of more than ordinary strength of character, with a well-balanced mind and sound judgment. He was fond of scientific investigations, and was remarkable for close observation and power of analysis. He died at his residence in Redding Centre, September 15th, 1859.

Among clergymen may be enumerated the following : Rev. Justus Hull, Rev. Lemuel Hull ; Rev. Thomas F. Davies, of Philadelphia ; Rev. William T. Hill, Presiding Elder of New Haven District ; Rev. Aaron K. Sanford, Presiding Elder of Pough-

---

* From an Address before the Connecticut Medical Convention, in 1853, by Rufus Blakeman, M.D.

keepsie District, New York Conference ; Rev. Aaron
S. Hill, of New Haven ; Rev. Morris Hill, of New
Haven ; Rev. Moses Hill, of Norwalk ; Rev. Hawley
Sanford, of Iowa ; Rev. Morris Sanford, of Iowa ;
Rev. Platt Treadwell ; Rev. Albert Miller, of Iowa ;
Rev. Leroy Stowe, of Milford, Conn.; and Rev. A.
B. Sanford, of Brooklyn, N. Y.

The following State Senators have been natives or
citizens of Redding : Thomas B. Fanton, elected in
1841 ; Lemuel Sanford, 1847 ; Cortez Merchant,
1855 ; Francis A. Sanford, 1865 ; James Sanford,
1870 ; Jonathan R. Sanford, 1877.

Thomas Sanford, former High Sheriff of the
county, and at one time nominee of the Democratic
party for Comptroller of the State ; Henry Sanford,
of New York, Superintendent of Adams Express
Company ; Aaron Sanford, of Newtown, present
High Sheriff of Fairfield County ; and Albert Hill,
City Engineer of New Haven, are natives of Redding.

APPENDIX I.

THE following recollections of those who attended church at the old Congregational meeting-house, before it was pulled down in 1836 to make room for the present edifice, have been kindly furnished by Thomas Sanford, Esq. They will be read with interest, as relating to a later period of the town's history than that covered by the preceding chapters.

Jesse Lacy, wife, son, and daughter, resided in the northeast part of the town of Easton, and had to go about five miles to meeting. The son, Deacon Rowland B. Lacy, now resides in Bridgeport.

Eli Lacy, wife, and daughter, from the same neighborhood.

Mrs. Ichabod Gilbert resided about two miles northeast of Redding Ridge. She was the grandmother of the Gilbert Brothers, of Bethel.

Deacon Lemuel Hawley, and niece, Miss Sarah M. Dutton, who afterward became the wife of Rev. Thomas Dutton.

Daniel Betts, wife, and two daughters.

Michael Jennings, wife, and daughter, Eliza, who became the wife of Mr. Thatcher, of Hartford.

Samuel S. Osborn and wife.

Joseph Hawley and wife.

Jedediah R. Hawley and wife.

Mrs. Abbott, the mother of the present Deacon T. M. Abbott, who was married about this time, and, together with his wife, were, and have been constant attendants at meeting.

Mr. and Mrs. Daniel A. Frost, and son, Ezra M. Frost, who now resides in Watertown, Ct.

Rev. Thomas F. Davies built the house just north of the Town House, and with his family attended church here till 1831, when he left to take charge of the Congregational church at Green's Farms.

Charles Wilson and family.

Leman Canfield and family.

Zalmon Read, an officer in the Revolutionary War, and family.

Deacon Samuel Read and family.

Henry Read and family.

Widow Betty Adams.

Calvin Jenkins and wife. He was a drummer in the Revolutionary army.

Mrs. Harry Lines and children.

Abraham Parsons, a soldier of Revolution, wife, and daughter.

Timothy Parsons and children.

The widow of Doctor Thomas Davies.

Deacon Lemuel Sanford and wife.

Widow Huldah Marvin and children.

Deacon Charles D. Smith, of this place, married the only daughter of Widow Marvin for his first wife.

Eli Read and wife.

Rev. Jonathan Bartlett and family.

Samuel J. Collins, wife, and two daughters. His youngest daughter is the wife of our present physician, Dr. Wakeman.

Jared Olmstead, a soldier in the War of 1812, and family.

Colonel Aaron Burr and family.

Jonathan R. Sanford and family.

Mrs. Benjamin Couch.

Mrs. John Goodyear and Jane Tillow.

Colonel Asahel Salmon, a soldier of the Revolution, and family. Colonel Salmon led the singing for several years.

Mrs. Daniel Sherwood.

Daniel Meeker's family.

Captain Lemuel Adams and family.

John Meeker and wife. He played the bass viol for years.

Azariah Meeker and wife, the grandfather of the present Azariah.

Harry Meeker and family.

Moses Meeker and family.

Captain John Gray and wife.

Joel Gray, wife, and daughter.

Mrs. Daniel Benedict and two daughters.

Captain John Davis, a soldier of Revolution, and two daughters.

Benjamin Meeker and wife.

Eli Starr Boughton, father of Benjamin S. Boughton, and family.

Samuel Meeker and wife.

George B. Phillips and family.

Cortez Merchant and family.

Mrs. Samuel S. Gray and children.

Mrs. Holmes.

Edward Couch, wife, and two boys. The boys now reside in Ridgefield—Edward J. and Simon.

Peter S. Coley and wife.

Alfred Gregory, wife, and children.

Eli Sanford, wife, and son, Hinman.

Daniel Barlow and wife.

Burr Meeker, a soldier in the War of 1812, and family ; and Miss Coley, who became the wife of Dr. L. N. Beardsley, of Milford, Ct.

Joel Barlow and family.

Henry and Joseph H. Meeker.

Ebenezer Sanford and Stephen Sanford.

Widow Esther Sanford and family.

Joshua Chapman and family.

David Chapman and family.

Daniel Chapman, 2d, and wife.

Daniel Chapman, grandfather of Daniel C. Rider, who with his family have been constant atendants at church.

Edward Merchant and wife.

Orson Merchant and family.

Joel Merchant, a soldier of the Revolution, wife, and son.

George Merchant and daughter, Eliza.

Zalmon Sanford and niece, Emily, afterward Mrs. Lonson Coley of Westport.

Captain Daniel Sanford and two sons—Marvin C. and Moses B.

Aaron Perry, wife, and two sons—Andrew S. and David.

John Couch and wife, and Yonge Lobdell, who afterward was a missionary in Asia. Also for a time a boy, who is now Rev. Augustus Jackson, of Washington, D. C.

Beach Whitehead and family.

John H. Lee and wife, and Jane Sherwood.

Noah H. Lindley and family, and his wife's mother, Mrs. Winton.

Isaac Coley and daughter, Betsey.

Lemuel Burr, grandfather of Lemuel B. Benedict.

Samuel Mallory ——

Eli Mallory, wife, and son, Frederick.

Aaron B. Hull.

Alfred Rockwell, wife, and son.

Thurston Lee and family.

Noah Lee and wife.

Azariah Coley's family.

The Darling family.

Widow Billy Comstock and her children.

Mrs. Cornelia Coley, and her children, who are now Mrs. George A. Hickok, of Bethel, and Mrs. Matthew Starr, of Norwalk.

Alonzo Byington and wife.

Joseph B. Goodsell and family, and J. B. Goodsell, Jr.

Burr Bennett and wife.

Samuel B. Goodsell and wife.

Aaron Byington and wife, Jane Darling, and William B. Skillenger.

Old Mr. Billy Morehouse.

Walker Bates and family. Mr. Bates at this time taught a select boarding and day school, and his scholars attended church.

Elias Bates and wife.

Bradley Hill and family.

Eliza A. Hull, sister, and brother John A.

Noah M. Lee and wife.

Stephen Jackson.

Zalmon B. Banks, wife, and family.

Deacon Joel Foster and family.

Mrs. Moses Dimon.

Charles Lewis (colored).

Mrs. Nathan Lee.

Captain Stephen Gray and wife.

Colonel Joseph W. Gorham and family.

Samuel Hull, wife, and granddaughter.

John Fairchild and family.

Ephraim Sanford and wife.

Enoch A. Sanford and family.

Bradley Sanford and wife.

David Sanford, wife, and son, George A.

Daniel Sanford and wife.

Joel, Ezra, and Irad Carter came to Redding about this time and attended church here.

Eli Gilbert, Milo Lee, and the Messrs. Sheltons, hatters, attended church.

APPENDIX II.

REPRESENTATIVES TO THE LEGISLATURE.

October, 1767. Col. John Read.
May, 1768. None.
October, 1768. Capt. Stephen Mead.
May, 1769. Col. John Read, Capt. Henry Lyon.
October, 1769. Capt. Henry Lyon.
May, 1770. Capt. Stephen Mead, Mr. Lemuel Sanford.
October, 1770. Col. John Read, Mr. Lemuel Sanford.
May, 1771. Col. John Read, Mr. Lemuel Sanford.
October, 1771. Mr. Hezekiah Sanford.
May, 1772. Col. John Read, Mr. Hezekiah Sanford.
October, 1772. Mr. Hezekiah Sanford.
May, 1773. Col. John Read, Mr. Hezekiah Sanford.
October, 1773. Mr. Lemuel Sanford, Mr. James Rogers.
May, 1774. Mr. William Hawley, Mr. Peter Fairchild.
October, 1774. Mr. Lemuel Sanford, Mr. William Hawley.
May, 1775. Mr. William Hawley.
October, 1775. Mr. Lemuel Sanford, Mr. William Hawley.
May, 1776. Mr. Hezekiah Sanford, Mr. Seth Sanford.
October, 1776. Mr. Samuel Sanford, Jr., Mr. Stephen
    Betts, Jr.
May, 1777. Mr. Lemuel Sanford, Mr. Daniel Sanford.
October, 1777. None attended.
January, 1778. Mr. Seth Sanford.
February, 1778. Mr. Lemuel Sanford.

May, 1778.   Mr. Lemuel Sanford, Mr. William Heron.

October, 1778.   Mr. Lemuel Sanford.

May, 1779.   Mr. Seth Sanford.

October, 1779.   Mr. William Hawley, Mr. William Heron.

May, 1780.   Mr. William Hawley, Mr. William Heron.

October, 1780.   Mr. Lemuel Sanford, Mr. Seth Sanford.

May, 1781.   *Unrecorded.*

October, 1781.   Capt. William Hawley.

May, 1782.   Mr. Stephen Betts.

October, 1782.   Mr. Lemuel Sanford, Mr. Stephen Betts.

May, 1783.   Mr. Stephen Betts, Mr. Thaddeus Benedict.

October, 1783.   Mr. Lemuel Sanford, Mr. Stephen Betts.

May, 1784.   Mr. Hezekiah Sanford, Mr. Thaddeus Benedict.

October, 1784.   Mr. Lemuel Sanford, Mr. William Heron.

May, 1785.   Mr. Hezekiah Sanford, Mr. William Heron.

October, 1785.   Mr. Hezekiah Sanford, Mr. William Heron.

May, 1786.   Mr. William Hawley.

October, 1786.   Mr. Hezekiah Sanford, Mr. William Heron.

May, 1787.   Mr. Lemuel Sanford, Mr. William Heron.

October, 1787.   Mr. William Heron.

May, 1788.   Mr. Lemuel Sanford, Mr. William Heron.

October, 1788.   Mr. Lemuel Sanford, Mr. William Heron.

May, 1789.   Mr. William Heron.

October, 1789.   Mr. Lemuel Sanford, Mr. William Heron.

May, 1790.   Mr. Thaddeus Benedict, Mr. William Heron.

October, 1790.   Mr. Thaddeus Benedict, Mr. Andrew L. Hill.

May, 1791.   Mr. Hezekiah Sanford, Mr. Andrew L. Hill.

October, 1791.   Mr. Hezekiah Sanford, Mr. Andrew L. Hill.

May, 1792.   Mr. Hezekiah Sanford, Mr. Andrew L. Hill.

October, 1792.   Mr. Hezekiah Sanford, Mr. Aaron Barlow.

May, 1793.   Mr. Hezekiah Sanford, Mr. Andrew L. Hill.

October, 1793.   Mr. Hezekiah Sanford, Mr. Simeon Munger.

May, 1794.   Mr. Thaddeus Benedict, Mr. Aaron Barlow.
October, 1794.   Mr. Thaddeus Benedict, Mr. Aaron Barlow.
May, 1795.   Mr. Thaddeus Benedict, Mr. Aaron Barlow.
October, 1795.   Mr. William Heron, Mr. Andrew L. Hill.
May, 1796.   Mr. William Heron, Mr. James Rogers.
October, 1796.   Mr. William Heron, Mr. James Rogers.
May, 1797.   Mr. Simeon Munger, Mr. Seth Samuel Smith.
October, 1797.   Mr. Simeon Munger, Mr. Seth Samuel Smith.
May, 1798.   Mr. Simeon Munger, Mr. Seth Samuel Smith.
May, 1799.   Mr. Simeon Munger, Mr. Stephen Jackson.
October, 1799.   Mr. Simeon Munger, Mr. Stephen Jackson.
May, 1800.   Mr. Simeon Munger, Mr. Seth Samuel Smith.
October, 1800.   Mr. Andrew L. Hill, Mr. Stephen Jackson.
May, 1801.   Mr. Andrew L. Hill, Mr. Stephen Jackson.
October, 1801.   Mr. Simeon Munger, Mr. Peter Sanford.
May, 1802.   Mr. S. Samuel Smith, Mr. Andrew L. Hill.
October, 1802.   Mr. Aaron Sanford, Mr. Joshua King.
May, 1803.   Mr. Seth S. Smith, Mr. Andrew L. Hill.
October, 1803.   Mr. Seth S. Smith, Mr. Andrew L. Hill.
May, 1804.   Mr. Seth S. Smith.
October, 1804.   Mr. Simeon Munger, Mr. Peter Sanford.
May, 1805.   Seth Samuel Smith, Andrew L. Hill.
October, 1805.   Simeon Munger, Peter Sanford.
May, 1806.   Andrew L. Hill, Simeon Munger.
October, 1806.   Andrew L. Hill, Simeon Munger.
May, 1807.   Andrew L. Hill, Simeon Munger.
October, 1807.   Seth Samuel Smith, Lemuel Sanford.
May, 1808.   Andrew L. Hill, Lemuel Sanford.
October, 1808.   Lemuel Sanford, Simeon Munger.
May, 1809.   Andrew L. Hill, Lemuel Sanford.
October, 1809.   Andrew L. Hill, Lemuel Sanford.

17

May, 1810.   Andrew L. Hill, Lemuel Sanford.
October, 1810.   Andrew L. Hill, Lemuel Sanford.
May, 1811.   Samuel Whiting, Peter Sanford.
October, 1811.   Andrew L. Hill, Samuel Whiting.
May, 1812.   Andrew L. Hill, Lemuel Sanford.
October, 1812.   Andrew L. Hill, Lemuel Sanford.
May, 1813.   Lemuel Sanford, Samuel Whiting.
October, 1813.   Lemuel Sanford, Samuel Whiting.
May, 1814.   Lemuel Sanford, Samuel Whiting.
October, 1814.   John Meeker, Lemuel Sanford.
May, 1815.   Jonathan R. Sanford, Samuel Whiting.
October, 1815.   Simeon Munger, Hezekiah Read, Jr.
May, 1816.   Isaac Beach, Hezekiah Read, Jr.
October, 1816.   Samuel Whiting, Hezekiah Read, Jr.
May, 1817.   Isaac Beach, Benjamin Meeker.
October, 1817.   Jonathan Meeker, John R. Hill.
May, 1818.   Billy Comstock, Aaron Sanford, Jr.
October, 1818.   William Sanford, John Meeker.
May, 1819.   Billy Comstock, Hezekiah Read, Jr.
1820.   Isaac Coley, Jonathan R. Sanford.
1821.   Daniel Barlow, Seth Wheeler.
1822.   Billy Comstock, John R. Hill.
1823.   John R. Hill, Aaron Sanford, Jr.
1824.   Ephraim Sanford, Rowland Fanton.
1825.   Benjamin Meeker, William Sanford.
1826.   Joel Merchant, Michael Jennings.
1827.   Thomas B. Fanton, Gershom Sherwood.
1828.   John M. Heron, William Sanford.
1829.   Aaron Sanford, Daniel Barlow.
1830.   Gershom Sherwood, Gurdon Bartram.
1831.   Jonathan R. Sanford, Jared Olmstead.
1832.   Ralph Sanford, Walker Bates.
1833.   Jacob Wanzer, Thaddeus B. Read.
1834.   Thomas B. Fanton, Bradley Hill.
1835.   T. B. Fanton, Walker Bates.

1836. Ralph Sanford, Burr Meeker.
1837. Timothy Parsons, Jesse Banks.
1838. Thomas B. Fanton, Aaron Perry.
1839. Thomas B. Fanton, Benjamin Meeker.
1840. Walker Bates, David S. Duncomb.
1841. Thaddeus M. Abbott, Morris Hill.
1842. Hezekiah Davis, John W. Sanford.
1843. Edward Starr, Jr., Barney Bartram.
1844. Charles Beach, Charles D. Smith.
1845. Peter S. Coley, Aaron R. Bartram.
1846. James Sanford, Harry Meeker.
1847. Bradley Hill, Samuel S. Osborn.
1848. Burr Bennett, Floyd Tucker.
1849. Daniel C. Rider, Henry Couch.
1850. Matthew Gregory, Rufus Mead.
1851. Milo Lee, Frederick D. Dimon.
1852. Aaron Burr, Aaron B. Hull.
1853. Ebenezer Wilson, Turney Sanford.
1854. Jonathan R. Sanford, Walker Bates.
1855. Cortez Merchant, Gurdon B. Lee.
1856. Thomas Sanford, Milo Lee.
1857. John O. St. John, David B. Sanford.
1858. James Sanford, Benjamin S. Boughton.
1859. John Edmond, Matthew Gregory.
1860. Jacob Shaw, Daniel S. Sanford.
1861. Edmund T. Dudley, Matthew Gregory.
1862. Walker Bates, George Osborn.
1863. John Edmond, David H. Mead.
1864. Walker Bates, Aaron Treadwell.
1865. Thomas B. Fanton, William Hill.
1866. Charles Osborne, Edward P. Shaw.
1867. David S. Johnson, William B. Hill.
1868. Francis A. Sanford, B. S. Boughton.
1869. Aaron H. Davis, William H. Hill.
1870. John S. Sanford, J. R. Sanford.

1871. E. F. Foster, Luzon Jelliff.
1872. Henry S. Osborn, Arthur B. Hill.
1873. Stebbins Baxter, Moses Hill.
1874. J. R. Sanford, Edward P. Shaw.
1875. Turney Sanford, Henry Burr Platt.
1876. James Sanford, Orrin Platt.
1877. Thomas Sanford, George F. Banks.
1878. ⌐ Azariah E. Meeker, Daniel Sanford.
1879. Harvey B. Rumsey, George Coley.
1880. David S. Bartram, Azariah Meeker.

Redding was made a Probate District in 1839. The Judges of Probate have been : Thomas B. Fanton, Jonathan R. Sanford, Thaddeus M. Abbott, and Lemuel Sanford, the latter being the present incumbent.

APPENDIX III.

PAY-ROLL OF CAPT. WILLIAM JUDD'S COMPANY, COL. WYLLY'S REGIMENT.

ENCAMPED AT READING, 1778-9.

Asa Chapman, Sergt.
Homer Phelps.
Joel Smith, Sergt.
Thomas Peck.
Elijah Porter.
William Lee, fifer.
Eleazer Porter.
D. Adams.
Timothy Keeler.
Levi Hamlin.
Elisha Holsten.
Stephen Chapman.
John Oakley.

Comr. Dunham, Jr.
Ebenezer Park.
Samuel Hotchkiss.
Ephraim Taylor.
Amos Barns.
—— Shaw.
Joseph Hill.
Benj. Potts.
David Heydon.
Ebenr. Park.
Abel Scipio.
Thomas Swift.
Luther Atkins.

APPENDIX IV.

Timothy Alling, Capt.
Robert Alling, Lt.
Stephen Alling, Lt.
Thomas Andrews, Lt.
Roger Alden, Capt.
Simeon Avery, Lt.
Ezekiel P. Belden, Capt.
Simeon Belden, Lt.
Caleb Bull, Capt.
Aaron Bull, Lt.
John H. Buell, Capt.
Phillip B. Bradley, Col.
Daniel Bradley, Lt.
Nathan Beers, Lt.
Nathaniel Bishop, Lt.
James Bennet, Lt.
Aaron Benjamin, Lt.
Abm. Baldwin, Chaplain
David Bushnell, Capt.
Isaac Munson, Surg. mate
William Beaumont, Lt.
Stephen Billings, Capt.
John Barnard, Capt.
David Beach, Lt.

John Ball, Lt.
Ebenr. Beardsley, surgeon.
Jona Burnall, D. C. M. G.
Gurdon Bill, marines.
Zebulon Butler, Col.
Edward Bulkley, Capt.
Stephen Betts, Capt.
Moses Cleaveland, Capt.
John. Cleaveland, En.
Elijah Chapman, Capt.
Albert Chapman, Major.
Lemuel Cliff, Capt.
Willis Cliff, Major.
Solomon Cowles, Com.
George Cotton, En.
Samuel Comstock, Capt.
William Colfax, Capt.
Giles Curtis, Lt.
Joseph Clark, En.
Eliph. Chamberlain, Capt.
Noah Coleman, Surgeon.
Thomas Converse, Capt.
Jesse Cook, Capt.
Abner Cole, En.

John Davenport, Major.
James Davenport, Com.
Pownall Denning, Lt.
Henry Daggett, Lt.
Samuel Deforest, Lt.
Richard Douglass, Capt.
James Dole, Lt. Horse.
John Dusher, Capt.
Martin Denslow.
David Dorrence, Capt.
John Ellis, Chaplain.
Edward Eels, Capt.
Charles Fanning, Lt.
Ebenezer Frothingham, Lt.
Thomas Farmer, Lt.
Silas Goodell, Lt.
William Glenny, Lt.
Ozias Goodrich, En.
Samuel Gibbs, Lt.
Nehemiah Gorham, Lt.
Eben. Gray, Lt.-Col.
Matthias Gregory.
Thos. Grosvenor, Lt.-Col.
Jesse Grant, Capt.
Jed. Huntington, B.-Gen.
Eben. Huntington, Lt.-Col.
Hezekiah Hubbard, Com.
Elijah Hubbard, Com.
Neh. Hubbard, Com.
William Higgins, Lt.
Jos. Higgins, Surg. mate.
Tallmadge Hall, Lt.
Philemon Hall, Lt.
Amos Hall, Lt.
Jona. Hart, Capt.

John Hart, En.
Chas. Hopkins, Lt.
David Humphreys, A. D. C.
Timothy Hosmer, Surgeon.
Elijah Humphreys, Capt.
Prentice Hosmer, Lt.
Elisha Hopkins, Capt.
John Hobart, Lt.
Samuel Hart, Lt.
Jaques Harman, En.
Gideon Hawley, Lt. Horse.
Jeronymus Hogeland, Capt.
Salmon Hubbell, Lt.
Asahel Hodges, Capt.
Peleg Heath, Lt.
Hez. Holdridge, Lt.-Col.
William Henshaw, Lt.
James Hyde, Lt.
Roger Hooker, Lt.
Jona. Johnson, Lt.-Col.
David Judson, Capt.
William Judd, Capt.
Elijah Jones, Lt. Horse.
Thaddeus Keeler, Lt.
Isaac Keeler, Lt.
Aaron Keeler, En.
Ephraim Kimberly, Capt.
Jacob Kingsbury, En.
Joshua Knapp, En.
Joshua King, Lt. Horse.
Amasa Keyes, Capt.
Eli Leavensworth, Major.
Elihu Lyman, En.
William Leverett, Lt.
Sibbens Loomis, Lt.

Seth Lewis, Com.

James Lord, Lt.

Noah Lee, Capt.

Asa Lyon, Lt.

William Lyon, Lt.

Return Meigs, Col.

John Meigs, Lt.

William Monson, Capt.

Theophilus Monson, Capt.

Charles Miller, Lt.

John Mansfield, Lt.

John Mix, Lt.

James Morris, Capt.

Eneas Monson, Sur mate.

Jasper Meade, Lt.

Samuel Mills, Lt.

John Miles, Lt.

Timothy Matthew, Surgeon.

John Noyes, Surgeon.

William Nichols, Lt.

Simeon Newell.

James Olmsted, Lt.

Sam. H. Parsons, Maj.-Gen.

Stephen Potter, Capt.

Solomon Pinto, En.

William Pike, Lt. Horse.

Ralph Pomroy, Lt.

Seth Phelps, Capt.

Abner Prior, Maj.

Reuben Pride, Lt.

David Phipps, Capt.

Jonas Prentice, Capt.

R. Peck.

Charles Pond, Capt.

Daniel Putnam, D. C.

Ebenezer Perkins, Capt.

Hezekiah Roberts, Capt.

Jedediah Rogers, Lt.

Joseph Rogers, Ens.

Peter Robinson, Capt.

Elias Robinson, Lt.

Cornelius Russell, Lt.

John Rose, Surgeon.

John Riley, Capt.

Aaron Rhea, Lt. Horse.

Samuel Richards, Lt.

Nehemiah Rice, Capt.

Josiah Root, Sur. mate.

Josiah Starr, Col.

David Starr, Capt.

Thomas Starr, Lt.

George Starr.

David Smith, Maj.

Ezra Smith, Lt.

Joel Smith, En.

Isaac Sherman, Lt.-Col.

John Sherman, Lt.

Thos. Y. Seymour, Capt.

Horace Seymour, Lt. Horse.

Aaron Seymour, Capt.

Benjamin Sutliff, Lt.

Elias Stillwell, Capt.

Reuben Sanderson, Lt.

Heman Swift, Col.

John Simpson, Surgeon.

Ezra Selden, Capt.

William Stanton, Capt.

John Sumner, Lt.-Col.

Thomas Skinner, Surgeon.

Abijah Savage, Capt.

Simon Thatcher, Capt.
David Strong, Capt.
David F. Sill, Lt.-Col.
Joseph Shaler, Lt.
Elisha Sheldon, Lt.-Col.
Jon. Trumbull, Lt.-Col.
John Trumbull, Col.
Ebenezer Farmer, Lt.
Tryal Farmer, Lt.
Timothy Taylor, Capt.
Josiah Tiffany, Lt.
Henry Ten Eycke, Capt.
John Trowbridge, Lt.
Isaiah Thompson, Capt.
John R. Troop, Lt.
Benjamin Tallmadge, Maj.
Samuel Wyllys, Col.
John P. Wyllys, Maj.
Jeremiah Wadsworth, Col.
Elijah Wadsworth, Capt.
Samuel B. Webb, Col.

John Webb, Capt.
William Watmaly, Engr.
Ebenezer Wales, Lt.
John White, Lt.
Joseph A. Wright, Maj.
Roger Wells, Capt.
Joshua Whitney, Lt.
Joseph Walker, Capt.
Peter Woodward, Lt.
Theodore Woodbridge, Maj.
Thaddeus Weed, Capt.
John P. Watrous, Surgeon.
Ames Walbridge, Maj.
Samuel W. Williams, Capt.
Erastus Wolcott, Capt.
Fred. Whiting, Lt. Horse.
Nathan F. Whiting, Lt.
Jeffery Whiting, Capt.
Robert Warner, Maj.
Joseph Wilcox, Lt.

FULLNAME INDEX

BARTLETT (Cont.)
Nathaniel 61 70 74 84-87 89 154 177-178 212 Rachel 178 Rev Mr 62 223 Roda 178 Russell 40 177-178
BARTRAM, Aaron 146 179 Aaron R 181 243 Ann 180 Anna 115 179-180 Barney 181 243 Belinda 179 Betsey 178-179 181 Betsey Nott 181 Charity 181 Chasie 179 Clarissa 179 Coley 181 Daniel 115 178 180-181 Daniel S 181 David 178-181 David S 167 171 244 Dolly 179 Eli 178-179 Elias 179 Elinor 179-180 Elizabeth 179 181 Ephraim 181 Esther 179-180 Eunice 178-180 Ezekiel 178-179 Ezra 178-179 Frederick 181 Gurdon 180-181 242 Hannah 178-179 Harry 179 Hepsy 178 Hulda 178 Huldah 179 Irena 179 Isaac 179 James 178-179 Jared 179 Jehu 179 Joel 178 Joel M 179 John 178 181

BARTRAM (Cont.)
Jonathan 178 Joseph 178-179 Julia 181 Julilla 180 Levi 180-181 181 Lodema 179 Lorraine 181 Lucy 179 Lucy A 181 Mabel 178 Mary 115 178-179 181 186 Milo 179 Molly 179 Mr 181 Noah 179 Olive 179 Oliver 181 Paul 34 115 178 186 Phebe 178-181 Polly 179 Ruth 74 178 Sally 181 Samuel 181 Sarah 178-179 Uriah 179-181 William 179 Willis 179
BATES, Aaron 182 Amaziah 182 Atty-gen 230 Chas H 169 Elias 182 238 Esther 182 Ezra 75 182 Hannah 182 Harriet 182 Henry W 168 John 182 Justus 182 Lydia 182 Martha 182 Mr 142 238 Nathan 182 Sarah 182 Seth P 170-171 Slawson 182 Smith 169 Tabitha 182 Walker 134 142 160 182 238 242-243 Waterman 157 167
BATTERSON, Stephen 75

COLEY (Cont.)
    Lenson 237 Miss 236
    Nathan 38-39 75
    Onesimus 202 Peter S
    236 243 Rachel 221
    William 169 Wm 172
COLFAX, William 245
COLLINS, Samuel J 235
    William F 124
COLVER, 131 Mr 132 157
    Nathaniel 130 157
COMSTOCK, 145 192
    Billy 44 146 237 242
    David C 88-89 Mary
    232 Moses 171 Samuel
    245 William King 232
CONNONRS, Mrs 216
CONVERSE, Thomas 245
COOK, Col 49 51 Jesse
    245 Phineas 123
CORCORAN, Jas 171
CORNWALL, Nathan 166
COSTELLO, Martin 167
COTTON, George 245
COUCH, Abigail 188
    Abraham 125 Adea 187
    Adria 188 Andrew D
    167 Benjamin 236 Capt
    7 9 12 25 29 Caroline
    190 Daniel 187 Darius
    228 Darius N 228
    Deborah 188 Ebenezer
    29 34 39 83 187
    Edward 189-190 236

COUCH (Cont.)
    Edward J 236 Eleanor
    189 Elijah 188
    Elizabeth 188-189
    Esther 189 Gen 229
    Hannah 188 Henry 243
    Hezekiah 189 Isabel
    188 Jessup 189-190
    John 129 188-189 237
    Jonathan 34 38 189
    Lydia 188 Maj-gen 189
    Mary 189 Moses 189
    Mrs 189 Nash 188-189
    Nathan 189 Priscilla
    190 Rebecca 188
    Samuel 7 10-13 30-31
    187-188 Sarah 188-189
    Seth 189 Simon 89 188-
    190 236 Simon A 190
    Simon Jr 188 Stephen
    188 Thesde 188
    Thomas 188-189
    Thomas Nash 188
COWDEN, George 222
COWLES, Solomon 245
CRAWFORD, 144 John
    122 127 John 2d 124
    William 150
CREVEY, George C 125
CROCKER, Daniel 87 89
    George 132 S L 228
CROFOOT, Dan'll 16
    Daniel 92-93
CROFUT, David 21

260

HAMILTON (Cont.)
Benjamin 34 79 Esther
79 Isaac 66 Molly 179
William 165
HAMLIN, Levi 244
HARMAN, Jaques 246
HARNEY, Martha 6
HARPIN, John 211 Mary
211
HARRIS, Henry D 165
Reuben 122-123
HART, John 246 Jona 246
Samuel 246
HAUGH, John 125
HAWKINS, 107
HAWLEY, Abigail 220
Bille 195 Eunice 186
195 Gideon 246
Hezekiah 196 Jedediah
R 234 John 220 Joseph
29 195 234 Lemuel 89
196 234 Lydia 195-196
217 Mary 178 195 Ruth
195 Sarah 211 William
37-39 42 114 195-196
217 239-240
HAZEN, 54 Col 70
HEATH, Peleg 246
HEBBARD, E S 122
HENDERSON, Samuel M
136
HENDRICK, Mary 74
HENSHAW, William 246
HERON, Elizabeth 199

HERON (Cont.)
Elosia 199 Esquire 50
John M 109 242 Lucy
199 Margaret 199
Mary 219 Maurice 199
Squire 51 197-199 219
Susan 199 William 37
44-45 144 150 156 199
240-241
HERRICK, W D 88-89
HEYDON, David 244
HIBBARD, Billy 123 E S
124
HICKOK, George A 238
HIDE, John 17
HIGGINS, Jos 246
William 246
HILL, Aaron S 127 147
233 Aaron Sanford 122
197 Abel 183 Abigail
196-197 Albert 233
Andrew L 43 217 240-
242 Arthur 141 Arthur
B 143 244 Betsey 197
217 Betsy 197 Bradley
175-176 197 238 242-
243 Burr 197 Daniel 33
139 183 David 196
Dimon 196 Eben 158
Ebenezer 133 196-197
Eleanor 196 Eliphalet
196 Elizabeth 196
Esther 196-197 Ezekiel
41 Fanny 217

HILL (Cont.)
Gershom 175 197
Hannah 208 Horace
197 Ignatius 196 Jabez
196-197 211 James 196
John 196 John L 147
John Lee 197 John R
46 118 121 125 147 210
217 242 John Read 197
Joseph 196-197 244
Lydia 197 Mabel 196-
197 Morris 124 127 197
233 243 Moses 147 196-
197 233 244 Mr 147
175 Nathaniel B 197
Peter 165 Phebe 183
Sanford 122 Sarah
196-197 211 Seth 196
Tho 17 Thomas 9 16
Will'm 16 William 17
93 147 196 -197 243
William B 243 William
H 243 William Hawley
197 William Jr 21 Wm
T 121-122 125 232
HILLARD, Zoa 211
HILLIARD, Isaac 151-152
Mr 151-152
HILTON, Daniel 4-5
HOBART, John 246 Rev
Mr 208
HOCH, Robert 165
HODGES, Asahel 246
HOFFMAN, John W 112

HOGELAND, Jeronymus
246
HOHMAN, Henry 172
HOLBROOK, Abigail 183
HOLDRIDGE, Hez 246
HOLLIS, George 125
HOLLISTER, Gideon H
205 230 Harriet 205
Mr 49-50 61 230
HOLMES, Mrs 236
HOLSTEN, Elisha 244
HONEYMAN, Joshua 98
HOOD, 229
HOOKER, 229 Roger 246
HOPKINS, Chas 246
Elisha 246
HORNE, John W 125
HOSMER, Prentice 246
Timothy 246
HOTCHKISS, Samuel 244
HOWE, 48 Lord 47
HOYT, Lucy 222 Phillip L
124 Thomas 4-5
HUBBARD, Elijah 246
Hezekiah 246 Neh 246
Reuben 112
HUBBELL, Elizabeth 232
Richard 5 Salmon 246
HUDSON, Dr 158
Erasmus 157 Joshua
136 Mr 157
HULL, Aaron 201 203
Aaron B 201-202 237
243

268

PENN, Mr 37
PERKINS, Ebenezer 247
PERRY, Aaron 237 243
Abagail 203 Andrew 56
Andrew S 237 Daniel
36 44 144 209 David
108 112 237 Deborah
209 Ebenezer 209
Elizabeth 209 Eunice
203 George 40 42 203
209 Grissel 209 Grizzle
204 Isaac 209-210 John
209 Joseph 209 Mary
209 Sarah 209 Thomas
209 Timothy 203 210
PHELPS, Homer 244 Seth
247
PHILLIPS, George B 236
PHINNEY, Mabel 194
Sarah 41
PHIPPS, David 247
PICKET, Nathan 21
PICKETT, Sarah 174
PIGOT, George 92 Mr 92
PIKE, William 247
PINTO, Solomon 247
PLATT, Abigail 210 Betty
115 Charles M 166
Daniel 210 Elizabeth
210 Eunice 210
Griswold 210 Henry
170 Henry Burr 244
Hezekiah 41 210 Isaac
115 John 210

PLATT (Cont.)
Jonas 115 210 Justus
210 Lucy 115 Mary 210
Nabbie 191 Obadiah
210 Orrin 244 Robert
210 Sanford J 170
Sarah 193 197 Timothy
193 197 210 William
210
PLUMB, Elijah G 112
POLK, Mr 227
POLLEY, G W 127
POMROY, Ralph 247
POND, Charles 247
POOR, Gen 54
POPE, 229
PORTER, Eleazer 244
Elijah 244
POTTER, Stephen 247
POTTS, Benj 244
POWELL, Mary 215
PRENTICE, Jonas 247
PRICE, Mary 193 Seth
193
PRIDE, Reuben 247
PRIOR, Abner 247
PUTNAM, 56-58 61-62 64-
65 85 154 158 193
Daniel 247 Gen 54-56
60-63 66 69 Maj Gen
70
RANDOLPH, John 131
READ, Aaron 89 150
Abigail 212 Anna 211

RUMSEY (Cont.)
Sarah 214 Seth Hull
214 William 214
RUSSELL, Cornelius 247
Eunice 177 John 123
Mary 218
RYAN, Jeremiah 39 75
Thomas 50
RYDER, James J 170
SAINTJOHN, 223 Abigail
215 Hiram 135-136 171
J O 135 Jacob B 170
John O 134 158 243
Peter 152 Samuel 136
SALMON, Asahel 62 144
236 Col 236
SALMONS, Asahel 75
SALTONSTALL, G 12
SANDERSON, Reuben
247
SANDFORD, E J 215
Ezekiel 215 Mr 117
SANFORD, 54 A B 233
Aaron 43 114-116 118
125 127 195 197 216-
217 233 241-242 Aaron
Jr 125 217 242 Aaron
K 217 232 Aaron S 143
Abel H 216 Abigail 178
218-221 Amanda 219
Andrew H 163 217
Anna 205 208 Anne
216 Annie 221
Augustus 220 Benj 144

SANFORD (Cont.)
Betsey 197 217 221
Betty 221 Bradley 146
238 Charles 217
Charlotte 217-218
Chloe 220 Clara 217
Daniel 50 139 142 145
150 217 220 237-239
244 Daniel S 243 David
145 217 220-221 238
David B 243 E A 146
Ebenezer 220 237 Eli
220-221 236 Elias 220
Elijah 220 Elizabeth 34
210 215 217 220-221
Emily 217 237 Enoch A
145 221 238 Ephraim
145 207 215-216 220-
221 238 242 Esther 216
220 237 Eunice 216-
217 Ezekiel 17 40 43
144 215-216 219 Ezra
220 Fanny 217 Francis
A 143 160 184 217 233
243 G A 146 George A
238 Hannah 116 216-
217 Harriet 217
Harriet M 217 Hawley
125 217 233 Henry 217
233 Hezekiah 38 40 42
115 216 239-240
Hinman 236 Huldah
216 220-221 J R 243-
244